Praise for *Falling in Love with Joseph Smith*

"Jane Barnes's startling, compelling book looks for treasure, much as the young Joseph Smith did, with the passion of a convert and the wild, sharp eye of someone determined to find it in the most unlikely places. This is a beautiful and utterly original book."
— Sara Miles, author of *Take This Bread: A Radical Conversion* and *Jesus Freak*

"This is a book about faith and irony, but don't let the title fool you. Hold on to your hats, because you're going to be falling in love with Joseph Smith, too!"
— Dennis Covington, author of the National Book Award finalist *Salvation on Sand Mountain*

"Jane Barnes offers a rollicking, visionary, and deeply personal exploration of the magnetic legacy of Joseph Smith and what his story can teach us about our own deeply American hunger for transcendence. In a moment when many Americans are realizing how little they know about Mormonism, Barnes shows us what non-Mormons can and should love about this uniquely American faith tradition."
— Joanna Brooks, author of *The Book of Mormon Girl*, associate professor, Department of English and Comparative Literature, San Diego State University

"Jane Barnes's fascination with Joseph Smith is an inward journey, an account of one person's attempt to articulate and to answer difficult questions about the mysterious Joseph, a man who puzzles and eludes her. Jane tracks her discovery according to a deeply felt but elusive imperative. *Falling in Love with Joseph Smith* made me think of one of my favorite hybrid books, Annie Dillard's *For the Time Being*—though this book is unique in its own way."
— Ann Beattie, PEN/Malamud Award–winning author, professor of Literature and Creative Writing, University of Virginia

"In this beautifully written, witty, fascinating book, Jane Barnes intertwines the explosive life of Joseph Smith, American prophet, and her own spiritual journey. As if channeling Mark Twain with a dash of Adrienne Rich and a mixture of Pilgrim and pioneer spirit, she breathes new life into the story of Mormon beginnings. And startlingly close and personal the story is, for those who know of Mormon ancestry and those who don't. Even the secular reader will recognize the American passion for self-transformation in this reimagining of Joseph's life and candid memoir of Barnes's own experience in the baby-boom generation. *Falling in Love with Joseph Smith* shows that Mormon roots are deep-set in ingenuity, seeking, appetite for life, and yearning for an afterlife."
— Alison Booth, professor of English, University of Virginia

"Out of a stone and the hat that surrounded it, Joseph Smith produced a book that launched a remarkable religion, [one] that continues to affect millions of people throughout the world. Therein lies the mystery of Mormonism. It has converted many and fascinated others, including Jane Barnes, who brilliantly employs the stone in the hat as the central metaphor for her ongoing love affair with one of the most enigmatic religious figures of modern times. She invites the reader to do what she did: pull the hat to the face to exclude ambient light that tends more to confuse than enlighten, and then peer into the darkness as the first step on an unpredictable journey into the persona of a modern prophet."

—Gregory A. Prince, coauthor of *David O. McKay and the Rise of Modern Mormonism*

"Jane Barnes has written an exuberant, honest, bighearted memoir of her own spiritual apprenticeship in mortality and love. Her unlikely crush on the nineteenth-century prophet allows her to see what many non-Mormons miss about Joseph Smith: that he is a great American original, 'more like Thelonious Monk in a rapture than Moses on the march.' Barnes longs for a God great and good enough to love Smith's—and her own—contradictions, to delight in the human imagination, and to share her own frank and buoyant wit. Jane Barnes is herself a great American original, with a voice I would follow across the desert. *Falling in Love with Joseph Smith* is her irresistible revelation of the human spirit."

—Lynn Powell, author of *Framing Innocence*

"Defying easy categorization, this book intermingles the life of Joseph Smith and the life of one of his most extraordinary admirers. Barnes is a highly literate, deeply sensitive woman who came of age in the tumultuous 1960s. Her style is masterful, characterized by succinct allusion, inventive metaphor, and lucid articulation of complex concepts. Her book is destined to take a place among the most distinguished interpretations of Mormonism's founder."

—Levi S. Peterson, author of *The Backslider* and professor emeritus of English, Weber State University

Falling
in Love
with
JOSEPH SMITH

JEREMY P. TARCHER/PENGUIN

a member of Penguin Group (USA) Inc.

New York

Falling
in Love
with

JOSEPH SMITH

My
Search
for
the
Real
Prophet

JANE BARNES

JEREMY P. TARCHER/PENGUIN
Published by the Penguin Group
Penguin Group (USA) Inc., 375 Hudson Street, New York, New York 10014, USA •
Penguin Group (Canada), 90 Eglinton Avenue East, Suite 700, Toronto, Ontario M4P 2Y3,
Canada (a division of Pearson Penguin Canada Inc.) • Penguin Books Ltd, 80 Strand,
London WC2R 0RL, England • Penguin Ireland, 25 St Stephen's Green, Dublin 2, Ireland
(a division of Penguin Books Ltd) • Penguin Group (Australia), 250 Camberwell Road,
Camberwell, Victoria 3124, Australia (a division of Pearson Australia Group Pty Ltd) •
Penguin Books India Pvt Ltd, 11 Community Centre, Panchsheel Park, New Delhi–110 017,
India • Penguin Group (NZ), 67 Apollo Drive, Rosedale, North Shore 0632, New Zealand
(a division of Pearson New Zealand Ltd) • Penguin Books (South Africa) (Pty) Ltd,
24 Sturdee Avenue, Rosebank, Johannesburg 2196, South Africa

Penguin Books Ltd, Registered Offices: 80 Strand, London WC2R 0RL, England

Most Tarcher/Penguin books are available at special quantity discounts for bulk
purchase for sales promotions, premiums, fund-raising, and educational needs.
Special books or book excerpts also can be created to fit specific needs.
For details, write Penguin Group (USA) Inc.
Special Markets, 375 Hudson Street, New York, NY 10014.

Library of Congress Cataloging-in-Publication Data

Barnes, Jane.
Falling in love with Joseph Smith : my search for the real prophet / Jane Barnes.
    p.   cm
Chapter 1 previously published in Dialogue (Stanford, Calif.),
volume 41, number 1 (Spring 2008).
ISBN 978-1-58542-925-7
1. Smith, Joseph, 1805–1844. 2. Barnes, Jane, 1942– 3. Mormon Church.
4. Conversion—Mormon Church. I. Title.
BX8695.S6B37   2012   2012018119
289.3092—dc23
[B]

Printed in the United States of America
1 3 5 7 9 10 8 6 4 2

Book design by Susan Walsh

For my daughters,

Maud and Nell

CONTENTS

ONE

Joseph Smith: Lost and Found

I was no stranger to the allure of conversion. I lived in the South, and had more than once found myself listening to some blistering preacher as I was driving down the highway. I often responded to the excoriations and palpitations, the chewy tentacles of guilt-tripping and sin-slathering, the baseless assertions bursting in showers of confession and raging tremolos. Yet I knew my mood would change completely if I ever made it to the firebreather's altar and took Christ as my savior. I'd be looking to join a witness protection program the next day. I might be susceptible, but I was the sort of willful, resistant seeker Sartre described as "crawling backwards on his knees to God." All my life I'd felt "hints and allegations," but even when I cast myself as bait onto the uncertain waters, I fled if I was nibbled.

Then, in 2003, I signed on as a writer for a PBS series about the Mormons. I'd been fascinated by the Mormon prophet, Joseph Smith, for some time, long enough to feel I wasn't going to be suddenly swept away by him. He aroused my enthusiasm, but he also inspired a deep, studious interest of a stabilizing sort. I'd met Joseph out of all Mormon context. I met him between

Emerson and the Beatles, between the American Revolution and the sixties, between the conservative New England tilt of my education and the ecstatic, destabilizing, boundary-busting, prolonged years of antiauthoritarian protest against the U.S. government. I met Joseph roaming the corridors of American history in Fawn Brodie's *No Man Knows My History*, portrayed as a genius who would be comfortable at the same table with P. T. Barnum, Walt Disney, and Norman Mailer—to name a few of the wildly imaginative national characters I'd been pitching for documentaries. Some people left the church when they read Brodie's skeptical biography of Joseph, but I flipped over him.

Somehow I had reached my forties without ever having met a single Mormon and knowing almost nothing about our homegrown prophet. I encountered Joseph amid the smoking ruins of Vietnam, Watergate, Nixon's impeachment, and the country's return to our primal dream of avarice. By that time "my" priests were Martin Luther King, Jr., and the Berrigan brothers, men who broke the law for a higher good. Fawn Brodie's Joseph was this kind of man. But the social activist priests always seemed more moral than faithful. Amid their good works, their contradictions and ironies somehow suggested that politics was what we had in a world from which God had withdrawn. Brodie made me feel that the same contradictions and ironies gave Joseph credibility as a modern man of faith.

Brodie's Joseph reawakened religious feelings I thought I'd lost forever. Not since I colored religious pictures as a child had I felt so close to a divine presence. His exuberant arc from boy conjurer into frontier prophet with gold plates gave me the most intense delight of which I was capable. Meeting the early Joseph fresh in middle age was like drinking from the fountain of youth. I was smitten by the boastful boy who looked into magic stones to track treasure chests zooming around beneath the earth. I loved the same boy for being filled with earnest wonder when the angel Moroni came to his bedroom one night and told him about the great work God had for him. Joseph's holy fairy tale seemed like a gospel written by Mark Twain. His story gave me the delight of reading Twain but more so, like the delight of human love, yet different. We do not normally think of God as tickling us until we break into helpless tears of laughter. But this was the God I felt in the early Joseph, a God with a touchingly, meltingly, divinely irreverent sense of humor. Here was a God who dared to clown around with his own image. He had created a story so comic, it defied disbelief.

When I met the Mormon revelator, I'd been working for Helen Whitney, the New York director/producer/writer, for a decade. Helen had increasingly been turning to the religious landscape as her focus. She, too, was fascinated by Fawn Brodie's biography. Her interest in Joseph was different than mine, but we were both baffled by the fact that his life wasn't more widely known. The nearly illiterate boy who created the Book of Mormon in three incandescent months lived for fifteen more years. The self-delighting, optimistic boy pilgrim became a self-dramatizing, conflicted seer who built cities, fought wars, initiated an extraordinary experiment in plural marriage, created bold new theology, flew in the face of every convention, and died in a horrific shoot-out. He was a transcendent representative of a proliferating American type—the self-proclaimed prophet— and the only one of his kind to found a church that was growing at the astonishing rate of approximately 280,000 converts a year worldwide. There was enough in Joseph's story for twenty movies.

In the early nineties, Helen and I proposed a film about his life to HBO. In the late nineties, we proposed a documentary about Joseph in Nauvoo, Illinois, to *American Experience*. Both times we were turned down. Then the 2002 Olympics in Salt Lake City announced the arrival of the Saints in business and politics. Yet their apparent assimilation was partial. The Mormons' acceptance has always moved two steps forward, one step back, even now that we have had two Mormon candidates for the 2012 presidential election, not to mention the smash Broadway musical *The Book of Mormon*. For reasons that aren't completely clear, whatever acceptance the Mormons have received has masked an enduring unease Americans feel toward Joseph Smith and his religion. In 2003, thanks to the Mormons' increased visibility and the unexplored tension beneath it, American television was ready for a major cultural assessment of the faith. Helen succeeded in persuading WGBH *Frontline* and *American Experience* that the moment was ripe for a series on the Mormons. We spent a year researching and writing a hundred-page treatment. Many writers leave during production (the filming period) once the treatment is finished and come back when it's time to write narration. I'd stayed on in earlier projects out of interest in the subjects and out of fascination with production: searching for characters and experts, interviewing, going on location, and staying involved with the shoots.

Working on *The Mormons* was no different, except that I was something of a pilgrim as well as a writer on this project. Maybe "pseudo-pilgrim" is a better term. As I've said, I felt my detachment was secure. The film was not about my idiosyncratic relation to the prophet. It was about the sweep of Mormon religion and history, from Joseph's founding revelations through the present. Nonetheless, as I went about the rest of my business, I expected I'd be in closer and closer communion with the prophet's burning core.

At first it didn't happen. Joseph Smith was everywhere and nowhere in mainstream Mormonism. He was present but still unaccounted for among the scholars poring over the prophet's massive biographical archives. The Joseph evoked by missionaries and in LDS churches across the country was a ceremonial figure: appropriate for the circumstances, but distancing. When faithful Mormons shared their Josephs with me, the traces of their personal connection were like shining instances of mica on a beach, riveting but not revealing. I began to feel the bulwark of Joseph's church for the first time. I was separated from him by the mighty fortress built around his holy flame. Standing in Temple Square and staring up at the figure of Moroni, carved in

22-karat gold leaf, I felt lost. Here, at ground zero of the Mormon faith in Salt Lake City, my fragile sense of the divine was buried under tons and tons of granite.

Where was the boy with his nose in his hat? It should never be forgotten that Joseph translated the Book of Mormon out of a hat. This was one of the most delightful events in all religious history, one accompanied by many beautiful supporting elements. Joseph began by seeking earthly treasure in his peep stone. Once he lifted his gaze to Heaven, he received gold plates and special spectacles called Urim and Thummim to help read what was on the plates. He did not translate by looking at them through his spectacles. He created a New World religion by putting his face in his hat, sometimes with his holy glasses, sometimes with his peep stone, and reading aloud sentences that unscrolled in the darkness under the brim. "Adorable" is the best word for this process. And for the unregenerate child in my heart, a rare, gorgeous chance for God to enter our fallen world. I have seen an illustration of this sacred process in which Joseph looks into a stovepipe hat and another in which he is about to clap a cowboy hat over his face. I have always imagined that he used a round, floppy hat of the sort boys wore in Winslow Homer paintings. But whatever kind of hat he used, the prophet who put his face in his hat is one who makes me feel religion is a joyous pastime. I believe Joseph sometimes even had a little fun at God's expense.

The young, greenhorn prophet had to have some priestly tool for his sacred translating of the gold plates; he elevated the hat he had at hand. Yet given his sensitivity to language, he could not have been oblivious to the uses of "hat" in his time: "old hat," "new hat," "high hat," "knocked into a cocked hat." There are arguments about whether "talking through one's hat" was in use during Joseph's day, but I don't think we should be afraid to imagine that the frontier revelator used a hat knowing it might be associated with "talking nonsense." He had an irreverent nature, and it has taken too long for that characteristic to be celebrated. "At the drop of a hat" was alive in the American West in Joseph's time to signal that a fight was going to start. "Throw your hat into the ring" was another phrase describing the joining of a political fight. I don't think Joseph was purposely announcing that he was going to start a battle using the Book of Mormon, but I think he might have enjoyed playing with words. Even if he didn't dwell on these resonances and connotations, he must have noticed the connection between "pulling a rabbit out of a hat" (very much in usage then) and pulling new scripture out of his own. If you feel God needs to update at least part of his image— the part that is pretty humorless—as I do, you will delight in this connection, too.

Yet it was hard to keep my own sense of Joseph's playfulness alive in Utah. How had Joseph's magical mystery tour launched the one true church? I was swamped by questions. How could the institution enforce its strict rules with such a riot at the root? Could the wildest story ever told justify the Mormons' use of excommunication? Why was irreverence such a divine quality to me? Why did I so rarely meet faithful Mormons who loved the sacred humor in Joseph's early story? Grown men and women held conferences to argue about whether peep stones really worked. No honest child could listen to those debates without a mix of repressed laughter and envy. *The peep stone worked for Joseph!* the child cries silently. *It worked for Joseph! I'd like to try a peep stone, too.*

I didn't really understand why it was such a scandal to have once mixed religion with magic. Weren't they at the very least on the same dramatic, emotional continuum? And why no conferences on Joseph's hat? One Mormon scholar did pick up his hat as we talked about Joseph's "inspired" translation; he paused and put his face in it momentarily, then returned to our discussion without missing a beat or changing his tone. His silent—and frisky—gesture showed he knew how funny Joseph must have looked as he dictated the Book of Mormon. His silence also spoke volumes about the sources of mockery Mormons had long endured. It was one of those interviews where I knew I should leave the unspoken alone. These weren't really laughing matters.

I found most faithful Mormons did not smile at Joseph's peep stones or many of the other details I enjoyed. But among Mormons I met who were leaving the church, there were those few who turned on Joseph and his founding stories as jokes. Raging against the angel Moroni and Hill Cumorah for being laughable, these apostates had a primal bitterness—as if they were tearing out the first taboo: the one forbidding them to admit that Joseph had an inspired sense of fun.

I don't submit this disrespectfully. The anarchic Joseph gave me one of my very few adult glimpses of God. As I worked on the film, I fought to keep that Joseph alive. I rebelled against the tendency to compare Joseph to ancient prophets or even to see him as a man of his time. He felt more like a contemporary, a naïve modernist. Starting with peep stones and treasure, then moving to angels and gold plates inscribed with ancient history, he mixed and remixed the elements of religious experience until he'd transformed them through fantastical vision, theatricality, and the written word into the Book of Mormon, one of the strangest works of scripture ever. I found it impenetrable. Yet millions had converted by reading its pages. I would be handicapped for several years by my inability to find a way into its soul. I didn't know enough about religion to consider the Book of Mormon either blasphemous or mystically inspired. Possibly because of my own ignorant disbelief that it could change people, I got some whiff of irony out of the vaguely biblical stories that included some whoppers like the one about the ancient people coming to the New World in submarines. Maybe I just assumed that the humorful young Joseph could not produce a completely humorless religious text. Whatever he'd written, it must have some sort of sophisticated distance, some kind of backpedaling archness toward true-blue, corn-fed piety. I believed Joseph was more like Thelonious Monk in a rapture than Moses on the march.

There are almost no dull moments in Mormon history. From its founding, the Mormon journey has brimmed with nonstop, heart-stopping dramas, which are almost entirely unknown to most Americans. As we researched the film, we were often told that the Mormons had lost the culture wars to the cowboys and Indians. This seems like a partial explanation for their absence from popular films and novels. Another part of the explanation has to be that Americans still haven't settled where or how the Mormons fit into our national mythology. Mormon identity is still a work-in-progress, and must remain so as long as so much of the story remains hotly debated.

During editing, as we wrote and rewrote lines of narration, we began our daily work by saying, "Abandon hope, all ye who enter here." As the Mormons crossed the prairie, they were enveloped in swarms of contested facts, which moved in overlapping clouds from one hive to the next: Kirtland, Ohio; Missouri; Nauvoo, Illinois. We spent hours seeking expert opinion just about whether Nauvoo's population "equaled," "rivaled," or "surpassed" Chicago's. It took Herculean research and distillation to get a clean line of documentary narration. Changing a comma, omitting a word often brought a new challenge and meant starting all over on a red-hot frontier where you could lose your bona fides if you called a tree by its wrong name.

Crossing the country with the early Saints gave me a chance to deepen what I knew about the older Joseph, the leader of the church. I had seen troubling complexity in his later self, but I'd never come to terms with it. A terrible melancholy hung over the second half of Joseph's life. The prophet was hurtling toward trouble or clawing his way out of it. He had enemies, but he was first among them. The older he got, the thinner he seemed to spread himself. The larger his church, the noisier the controversy, the more people he was for too many others.

As he hurtled through Missouri and into Nauvoo, there were countless streams of consciousness pressing their disparate claims on Joseph's revelatory powers. He was working as a lawyer, architect, army general, quartermaster, presidential candidate, mayor, medical healer, hotelier, and prophet. I was moved and fascinated by Joseph's visions of his brother Alvin in the afterlife, an event that gradually led to his envisioning baptism for the dead. I was intrigued by that ritual and by Joseph's ideas about progression to Godhood. I believed he was profoundly serious about polygamy. Plural marriage, like a lot of his later theology, was focused as much on the dead as the living. Yet his powerful desire to hallow death lacked the centripetal force of his earlier drive to write the Book of Mormon.

Things were flying apart, not together. It turns out that many of the most devastating criticisms of Joseph arose during this time and then were projected back onto his youth by hostile biographers: that he was power hungry, a liar, a con man, a sexual predator, a madman. I felt there were still enough firsthand accounts to see an exuberant and joyful innocent in Joseph's youth, but I had no idea how that boy connected to the man. During the Nauvoo period at least ten of his lives weren't speaking to each other. Indeed, his warring parts were shouting back and forth. How could the center hold? Finally, he did not seem to care if it did. He lied about polygamy from the pulpit and burned a newspaper press to punish his enemies for trying to expose him. A few days later Joseph was murdered in his jail cell at Carthage, Illinois.

We went back to Utah for the last shoot in January 2006. My job was clear-cut, but some joy had gone out of me. My attention had been undermined by watching Joseph self-destruct. The possibility that he was a charlatan was real to me for the first time. I constantly thought of Wordsworth's lines predicting that everything wonderful would come to a bad end in modern life: "We Poets in our youth begin in gladness; / But thereof come in the end despondency and madness." Actually, I remembered the lines as Robert Lowell deliberately misquoted them: "We poets in our youth begin in sadness," lines underscoring how our despair had deepened since early olden times. Joseph Smith couldn't change my life. What had I been thinking?

Soon I noticed I was losing personal things: hairbrush, glasses, cell phone. I couldn't take the time to look for them. Every minute on a shoot costs money. Every second has been scheduled. The producer and the cameraman (and their technical crew) have to focus at peak concentration for twelve to fourteen hours a day—day after day—for weeks. I was a floater with the car. I sat in a cubicle at the Alta Club in Salt Lake City, working on interview questions, doing new research, on call at every minute for anything from Scotch tape to an assessment of the twentieth-century tithe. There wasn't a free minute to look for lost stuff. Weirdly enough, things kept turning up. I found my hairbrush, my glasses, my cell phone in my briefcase or pocketbook or some other place I had torn apart to no avail just before I left for work.

I did not think to use the word "miraculous" until one particular snowy morning. As I sat down in my cubicle, I heard a woman's voice in the front lobby, calling out tentatively, "Hello . . . Hello? Has anyone lost a little phone book?" Fear and trembling overtook me. I looked, and my little phone book wasn't anywhere. It contained the irreplaceable work of several years: the unlisted numbers, home-phone numbers, weekend-retreat numbers, e-mail addresses, faxes, all the private information without which you cannot reach important people or anonymous sources or the as yet undiscovered champs of your documentary film. "Hello, hello . . ." I shouted back, and the angelic stranger followed my quaking voice into my cubby, holding out the little damp phone book. She had been at the red light when I crossed and saw me drop the book; she jumped out of her car, grabbed the thing, parked, and followed me into the club. I was lost without knowing it, and now I was found without having lifted a finger.

A new awareness followed me back home to Virginia, where I started organizing a shoot with a noted Mormon professor, his family, and their congregation outside Richmond. I needed to "scout" his home and church for light, space, availability of different shots, permissions, all the things that need to be determined before the camera comes. I could drive most of the way from Charlottesville on Route 64, but once I got off into the countryside, I knew the roads were a mess of spaghetti. The church, where I was to meet the scholar and his family, was in the mess. I had spoken to this man several times and knew his books, brilliant works about the power and importance of Joseph's theology—and about the hysterical resistance to it. When I asked him for help through the pasta, his written instructions were models of detailed clarity.

Yet, as soon as I got off Route 64—though I did my best to follow his map—I got lost. I called him from the road, and he kindly talked me back onto the right path. I was lost again in moments and had to phone him once more; he repeatedly helped me find my way. I was beginning to panic. I felt I might be lost all afternoon. I'd miss the service, be a total inconvenience, give our project a poor introduction. And then I rounded a corner and saw the T at the end of the road ahead, the place, he'd told me, where I could go only right or left. I was back on track. I was found. The words "lost and found, lost and found" went through my mind, and they were the last words before something like lightning struck my brain. I had a terrible headache; I was sobbing in darkness; I knew my own death completely.

As I wept, waiting for the worst to pass, people began honking their horns behind me. I wiped my eyes, put the car back into gear, started forward. I've always feared death, more than illness, more than incapacity. I'd had intuitions of the darkness before, but never one so profound and black. Gradually, though, I realized this dark was not so bleak. It was rich. The richness *was* the dark. It was saying something to me, and I struggled to hear the words. I felt the presence of Joseph Smith and heard something that I could only call a voice. I knew it wasn't Joseph's voice. It wasn't human. This voice was like a muscular swirl in a velvet tent. The richness didn't speak my language. But then suddenly, without a word being spoken, I understood. The richness was the knowledge that everything on earth was a half-finished sentence, which would be completed on the other side. *I was having a conversion!*

I began driving as if I'd lived in the spaghetti all my life, turning before I'd even read the street signs and racing toward the church in full confidence that I'd be there in time. Yet I was still afraid. I was terrified of life and death, the road ahead, the road behind, but I'd always been afraid of them. Now I had a new fear. I was terrified of walking into the Mormon Church and joining it. I was backpedaling in a primal panic. I'd been out with the missionaries and knew people converted all the time for much less than what I'd just experienced. Alex Caldiero, a Sicilian poet and performance artist, had asked missionaries in for some lessons. The next thing he knew, the light in the room began to change, and not long after that he was in the middle of a conversion. A man in Ghana tracked the picture on a page torn out of the Book of Mormon back to Salt Lake City through his dreams. He converted before the church accepted blacks in their priesthood. I was, all over again, the sort of tinderbox that could burst into flames at a moment's notice. I was subject to a blazing revelation announcing I wanted to convert to Mormonism.

I had always fallen in love and fascination with people, books, places. But I *couldn't* join a church. I did not believe in beliefs. I believed in intuitions, revelations, even answers, but they were all provisional. I could not pledge allegiance to the great movements of the spirit. They might change and enlarge us; we might position ourselves so that we were in the right place at the right time; we might be grateful when they came, but we couldn't command, placate, or even serve the muscular swirl in the velvet tent. I talked to myself sternly as I bore down on the LDS Church on the side of the road ahead of me. By the time I arrived, I was calm enough to perform in my role as a professional media observer. I was saved from being saved.

I thought about the experience of my near-conversion many times afterward. I tried to get its power under some kind of management. I told myself that after the fear I felt on the road lifted, the reassurance sank into my aquifer. The edge of my death terror was not so serrated, not so cutting. For this I would be grateful for the rest of my life. Joseph was as colorful as fireworks on the Fourth of July, as old-fashioned as Tom and Huck, and as much one of us as Holden Caulfield if he'd struggled in the priesthood. Joseph had left his indelible stamp on American religion by creating a church out of native pandemonium. Such was my elegiac way of talking to myself as I worked to put Joseph and my conversion moment on the shelf with other scrapbooks. Yet I was haunted by a sense he still had much to teach me about God.

I was scared of the mess he became, but over time I was increasingly intrigued by what had gone wrong. I didn't know

how any modern person got through life without finding themselves inside the particle accelerator: the device in which people's energies were constantly released by having their atoms
collide at the speed of light. In my own life, I'd come to believe this perpetual shattering was what modern people call
home. I felt Joseph had lived in such a home, that his life had
always been in a radical state of change: psychological, moral,
and spiritual. How had he stayed connected to God throughout?
Had he? The more I tried to shut the cover on an adventure
well lived, the more strongly Joseph Smith called out. The more
I read other people's conversion stories, the more anxiously I
avoided my own. The more I wouldn't join a church, the more
my fate felt sealed. Finally, I saw I'd get my freedom back only
by giving the prophet his due. This book describes how falling
in love with Joseph Smith took me into conversion and out the
other side.

TWO

The Return of the Repressed

Our history has sailed on spring tides of conversion. Americans have always desired the experience of things for themselves, and conversion was the fast track to ultimate reality. Conversion was also our first performance art, our first self-dramatizing monologue, a way up the ladder of interior success. As their "errand into the wilderness" unfolded, the Puritan faith required new members to write conversion narratives testifying to their experience of God. That was central and had to be personally affirmed. No one should stray from the community's purpose. Like the college essay of our own day, a convincing account meant acceptance as one of the elect and a role in the leadership.

Hundreds joined Jonathan Edwards's Congregational Church during the First Great Awakening in the eighteenth century. He worked on people's fear of damnation in a world and culture today's therapists would regard as a model of dysfunction. The point of that bygone Christianity was to crush the sort of self-esteem we're always pushing. Edwards's sermons provoked tears, and people cried at least in part with ecstasy at being called "great heaps of light chaff." When his congregation began to moan, he moved them to conversion with descriptions of God tossing people into hell according to His whim.

Less than a half century later, the American Revolution had put an end to state religion. People were free to worship whatever they wanted. New Protestant sects like the Shakers, Free Will Baptists, and Universalists multiplied along with the Methodists, Anglicans, and Presbyterians who were already established. There was a Second Great Awakening, a wild, far-reaching series of revivals that inspired thousands from all along the eastern United States. The outpouring of spirit passed from New England through the so-called Burned-over District in western New York State and down through Appalachia. We would have felt more at home in these gatherings, which resembled outdoor rock concerts. Exhibitionism, talent, sex, and the very early signs of advertising joined forces on behalf of personal salvation. There was a plethora of prophets: preachers wearing bear suits, a Jesus in Kentucky, and a Devil imposter named Crazy Cow in Pennsylvania. Camp meetings went on for days. Crowds swelled to twenty thousand. There was preaching, music, drinking, dancing, swooning, and speaking in tongues. Conversions soared.

Enter Joseph Smith, born in Sharon, Vermont, in 1805. As a teenager, he responded to the evangelical furor around him with ambivalence. He was open to his time, but he also made something very new and different from the influences he soaked up. Mormonism is often called "the American religion," perhaps because so many shades and nuances of American religious feeling streamed through the prophet from both sides of his gene pool. His family had been incorrigible seekers through more than a century of religious conformity in the new country. On his father's side, Joseph went back to Robert Smith, who'd sailed to Massachusetts with the Puritans in 1638. Robert was active in the early Puritan Congregational Church in Topsfield, though he never took the necessary step of joining through personal conversion.

Robert's son Samuel and grandson Samuel Jr. were also churchgoers, but also not members. Yet both were men of property and leaders. Such men usually felt compelled to convert. Nathaniel Hawthorne (the prophet's contemporary) described the early Puritans "as a people amongst whom religion and law were almost identical." Colonial magistrate Governor Thomas Dudley drove the idea home in lines of no-nonsense poetry: "Let men of God in courts and church watch / Oe'r such as would a toleration hatch." Nonmembership was suspicious among the able-bodied. In *Radical Origins*, his book about Mormon colonial forefathers, Professor Val Rust suggests the freethinking Smiths harbored inclinations that were too much for hidebound Topsfield. They must have also had some extra diplomatic polish or personal appeal to be so successful as outsiders.

When the rules loosened up slightly, Asael, Samuel Jr.'s son, did express his radical side by joining the Universalists, who disparaged Calvinist notions of election and offered conversion to everyone. This was a move away from the supernatural and a step in the direction of reason. In the more precise words of Richard Bushman, Joseph's Smith preeminent contemporary biographer, "Asael's Universalism was a form of vernacular rationalism, an offspring of the Enlightenment." In a culture that was all religion all the time, the Smith family ran the gamut of independent thought, a quality the prophet also enjoyed—but at much higher prices.

Through his mother, Lucy Mack Smith, Joseph went back to the first Pilgrims, Separatists who preferred risking their lives on the Atlantic to continuing as members of the Church of England. The Macks were incredible yeoman tigers. Even when they were failing, as they often were, they hurled themselves at the experience. Joseph's maternal grandfather, Solomon Mack, was a poster boy for the exuberant, unstoppable energy of the eighteenth-century self-made man. He was crushed by trees, horses, and millstones, and he fought in the American Revolution. He lost money, owed money, made money, and started the cycle again several times. Energy came with the Macks, but also strong feelings, intuition, general at-homeness with the mysterious beyond. Lucy's sister Lovisa had what we would call a near-death experience during which she saw the Savior through a veil "as thick as a spider's web." At sixteen, Lucy's brother Jason joined a sect and became a Seeker who lived in imitation of the early Christians. He devoted his entire life to converting others to his faith. Lucy herself had rich dreams and visions, which she studied for clues to her religious life. This younger generation came by their spiritual gifts honestly from a father who in some ways outdid them all. When, at the eleventh hour, he saw that his trials had been sent by God to humble him, Solomon Mack underwent a conventional evangelical conversion in 1811. He finished his life as a writer, the author of a stirring account of his final change of heart.

Like most people in the nineteenth century, both sides of Joseph's family were defined by conversion: the Smiths by making their separate peace with it and the Macks by obsessing about it. When Joseph came of age in 1820, people were converting publicly by the hundreds at the revivals in the Burned-over District, where his family then lived in upstate New York. Conversion was like the draft on the eve of World War II. People understood what it meant. It was a duty, a fulfillment, and a redemption. In 1820, "conversion was compelled by a set of clear ideas about the innate sinfulness of humans after Adam's fall, the omnipotence of God—his awful power and his mercy—and, finally, the promise of salvation for fallen humankind through Christ's death on the cross."

At fifteen, Joseph had some sins to worry about. He smoked, he drank, he fooled around with magic. But the sins that probably occupied him most were those of the person he was closest to: his father. Joseph Sr. was a drinking man who adored his family as certain large-hearted failures do. When he and Lucy were first married, he supported himself by teaching school and "merchandizing," running a little shop. He dreamt of bigger things. He got involved in an unlikely get-rich-quick scheme to sell gingerroot from Randolph, Vermont, to the Chinese in

China. In so trying, he lost the family's savings, sentencing himself and his four older boys to back-breaking labor on a series of hardscrabble farms. Though bad weather and poor luck forced the family to move on more than once, they were hard workers and finally started to make some success of their rented land once they reached Palmyra, New York, in 1816.

Joseph Sr.'s wife and their children went to church quite frequently, often to different ones. Joseph Sr. never. However, if his self-help program sometimes included falling off the wagon one day at a time, he was also a genuine folk visionary. Joseph Sr. always had religion on his mind. He wondered about the nature of God. He contemplated the arguments between different sects. He had flirted with Asael's Universalism, but it never stuck. Over time, Lucy wrote in her *History of Joseph Smith*, her husband "would not subscribe to any particular system of faith, but contended for the ancient order, as established by our Lord and Savior Jesus Christ and His Apostles." This Restorationist view was quite common, but Joseph Sr. gave it special meaning for his family through his remarkable dreams. In her family biography, Lucy describes her husband's dreams in a poetic language that is quite different than her own crisp yet colorful style. Presumably, the poetry is her husband's. Her dedication to collecting his visions reflects the passion for the truth she shared with her son Joseph.

Though Joseph Sr. was a family man, someone who was (seemingly) rarely alone, he is a solitary seeker in his dreams, traveling again and again "in an open, barren field." The traveler's guide tells the pilgrim, "This field is the world, which now lieth inanimate and dumb, in regard to the true religion, or plan of salvation." As the dreams develop, the guide urges Joseph Sr. "to travel on" so that he will find nourishment. Yet the sanctuaries he finds all seem like the churches that he cannot accept—nor they him. The pilgrim finally dreams he has been shut out of the meetinghouse where everyone is being judged on the Last Day. His flesh begins to "wither to the bone" as he stands there. He cries out in "the agony of my soul, 'Oh, Lord God, I beseech thee, in the name of Jesus Christ, to forgive my sins.'" Joseph Sr. is "now made whole," and the door to the meetinghouse opens to this unorthodox Christian.

In the midst of his hard life, the father's personal faith flowered in his rich, symbol-soaked psyche. In his family's mix of independence, freethinking, and religious verve, his father's dreams lent a sort of finishing touch to Joseph's prophetic makeup. It was literally true, as Dan Vogel points out in his award-winning biography *Joseph Smith: The Making of a Prophet*, that the boy had his first vision soon after his father had his last. But in case he needed an ecstatic model of a penitent who wandered freely between this world and another, the searching boy had it in his father.

At fourteen, Joseph went into the grove to pray and ask God which of all the sects was right. At that point, his mother, two of his brothers, and a sister had converted to the Presbyterian Church. His father was on his own, and Joseph was interested in the Methodists. "But so great were the confusion and strife among the different denominations that it was impossible for a person, young as I was, and so unacquainted with men and things, to come to any certain conclusion who was right and who was wrong," he wrote. When Joseph knelt down and poured out his feelings to his Maker, he described himself as "greatly excited" by "the cry and tumult" of his confusing thoughts. He was desperate for an answer. He was given a sensational response. He received his First Vision, the celestial visitation that clearly put Joseph on his prophetic path.

A great shaft of light filled the forest. God appeared with his son, Jesus Christ, enveloping Joseph in radiance as the Lord told him his sins were forgiven. God also made known "that all the creeds were an abomination," and that the boy was forbidden to join any of them. Joseph's destiny was now sealed, as he started the journey that would include the angel Moroni, the gold plates, the Book of Mormon, and the gradual transformation of his extraordinary personal conversion into a religion, a church, and a rich, unruly, colorful literature.

Joseph lived in the age of print as we know it. In a surprisingly farsighted way, poorly educated as he was, he understood that he lived in a culture of books. Somehow even before he knew he would be a writer, he grasped intuitively that the Christian truth was in danger of becoming only one truth among others. Scripture would have to have a champion to enshrine it. Early on, Joseph knew he would have to be a contender in a battle of the books. Otherwise he would never have written one. Ultimately, over the course of his short life, Joseph wrote an enormous amount about his beliefs, including works of new scripture, as well as a history of the church, sermons, speeches, and letters. This work shows remarkable development for one who started out with so little literary background, but it is also filled with inconsistencies and contradictions.

The first layer of rich, unruly Mormon literature consists of Joseph's writing. There's another layer in the newspapers covering the sudden eruption of Smith's controversial church. Then, as time passed and the Mormon drama grew, reporters infiltrated the community for exposés in national magazines; Joseph's enemies published hostile interviews, articles, and books; and the church put out its own adulatory publications. Joseph's associates and family wrote memoirs about the prophet; pioneer followers described him in personal journals. Vast archives collected Joseph's correspondence with his family and friends, letters from contemporary converts and members of his church. Between the time of Joseph's death and the middle of the twentieth century, these layers had gone through a history like that of braided rugs. First, the materials at hand were combined through necessity according to a time-tried design. Slowly but surely, there was enough space and foundation to involve art in braided rugs. Then when craft gave way to every man for himself, every artist had his own design for every rug. Today much of what has been written and is being written by Mormons and non-Mormons about the church and its history is a riveting display of ingenuity in pursuit of the mysterious.

Enter Jane Barnes, born in New York City in 1942. My family definitely was not defined by conversion. I don't even know now whether my parents were raised with any religion. They weren't atheists, at least not vocal ones, but I don't know if they thought about religion enough to say they were agnostics. There were no revivals in Providence, Rhode Island, where we moved soon after my birth. I don't think I heard the word "sect" until I took a religion course in college. If I went to a friend's house and their parents said grace before the meal, I felt sort of sorry for them for being so behind the times. My child's logic here was that what my family did was smartest and best; we didn't say grace; there must be a reason; the only one I could think of had to do with being more or less up-to-date. The family in *Little Women* might have said grace (for all I knew), but we didn't. We were modern.

Grace was old-fashioned to me, but God wasn't. I had no idea the two were connected. Yet as a child in Providence, I was a believer. My older brother and sister grumbled when my parents made us walk up the hill to the Episcopalian church on Sundays. I can't tell you which parent cared enough to make us go. But I loved the services and the classes afterward. I loved coloring pictures of camels and robed men in sandals and listening hard to Sister Pearly Voice. She really caught my attention when she said God was with each of us at all times. Actually, she made the more extraordinary claim that He *loved* every one of us. I started doing the math in my own primitive way. There were problems all around. Just take our family. Even with two parents trying to do God's work with four children, I felt that I personally could have used more love. But multiply that by the number of people in church on a Sunday morning. Even if the minister had the sudden, invisible powers of a jet plane, he could hardly have zoomed around fast enough to love every person simultaneously.

Just about that time my parents told us we were moving to Washington, D.C. When we did, they no longer enforced church-going. I was still ardent. I was eight. I was pretty taken up with the problem (the "mystery," according to Sister Pearly Voice) of how God could love everyone all the time simultaneously. On Sundays, while the rest of my family read newspapers around the breakfast table, I traveled from Georgetown by taxi to St. John's near the White House. I soon felt like the odd man out. Daddy had come home from World War II and joined the State Department. I didn't want to miss one of his anti-Communist riffs while I was off at church. How could I save America if I didn't know what challenges the free world faced? I wanted to be part of my tribe; I wanted to care about what they cared about; I wanted to fight their battles with them.

But I also had a persistent religious drive that was all my own. At night, I now put myself to sleep by imagining that I was God looking down on a little street of houses, going from one to the next, lifting the roofs and waggling my magic fingers over the families inside to calm them for a good night's sleep. This was presumably my way of handling my anxiety about God's real ability to fulfill His claim to love each and every one of us all the time. World population was rising, even I knew that. There were billions of us! So let Him have his mad ambition, I'd take care of what I could actually manage. This devout part of me did not give up easily, but when I worked hard to win a Bible for memorizing verses in Sunday school, winning suddenly felt empty. It was just success for success's sake. I felt I was betraying God with my words.

The taxi may have been an even bigger factor. I knew it was weird for an eight-year-old child to pay strangers to drive her around in search of answers to the meaning of life and death. I didn't want to be so weird. I was going to have to stuff God someplace where He didn't hurt my social life. It wasn't easy to make the break, though strangely, making the break absolutely, cutting God off completely, was easier than having dribs and drabs of contact. So that's what I did. Then once I stuffed God, I didn't feel as comfortable with my family on Sunday mornings as I expected. Though it was good to be back with my tribe, they didn't have all the answers, either. I'd gotten out of the taxi, but I was still an uprooted pilgrim. I began moving around in books, shopping for big ideas. Later I often fell in love with people who seemed to have hold of some greater truth, one which I could find in myself by learning it from them.

Whenever I was truly smitten, I was knocked flat by the flood of impressions pouring over me. Yet I was also given certain powers to regain my footing. I had the power of obsession, with its steep learning curve and special intuitions of what was going on in my beloved's mind and heart. These intuitions were inchoate, yet peppery, not like the usual things my friends said about people they fell in love with: "He's so handsome!" "He's a gentle person." "He's got a good head on his shoulders." I felt I was lying down in a waterfall, watching salmon leap upstream through a bluish veil. I was pretty silent when others dished. What could I say? "Glimpsed a curled shadow!" "Hey, here comes an incongruous nuance!"

Come to think of it, my intuitions were sort of like the muscular swirl in the velvet tent that I'd felt on the road to Richmond. They had a divine spark to them! They certainly had a divine power of discernment. I fell in love with my former husband because he had charge of the truths of literary power. Since I myself also wanted to be a writer, there was a big work for the muscular swirl in my velvet tent. I had to differentiate his important qualities from his lesser ones, which was hard to do in a man with a passion for words and opinions on everything. He'd been raised Catholic and wanted to be married in the Catholic Church. I guessed this meant religion had some importance to him. At that time, as the non-Catholic, I had to sign a paper saying I would not interfere with our children's Catholic religious education. As it turned out, my husband slept late on Sundays, and the only way our two daughters would have had even the drip of religious education they got was by my taking them to the local Catholic church.

The girls were probably four and six. They hated church. I wasn't that comfortable myself, as a result of some ghostly hangover from my childhood, when our Irish maids were Catholic. Because we were taught to see all our servants as characters in our family's colorful narrative, I thought of Mary as my friend, free of religious disadvantage. But when, at the age of nine, I attended her wedding to Pat in a huge, architecturally overwrought D.C. cathedral, I was shocked by the operatic soprano aria. It seemed in terrible taste, and I was haunted by aesthetic unease as I sat in a pew at Holy Comforter in Charlottesville, trying to shush my complaining children.

When I tried to take the girls to an Episcopalian church, they also protested. They said God was boring, and they had a point. Also, I lacked whatever it was that some mothers had, the authority or grouchiness or grit just to push them into Sunday school no matter what the little heathens thought. So as if I were giving them the biggest free pass ever, I said they didn't have to go to church, but we would read the Bible together on Sunday mornings. That was a disaster. We hadn't even gotten through Genesis, when my oldest daughter, Maud, figured out she was going to die. She might have been alerted by God's telling the serpent that it would eat dust for the rest of its days. She could have confused it with "biting the dust," which conceivably she'd heard in cartoons. Doesn't matter. Maud saw what she was facing, and then she told her younger sister, Nell, that she would die, too. There was enough wailing and tearing of hair and gnashing of teeth to wake their father.

"Who will feed us?" Nell wanted to know as he joined us in his bathrobe. "Does God know where I keep my clothes?"

She took a breath and then came through with the killer, "Will we all die together?"

Their dad brought up their grandmother, who'd died a year

before. Apparently, he intended to argue from nature. Death wasn't bad, he explained gently, it was natural. I could have told him that he was making a mistake.

He had given the children tremendous new purchase on the abyss. Their eyes lit up. Maud made herself cry just by saying "Grandma," a family member who they had previously thought had *uniquely* passed away. Now they understood that after "Grandma," the deluge: their father, mother, uncles, aunts, themselves! On and on. It seemed like we were grief counseling round the clock to get them to eat and go to bed. Their father, the lapsed Catholic whose responsibility this whole crisis was, finally came up with the idea that when we died, we'd all go into God's brain. Perhaps because there was such a high value on being smart in our house, Maud and Nell began to calm down again. There were dark problems ahead, to be sure, but they at least had the confidence of knowing the smartest Being in the universe was on the case.

The experience taught me that a little religious exposure was a terrible thing for the ignorant. Our children would now never get more of it. Meanwhile, this unacceptable brush with their deaths poured gas on my personal eternal flame. Fear of my own death always burned inside me, often uncontrollably, most uncontrollably when I met new people at big, noisy parties. We'd be smiling and yelling to be heard over the roar, chopping the air with our hands, trying to signal some great individuality of our own, some special reason to stand out in a room of automatons gesticulating cheerlessly. We might disappear at any moment, and here we were breaking invisible rocks in an ant farm. Why weren't these strangers screaming? Why wasn't I?

Now fear of my children's deaths magnified my fear of my own by a factor of a trillion. If I let the thought enter my mind for a second, I had to move quickly to get away from it. But I would have lost the power to walk. I felt like my legs were disappearing one at a time. I'd put a shoe on the ground; my foot, followed by my ankle, calf, and knee, slowly went into quicksand. I was on a dusty moon without a space suit. I had to will my other foot forward, though it, too, began to disappear. It took about a day to get across the front hall to the door. Given the threat that those I loved and I myself were living under, this sort of slow motion did not seem deluded. The basic facts of life and death were insane. I understood men who thought they were receiving messages from aliens through their gold fillings. I was envious of them. I wished any extraterrestrial anything would contact me. I called on my childhood God. I'd repressed him so deeply, He sent no answer. That's when my adult searching began.

I was familiar with the Dalai Lama's caution to American students of Buddhism: People "should stay in their own tradition." Though I had grown increasingly mystified by Christ and could not believe he was actually God's son, I got that there was a Christian tradition. My roots made me part of it. I was some kind of a Christian, though I clearly wasn't going to be a Catholic. I stuck my nose back into the Episcopalian church for a more serious second look. This was the 1970s. The church was heavily focused on social justice. Of course that was good. I, too, wanted to end war, save minorities, and found a nonprofit to end all nonprofits. But what about death? I wanted a person of God to stand up there and describe how terrifying human disappearance was. I wanted Bosch's *Garden of Earthly Delights*, Dante's *Inferno*, Sartre's *No Exit*. I wanted to be convinced that the minister truly understood death and its horrifying implications. Then I wanted my clergy to show me with equal imagination and intensity how their God was equal to the task of conquering death, suffering, and nothingness. Maud and Nell were right. The sermons were boring. Still, I clung to the hope that I'd find life in them. I went back several times until a well-meaning, scruffy youngster stood in the pulpit and explained the crucifixion this way: "Pontius Pilate had turned the thermostat back to zero on Jesus." This boy preacher thought God was in the forced air-heating system. No, no, it was too awful, much more terrifying than I'd realized.

I gave up finding help in the church of my childhood. I started a slow mosey through the menu of contemporary religious offerings. Over the years, I tried the Unitarian Church (too cool) and the ecstatic Protestants (too hot). Though I was a wavering Christian, I found when I studied Zen that the longer I meditated, the more I wanted to pray; the more I wanted to pray, the less I had to say. At some point, a friend introduced me to the Pathwork, a group in nearby Madison County that formed around Eva Pierrakos, a channel with a Jewish background. She had died in 1979, only a few years before. From every report,

Eva, the daughter of the novelist Jakob Wassermann, whose circle included Thomas Mann, was a fascinating person. Eva's family fled to Switzerland to escape the anti-Semitic brutalities of World War II. She studied with Jung, discovered her gifts in automatic writing, studied dance, and moved to the United States, where she met her husband, John Pierrakos. He was a psychiatrist involved in core energetic body work; and once Eva integrated his theories, she was ready to be a vehicle for the Guide. This was a far-seeing and rather educated entity that spoke to Eva during her trance states. Some of the people carrying on her work in Madison County had attended the actual lectures on psychosexual-spiritual growth, which Eva's Guide delivered in lower Manhattan during the late 1950s.

Her friends were cosmopolitan, intelligent, attractive; they made Eva feel so close, I was almost overwhelmed by the vulnerability of the whole enterprise—its vulnerability, that is, to satire. I found the idea of a non-insane person sitting in a straight-backed chair, as Eva reportedly did, slowly closing her eyes, letting her breath change, and then speaking in the voice of her channel . . . Well, I found it funny on the verge of heartbreaking. Yet the laughter that often tickled the back of my throat like an unfulfilled sneeze had no edge. The pain that came into my heart was very tender and protective, and I had to admit that I rather admired Eva and her followers for wearing their off-the-wall faith in the supernatural on their sleeves.

Somewhat later, as I read about Joseph Smith for the first time, his story infected me with some of the same feelings I'd felt for Eva, though multiplied many times over. The joy he gave made me feel hilarity on the verge of divine ecstasy. It didn't at first occur to me that this way might lie actual belief. In truth, at the end of making the film, when I was stopped in traffic by the head-splitting revelation I've described, it took a moment for me to realize those dire feelings of misery had anything to do with the God of joy. The God I met on the road to Richmond came at me with a vengeance, shape-shifting into another Joseph Smith. This Joseph was dark as well as funny, electric as a live fish, surrounded by skulls: ironic. In a matter of moments I knew my death. I heard the reassurance about the afterlife, and I also thought to my horror, *I am having a conversion.*

THREE

The Angel, the Plates, and the Power of Joseph's Charms

I *am having a conversion?* I'd had other thunderclaps like this before. They were serious business, like the whack a Zen master gives his student, telling him to wake up. Practice is serious! It's your life! I'd gone through mine experiencing such whacks: *This is the man I'm going to marry! That's the right therapist for me! I'm going to write a novel about Lenin's wife!* I respected these thunderclap whacks. I'd used them as guides during the disruptions of life in the particle accelerator. But *I'm having a conversion?* I was certainly having something. I well knew nothing might come in its wake, but deep down I also sensed that conversion might be my type. A friend of mine once told me I "wanted the meaning of life for breakfast." She felt it was "a problem," since I never finally seemed to get the full answers I craved. The desire to know the ultimate was the reason I'd been married, gone through therapy, and written a novel about Lenin's wife. I wasn't completely surprised to find myself gripped by the idea of conversion. Weirdly or happily, despite all the differences between Joseph's time and mine, there was a timeless attraction to conversion, which the prophet and I probably shared. In my day as in his, "Conversion was an experience. It was not simply something that people believed—though belief or faith was essential to it—but something that happened to them, a real, intensely emotional event they went through and experienced as a profound psychological transformation that left them with a fundamentally altered sense of self."

I definitely had something I wanted from religion and Joseph was religion red in tooth and claw. His story consisted of every primitive thing that went into the start of a religion: the big bang moment of God exploding through matter; an unlikely innocent's unlikely report of the event; the instant blowback from deadbeat hoi polloi and spiritual heavy hitters. A barroom brawl for pious people erupts; yet when the prophet dies, the supernatural uproar moves into the hands of bureaucrats, who form an enduring church task force. Joseph's founding of Mormonism is a laboratory of every attracting and puzzling facet of religion. Can God be felt only by innocents? Or does He fly in willy-nilly? Is there faith without the supernatural? Can a person be free and religious, too? If you do believe, do you have to go to church? If I was having a conversion, could it only be through knowing Joseph Smith? Yes. I had to trust this man, figure out whether I was responding to a truth in him or just out gallivanting with the outrageous. My feelings were like those I'd previously felt for a beloved who stood for some buried part of myself. I didn't imagine that knowing Joseph was going help me surface my inner prophet. I did feel I would never have such a personally compelling chance to resolve my feelings about God.

Yet all I'd ever have was his admittedly rich, exhausting paper trail. No actual lovers' quarrels, no adolescent, all-night self-disclosure or postmortem meta-conversations to give me his explanation for the mad controversy surrounding him. I was going to have to write Joseph's biography—but it would have to be an autobiographical biography. His life and my conversion were inseparable. My portrait of Joseph would cast a shadow in whatever shape my conversion finally took. I would need to mix pieces of his portrait with pieces of my own, mingling his history with my personal emotion, running his religious growth along a parallel track of my own, starting with his childhood.

If only Mark Twain had written a book about the young Joseph! Our greatest humorist might be known for his impudent attitude toward God and a number of immortal jokes at the Mormons' expense. But his droll, poetic tone would be perfect for capturing Joseph's youthful path to God. Open the books anywhere in Joseph's childhood: you can't miss the boy's resemblance to Tom and Huck. In upstate New York, where the Smiths finally settle, the sun's just up in the great American morning. Nature is buzzing with creatures, plants, and every promise. There's no more state religion. God belongs to Everyman now. The hidden world is teeming with spirits, some friendly, some not, all signs pointing the way on the pilgrim path. There's an angel behind every blade of grass, urging it to "Grow! Grow!"

Before the reign of science and its four trillion facts, in the delightful anarchy of Joseph's boyhood, many adults were still children. For both Joseph Sr. and Joseph Jr. the unseen was as much a stomping ground for angels as for dead Indian kings and Captain Kidd's gold treasure that was said to be buried in the banks of the New York's Susquehanna River. But a man didn't have to go so far to find barrels and barrels of gold in Palmyra. Joseph Sr. had visions of barrels in Hill Cumorah and trunks of gold in his neighbors' backyards. Between father and son, Joseph Jr. may have been more grown-up about these kinds of visions. As a friend said of him, he does not "pretend that he sees them (spirits and angels) with his natural but his spiritual eyes; and he says he can see them as well with his eyes shut, as with them open."

The Smiths shared their neighbors' worldview, but they weren't like other families. The Smiths were more alive than Tom Sawyer's proper Aunt Polly and more stable than Huck's hideous father. In spite of the Smiths' poverty, they were remarkably close and affectionate. They were quirky, very individual, yet they weren't particularly competitive with one another. The father was a poet, and the mother a heroine. Lucy Smith was a vital, supportive, tough woman. Her biography of her son is a gem. She first called the book *The History of Mother Smith, by Herself.* Not a shy title, but one showing glad pride in her own sterling qualities and all she'd lived through. First published in 1853, the book was renamed for a new edition prepared by the church in 1901. Now it was called *History of Joseph Smith, By His Mother, Lucy Mack Smith.* In print, a touch of her artless self-regard had been subdued. Nonetheless, I surmise that her children had the advantage of growing up with a mother who didn't doubt herself, one who wouldn't criticize her child any more than she would find fault with her own dear person. If Lucy loved you, she was insulted if you didn't love you, too.

Perhaps her rose-tinted glasses kept her from writing much about her husband's magic practices. Other erudite sources make it clear that Joseph Sr. raised their boys with an excellent education in looking for treasure, right along with readings from scripture. As Michael Quinn observes in *Early Mormonism and the Magic World View*, "Magic and treasure-seeking were an integral part of the Smith family's religious quest." From early on, Joseph Sr. and Joseph Jr. worked together. The father had divining rods that trembled when they sensed gold. Then he would circle the place with witch hazel sticks to ward off evil spirits. Not that he found much that way—if anything. Joseph Sr. also believed in the power of peep stones to locate treasure, but he didn't have much luck with them, either. Peep stones were unusually shaped or colored stones that, although completely opaque, had powers of special sight in the hands of the right person. Joseph Sr. had embarrassed himself more than once by putting a magic stone in his hat and then his face in afterward (according to a method used by other well-respected scryers). He'd see treasure in the stones, but not where it was hidden. The method had not been good to him, but Joseph Jr. used it to greater and greater avail as he developed.

Gradually, the boy's reputation outshone his father's and

older brothers'. Joseph's abilities did not create hard feelings among the men. But Joseph Jr. suffered when his father acted below his proper dignity—as when the older man made a fool of himself in public after he'd taken too much whiskey on board. I think fondly of one such occasion when Joseph Sr. went around throwing spells down the barrels of his friends' guns at a turkey shoot. Hard to tell exactly what he had in mind. Wanted to get all the birds for himself? Wanted no birds to be shot at all?

The boy had always somehow known he would have to carry his beloved Pa, and maybe his whole hard-luck family, but that was fine with him. He understood he had mysterious gifts. Joseph had his father's deep religious feeling, and his "cheery, good nature" attracted love. Maybe it was because he himself loved others so easily. Maybe it was because he had such a way with words. He didn't know spelling, couldn't read well. He was ignorant, but had a rich imagination. His stories spilled out of him in prayer and necromancy. He needed the first as much as he needed the second. When he prayed, the magic happened; when he put his face in his hat for a group of greedy treasure seekers, he felt his power.

All his life, God came to the boy when he prayed. He had come as a voice, as light, as a being. Then the day in the grove, God terrified him by appearing in a shaft of radiance. Joseph often played that experience in his mind. It changed so that sometimes it seemed that only God had been bathed in the great light. Sometimes it seemed that there were angels. Sometimes

God was there together with his Son. The important thing never changed, though. Joseph's prayer *had been* answered, and not in a small way. He had asked for a sign, and he, Joseph Smith, Jr., had a vision. There were people who didn't believe him. But they didn't matter. His peep stone had brought him followers. These men looked at him in a way that made the boy feel like he had treasure written all over him. That made him do things he regretted, as I imagine him burying the tail feather ahead of a certain meeting with a pack of local gold diggers.

When he met with the men, Joseph could just about see them licking their chops over the gold he'd help them find in the earth. He kept cool, so cool he almost made himself laugh. He stared quietly into his hat at his peep stone, from which so many blessings had flowed. He dragged the performance out until he could feel his audience quivering with the suspense. Then Joseph looked up into the trusting eyes of these grown men and very quietly, with an almost scholarly precision, told them where to dig. *But!* he cried, stopping them with an artfully raised finger, when they dug, they would know for sure they were at the right spot *because*, as the good Josiah Stowel told the Brainbridge court in 1826, they'd find a certain tail feather marking just where the treasure chest was buried. When they dug, *all* they found was the feather. Joseph couldn't believe what they were saying. He stuck his face in his hat one more time. When he emerged, the boy sounded *shocked*, terribly, terribly shocked to report that an evil spirit made the money move down out of reach at the last moment. The men looked at one another with amazement, shaking their heads and murmuring over the kid's talent.

His successes went to his head. Joseph admitted this in his prayers, yet he couldn't see the harm in playing games for money. Once in a while he actually found an old coin or two. He did better than most treasure diggers. It wasn't impossible, though, that some of the other things he did might be considered sinful. Ever since God appeared to him in the grove, he was easily bored by ordinary digging. Boredom made him show off in front of Sally Chase. He told her and her brother, Willard, that there was gold under the ground in their backyard. When Joseph started to dig, he actually saw the precious metal a few feet down. God was close to him then, he knew that. But when Joseph dug farther and came up with nothing, he saw Sally suppressing a smile. She must be in love with him! Well, if she wasn't, she would be by the time he was finished.

Joseph laid down his shovel with a self-important sigh. He told Sally the gold was embedded in such a way that he would need to sacrifice an animal. They'd all seen a traveling necromancer do that recently before bringing up his treasure. Sally dipped her head with mild, flirty mockery. Her doubt inspired Joseph. He called his powers of persuasion to him as he walked over to the sheep pen where her father was standing by the fence. Joseph revealed to him that he'd found a treasure so valuable only a blood sacrifice could ensure success. Sally's father was a bigger fool than Joseph realized. He *offered* him the family's black sheep. It wasn't the boy's fault, was it, that her Pa gave up the bad-luck sheep so willingly? Joseph took the sheep in circles around the place where he'd been digging. He waved a rusty sword he'd inherited from a traveling necromancer and chanted stuff he'd heard the older magician use. The poor sheep began to look over at the boy as if to say, "Who's the dumb one here, lad?" The look wounded Joseph deeply. What he did next was wrong, and he knew it. But he'd gone too far to stop. He slit the sheep's throat and let the blood drip over the place where the gold was buried. Sally watched with a look of disgust in her eyes. He felt nothing but misery as he went back and dug, dug, dug, but found nothing. He felt so low, he could not speak, could not lift his head though Sally called out a faint "Good-bye" as she and her brother left Joseph at his hopeless task. He could hear their laughter as they moved off. He forbade what felt like tears to leave his eyelids. When he looked up and saw Sally and Willard had gone into their farmhouse, Joseph threw the shovel on the ground, muttering for anyone who might be listening: The gold had been charmed away by a king in a cave in Cumorah!

For months to come, Joseph asked forgiveness on his knees before bedtime. He begged God to understand that he meant to do nothing "malignant," but had only shown "the weakness" of youth. He knew he had been guilty of "levity," and he used that grandiose word because it carried a little of the real seriousness of his crime. He was guilty of having fun at others' expense. Worse, he who felt that magic was a form of God's work, a way of discerning things unseen, he, Joseph Smith, Jr., had used magic for improper, unreligious ends. As he prayed, he blushed with the memory of the tail feather, which after all was just an innocent prank compared with killing the poor sheep. In that, he'd shown a wicked willfulness at utter odds with the character appropriate to one who was called of God as he was.

Along with forgiveness, the boy pleaded night after anxious night for another manifestation such as he had received in the grove. It didn't have to be so sensational. It could be a mouse, a tiny mouse of a manifestation, a mosquito of one. Joseph went for days without the Lord's reassurance. He had betrayed his call. And then, just when he believed his soul was doomed to be a shriveled prune, the heavens opened and it poured. He could not believe what was happening. The room was filled with light. There was a being there in the room with him. When God and Jesus appeared to him in the grove, they had obviously been otherworldly creatures. The being now presenting itself was as real as his brothers, so real in a human sense that Joseph looked at the beds around him to check who among the boys was playing a trick on him. All of his brothers were asleep in their beds.

Then the being told Joseph he was the angel Moroni. Joseph could hardly breathe. He was faint of heart, yet somehow not surprised in the moment. He knew he was meant for something marvelous. He prayed for the strength to bear what was happening as the angel told him that God did have a work for him, one that would nourish *the entire world*! There were gold plates in the message, a history book written by the ancient people. It was a book so wonderful that it contained the Savior's account of the gospel as he'd told it to the bygone authors!

Yet the boy could not just go out and dig up the plates. By now, the strain on his courage made Joseph wonder if he could stay on his feet while the angel went on giving instructions. The boy's attention was waning. The first time through, he grasped that he must not seek the plates with an idea of getting rich. Then he felt so dizzy, he fell back on his bed. Later, when he came to, Moroni was not there. Joseph feared he would not come again. But the angel returned and repeated his message a second time. Joseph strained to hear what he had missed before. Now he heard that he should not seek the plates for his own personal gain, but also that he must grow in worthiness until he was ready to go and dig them up. Once again, Joseph grew dizzy and fell onto his bed. The angel came three times that night to deliver his message, and by the third time the boy was finally prepared to hear and absorb all his words. When the light of the last visitation faded, dawn was breaking.

Joseph's life had been changed in ways almost beyond his ability to bear. He embraced his work, though it made him feel terribly alone. He understood what he was meant to do; and it seemed entirely beyond him. He feared that he would never feel lost in simple boyhood joy again. The burden of his new mission weighed on him so heavily, he followed Moroni's instructions and told his father and mother and finally all his siblings. The whole family was transformed by the story of

Joseph's God-sent destiny. There were many cautions among
the Smiths about keeping Joseph's news secret, and many promises to be mute. There were also many slips. Not to single out
anyone in particular, but Joseph Sr. may have slipped first, then
again and again. He was said to have boasted to the neighbors
about his son finding a "gold Bible" and of visits to Joseph by
a Spirit. He apparently could not keep himself from telling
how the Spirit instructed Joseph to dress in black clothes and
borrow a black horse to go and get the plates. Joseph Sr.'s vivid
imagination struck a chord with other men, who spread the
word to still others, who carried the stories north, south, east,
and west.

As a writer, trying to capture the sacred irreverence of
Joseph's youth, I felt more and more forlorn that Mark Twain was
the only writer who could have really wrangled the rambunc-
tious young prophet into print. Technically, Mark Twain and
Joseph Smith were born about a generation apart (the former's
dates are 1835–1910; the latter's are 1805–1844). But their fron-
tiers weren't that different. Twain's gallery of American boys just
wasn't complete without young Joseph Smith. There was Tom,
the conventional boy with a gorgeous imagination and heart, and
there was his "antithesis," Huck, the wounded outsider with a
soul. But Joseph, the religious visionary with no regard for the
rules, was another iconic American type, a combination of both
boys and more. Just imagine how Tom and Huck would have
taken to Joseph's magic practices! And once Joseph started talking about gold plates, an angel, and the possibility of his writing

a new Gold Bible, Tom and Huck would have been all ears as the reports of Joseph's successes made their way into the Midwest.

Very soon Tom and Huck were seething with envy. I know because I finally had to write them into the story myself. They were a little older than they were in the books that would make them famous. Those books still had to be written. But Tom and Huck had such good feelings about their own talents that they got really sick of hearing about Joseph's stardom. They finally jumped a boat going east so they could meet the competition and see for themselves what he was like. In Palmyra, Tom and Huck soon began to look around Main Street for someone who could give them information. Just then, sauntering their way, they saw a rather handsome youth dressed in ragged clothes with a battered old hat on his head. He walked right up to the new boys to find out about what had brought them into town. Tom asked him if he knew Joseph Smith. The stranger said he did not, but wondered why Tom wanted to talk to him.

Tom said, "We kept hearing about him in Missouri where we're from. We'd like to get hold of one of those peep stones he uses to get gold."

The stranger said, "How about the angel Moroni?"

Tom laughed. "We heard about Macaroni, too."

"You heard about the angel Macaroni all the way out in Missouri?"

"All the way acrost Missouri, in Hannibal," Huck said.

"Never heard of Hannibal," the stranger said kindly. "But

you've heard of Joe Smith and Palmyra. Now I'd say that's making a name for yourself. I guess you won't mind if I tell you I'm Joseph Smith."

At first, when Joseph stuck out his hand, they wouldn't shake it. "Ah, c'mon," Joseph said. "You'd have done the same in my place." The boys knew he was right. So they gave up their grudge and shook hands with Joseph, who said he'd show them Hill Cumorah.

That's how they got started off in the poetic light of early evening. Took no time before Tom gave an account of himself, mainly a summary of how he wanted to start his own business, one that would help put Hannibal on the map and give his friends jobs. Huck said Tom needed money because he wanted to marry. Huck himself could never marry; he could never even hold a steady job, but that didn't mean he didn't have a soul. He thought maybe that was supposed to be his life's work, the care and feeding of his soul. It was job enough to keep himself out of prison, dreaming dreams that other men gave up without realizing what they'd lost till their lives were almost gone.

The boys came to a lovely dimpled slope of Hill Cumorah. They sat down in a row in rising moonlight. Tom rolled a cigarette and passed it around. Sitting on the uphill side of the hollow, Joseph leaned back and pulled a bottle half full with whiskey from under a rock. The messy cigarette and whiskey went around the circle while Joseph got started on his own story. Tom and Huck had never met any boy like him! He had as much trouble in church as Tom himself. But with all his searching for God and

using any means, Joseph might have outdone Huck when it came
to bending the rules for a higher purpose.

"I've wanted money just like you two. But I bet you'd never
say it's all you wanted. Even if it had been, I put everything on
the table when I went into the grove and prayed, asking God to
tell me what church was true. I was practically murdered by
some demon before I got an answer. This was no dream. I really
thought I'd be dead if I didn't fight for my life. Next thing I knew,
God's shining down on me and Christ's with him. That's when
he told me all the churches were wrong. I was going to have to
start a new one."

"Well," said Tom, blowing smoke rings, "he gave you a break
there. If you make up your own church, you could keep the
service to a minimum."

"This is bigger than that. I'm starting a new religion."

Silence fell. Both Tom and Huck took hits from the whiskey
bottle. Soft whistles. Tom asked if Joseph needed investors. Joseph said no thanks, but maybe down the road. Huck asked
about the demon "what nearly killed you." Joseph swore he hadn't
been back. Since the hour in the grove, the angel Moroni had
come to his bedroom, not just once, but three times, and each
time he told Joseph about gold plates buried at the top of Hill
Cumorah.

"Are they there now?" Tom asked.

Joseph nodded.

"Well, what are we waiting for?" the young entrepreneur
wanted to know.

Joseph said he'd take them to the place, but they couldn't look at the plates. Some years before, he'd broken his promise not to touch them until he was morally ready. "I was greedy. I went to take the plates out to sell. I dug them up, but when I tried to take them away, I got a terrible shock. A toad the size of a man struck me with a rusty sword."

Tom burst out laughing, "What had you been drinking?"

Huck cut in, "Or dreaming."

Joseph pulled Huck to his feet. "You think you're such a big deal loafing around with your soul. C'mon, Tom. I think there's a reason you boys turned up here tonight. You boys are still praying your whiskers are going to grow. Meanwhile, I'm facing my biggest test ever. God wants you to understand there's more to being a man than boasting and spitting. There's more to life than the world. There's heaven and earth. Heaven! Heaven and earth!" he cried.

Tom and Huck weren't having any less fun because of Joseph's turn to the serious. Watching his unsteady progress up the hill, their hearts swelled with affection. Prophet he might be, but he was their kind of prophet. They followed Joseph to a well-hidden spot at the top of Hill Cumorah. Suddenly he spread his arms to forbid them from going any farther.

"The plates are here!" he murmured.

Tom and Huck peered over Joseph's spread-eagled arms. They could see a few moldy old boulders, a bush or two, a faint path that might have been made by deer.

"Aren't you going to show 'em to us?" Tom asked.

"You'd die if I did."

Joseph gave each boy a candle. Tom lit them as Joseph sank to his knees. They must hold the lit candle in one hand and put their free hand over the flame, not close, but enough to feel the heat while they took a solemn oath. Tom and Huck respected solemn oaths more than anything, especially ones pledged under a moon late at night. Joseph began to pray, "When the great book of history is written, all the pages of all the books will flow into one. As you leave, remember this sacred night we spent together. But you must be ready to keep this secret almost until your deathbeds. Later when the word goes out that Christ's restoration is real, stand by me against my enemies. When you hear me reviled, stand by the work of Joseph Smith Junior. Recall to them how we were once free fellows together and that I was a regular boy like both of you. If you do this for me, the great Author of all events will record your testimony. And tonight I ask that He also situate you in a front-row seat for the Judgment."

When Joseph was done, the young prophet seemed exhausted. He might have even slept there on the ground, but Tom and Huck put his arms around their shoulders and slowly wended their way back to the Smith family cabin. When they saw he was safely inside, the boys took off on their own to find a place to sleep. They found an old shed filled with hay. It was warm in there, and they made themselves so comfortable they would have smoked again if the place was not such a fire hazard. They made do with what was left in the whiskey bottle. They had much to say about Joseph's gifts and the gold plates. It was hard for them to get beyond their enthusiasm for Joseph's imaginative audacity. Why hadn't they ever known about seer stones? They rued all the time they'd wasted before they'd heard about treasure digging. What a boy this Joseph was with his big heart and brains and humor. Tom and Huck howled over "the toad with a rusty sword." They laughed until happy tears ran down their cheeks, and after they quieted down a while, they made themselves laugh and cry again by reminding each other how "the toad the size of a man struck Joseph with a rusty sword."

Well, finally they were laughed out and knew they couldn't put off the problem any longer. Huck was the one to bring it up. He'd been in what you might call bigger moral trouble than Tom, and he knew how a boy's goodness could get all turned around upside down and backward when he was trying to do something a little too big for his britches. Huck said he worried that Joseph had painted himself into a corner. How could he ever make good on his promise to deliver the plates?

That was the end of sleep for Tom and Huck. They were up for hours turning over Joseph's fix.

Huck said, "You can't pray a lie. I know that."

Tom said, "When he looks inside his soul, he's imagining as often as he's praying."

Huck said, "Maybe he did see the plates on a night like this—under a moon that made things seem different than they really are."

Tom said, "If he didn't see them for real, he's going to catch it."

They went round and round on that point of Joseph's imagination, the inside and the outside of it, and whether the plates really existed. Whether Joseph could restore the days of Christ like he said. It got to be dawn before they reminded each other that Joseph had said the gold plates were "thin as tin." It made sense: his father was a cooper, wasn't he, among his other trades? There must be tin lying around for making barrel hoops and sap buckets. Maybe all of Joseph's talk about history had been a hint. A big hint! It had been his way of saying he needed some help here, help the boys knew they could give him. If they worked fast, they could collect enough tin to cut out a model and bury it on the top of Hill Cumorah in the place where Joseph had shown them the plates were!

I felt I should now leave Tom and Huck, drawing a curtain of tact across this sensitive moment—one which has shaped the lives of literally millions of people at home and around the globe. Whatever Tom and Huck decided that night, I knew they did it from affection and compassion for their gifted Joseph's plight. After the solemn oath, they were friends forever. My tale should have ended here—except I tarried. I couldn't resist going around town listening in on conversations among the townsfolk about their homegrown prophet. People were very even in their yeas and nays, as passionately for Joseph Smith as against him. There wasn't even agreement on what the young man looked like or if he was intelligent.

Before I finally departed, I was irresistibly tempted to go back to Hill Cumorah. I don't know exactly why. I really didn't want to know what Tom and Huck had done. I didn't want to be responsible. But my wish was not granted. I'd gone about a quarter of the way up the hill when I began to hear shouting and the sound of saplings being snapped and bushes overrun. And soon enough, Tom and Huck came stumbling into the clearing, panicked and distraught, their faces white and eyes like fried eggs. Their desperation told me they'd met with some overwhelming power at the top of Hill Cumorah. It was as if Tom and Huck, survivors of so many mortal terrors, had pushed too far and wakened Yahweh where he slept. As they raced by me, I could just make out their frightened words. They were screaming over and over, "Run, run, get away while you can. There's a toad with a rusty sword. We were struck by a toad the size of a man . . . with a rusty sword. . . . A toad man, rusty sword, struck . . ."

FOUR

La Vita Nuova

In my happiest memories of my childhood, part of me seemed to have a toe in the America of Tom and Huck. Those holy hours have never been extinguished. Even now I feel a part of me is Tom and Huck's age. In the summers after we got out of grade school, even after we moved to Washington, D.C., our mother would take us to our family's converted barn on Narragansett Bay in Saunderstown, Rhode Island. The property was part of an old Colonial plantation where as children we had everything we could ever want: a bull in the upper meadows, a pine forest with an owl, a slave graveyard, and a circular stone structure as tall as a man in the lower woods. (We sometimes smoked there because all the mothers told us not to.)

There was always a gang of children seemingly between six and eleven. No babies, no teenagers. There were wars between boys and girls and cliques that came and went. But occasionally we ended up in the large meadow above the original farmhouse at sunset. It was filled with huge boulders laid out like sleeping elephants. Trees hid the road. Some loving spirit cohered, and we played a game we made up as we went along. It was a pastime with no rules, with vaguely stirring, constantly shifting goals like capture the flag without a flag. Plots abounded and were confounded or maybe not as couriers returned from the slave graveyard with new rumors of some mysterious excitement. Every bit of stealth, every ounce of valor was hallowed by unseen angels affirming the great urgency of it all. We were part of a vast beauty, baptized by golden evening sunlight. We weren't any age in particular; we were children in general. We had powers beyond any grades we earned in school. We were part of a great design. The air on our skin was religious. As C. S. Lewis wrote in *Mere Christianity*, that early joy is "not a deception." In such stuff oceanic feeling resides, and from it believers like Lewis feel the new life of conversion is supposed to come.

Joseph had blasted me back in touch with my sacred roots of joy. I just wondered how I could follow up. Whether I could go the distance. Be whole in awe and terror. Grow something magnificent from my personal cutting of deep childhood joy. You heard about people doing such a thing. But that conversion also meant death and rebirth, some sort of huge interior reconciliation, which seemed beyond me even as I set off in its direction. I'd be lucky just to get my ball of religious dough to rise. Maybe I could handle going from natural life to spiritual life. That seemed possible.

Though I'd never watched anyone close to me find God, Saul's sudden conversion felt incredibly familiar. His story of out-of-the-blue rapid change was practically in the water supply. "The road to Damascus" had always been a cliché I depended on, and it may have been some unconscious model for my own near-conversion experience on the road to Richmond. William James believed Saul's kind of "crisis" conversion was the most "interesting" kind, more interesting than Saint Augustine's long and winding path to his final commitment to a new Christian life. James devoted more space to crisis conversions in his enduringly fascinating *Varieties of Religious Experience*, though many of his testimonies were by people who knew enough about Christianity to know what to do once the first wave of intensity had passed. I did not. I was ignorant.

My tatterdemalion credentials drew me closer to Joseph. Most people I knew treated him like a terrible scandal, though a lot of these people, many of them my good friends, really didn't know much of anything at all about the frontier seer. Most secular intellectuals lined up behind Christopher Hitchens, rolling his eyes in *Slate* and snidely dismissing Joseph Smith as "a fraud and conjurer well known to the authorities in upstate New York." Pronounced on the eve of Romney's second run as a presidential candidate, Hitchens's comments made me feel he hadn't read anything new about Smith or his church since the 1980s. Though I hadn't found much deep feeling for Joseph in the Mormon rank and file and too much hagiography in church-produced biographies, there was a long, noble history of Mormon intellectuals extending the research and struggling to come to terms with their prophet's complex nature. Not to confuse Jesus with Joseph, just to compare their biographical trajectories for a moment: Christ's life has been so swarmed with commentary, the *feel* of religion has all but been squeezed out of it for me. Joseph's life still simmers in the vital, chaotic, wondrous aftermath of his big bang encounter with God. The facts about Joseph are still being unearthed; and as messy as Joseph continues to be, he's still in on the *mysterium tremendum*.

Loosely speaking, Joseph's life divides into two parts: his youth, which culminates in the Book of Mormon, and his maturity as the volatile leader of his new church. Biographers of Joseph agree about the basic circumstances of his developing years. He's a cheerful, mischievous boy. When he is eight, a life-threatening surgery on his infected shinbone leaves him with a permanent limp. The family spends more time reading the Bible than going to church. The Smiths are surrounded by revivals, self-dramatizing prophets, and many emotional conversions. Joseph's uneducated but has "a fertile imagination" and a "meditative" mind. No stranger to the appeal of dead Indians and gold, Joseph goes after them with magic stones. God is also calling him to a great work through dramatic visions. The boy moves back and forth between his earthly quest and his divine one. Gradually, though, he sets his magical pursuits aside for transforming experiences with the angel Moroni, the gold plates, and the Book of Mormon. Depending on whether writers shade the basic account toward the dark or the light, Joseph becomes a cynic or a visionary, a money grubber or a religious seeker, a fraud or a prophet of God.

There are no reports of Joseph as a boy from his boyhood itself. His childhood exists only in memoirs or retrospective journals, his own included. Joseph did not keep a diary during the extravagant years when he was coming of age. Those were years when Joseph was becoming a prophet without having the slightest idea how one would operate in his own day. He was basing himself on the Old Testament prophets, but he didn't really know how they operated, either. He finally started a journal in November 1832. He was twenty-seven. As soon as he started a journal, he wrote entries recalling his prophetic story: his hour in the grove when God appeared to him; the angel's visit and his revelation of the gold plates; his digging up the Nephite record; his translating it with the help of spectacles prepared by the Lord. Joseph understood the need to present a particular self in his journal. He wasn't so sure of the art, since he left contradictory accounts of some key events. Much is made of his contradictions, especially those involving the First Vision. Sometimes Christ is in the grove with God, sometimes he's not. Forgiveness of sin matters, then it doesn't in another version. Joseph's mention of specific revivals on different dates skews the official chronology.

There are eight versions of the First Vision, the first in 1832, the last in 1843. The official version is the one written in 1838 and appears in the *History of the Church* and was canonized as scripture in 1880. Over the years, the First Vision went through drafts in Joseph's mind. His artistic human imagination was so often in view that Fawn Brodie believed Joseph missed his calling as a great novelist. But for her, this precluded a religious calling. She did not consider that while scripture may be God's personal genre, it, too, must be written by a particular person in history. And that person in this case was Joseph Smith, prophet of God and Promethean improv artist. He tried his story one way and then another. It's never finished in his journal.

When Joseph published his "official" account of the First Vision, which differed from the story he'd told around town, his detractors jumped on him for being a liar. Storytelling requires certain dishonesties: articulating, shaping, polishing among them. That Joseph would be a fabulator isn't so surprising. The frontier was full of fabulation and people riffing on it. But it was amazing that the nearly illiterate Joseph was a *writer*, that the stories he told were destined for the page. From the beginning, his story of his place in God's universe was very bold: Joseph prayed for the truth and God appeared to him. That Christ came and went at all in the boy's experience was extraordinary, until we watch him become a prophet who alters Christ's role absolutely in the Book of Mormon. Before Joseph was capable of that, he served a long apprenticeship in living the double life of a writer, a person whose experience sometimes ran parallel to his imagination, and sometimes was a product of his imagination.

From his early teenage years on, he'd enjoyed some sort of overwhelming inner upwelling of words and religious visions. Gradually he began to tell people around him the story about what he was going through with God. But he always had more inside him than he could express. That he dared express it at all was marvelous. Once he began, he must have realized that bringing it out meant that more came. There were years when the word was made flesh through him. Print poured into his hat. Somehow he received a book of revolutionary scripture. His revelations began then, too, haltingly—one here, one there, gaining steam, so people around him wrote them down.

We have his stream-of-consciousness account of the angel's visit in his 1832 diary entry called "A History of the Life of Joseph Smith." When we compare it with the "official" 1838 version in the *History of the Church*, we can see how much Joseph had learned about writing his personal story. (The Book of Mormon, his history of Christ, was published in 1830.) The first description was an unpunctuated jumble. The second was a work of literature filled with artful details. It started, "While I was thus in the act of calling upon God, I discovered a light appearing in my room, which continued to increase until the room was lighter than at noonday, when immediately a personage appeared at my bedside, standing in the air, for his feet did not touch the ground."

The first part of Joseph's story has a separate life from that of the Book of Mormon. The tale of the angel Moroni, the gold plates, the holy spectacles, the getting of the plates and their translation fit into a perfect telegram for public consumption. For that, Joseph would have had some sort of a place in history even without the Book of Mormon, which, however, did change religious history. There is a joy and innocence to the early story that seems part of some tradition of shepherds in fields and visitations from heaven in the night. It's vaguely biblical, but also weirdly American, if only because it's a frontier boy who is telling it. He was not just any frontier boy, because he understood the religious power in a story. He chose to bring a foreign narrative to his native shore. I felt its religious call and saw no contradiction in his telling and retelling his stories to himself, trying one emphasis and then another. A pious Mormon might say that God had to be the author of the angel and the gold plates or Joseph was not His prophet. A skeptic might agree, but then point out that since Joseph was so clearly the author, there was no prophet in the mix. To a pious Mormon, I was a sinner for seeing art in Joseph's sacred story. To the skeptic, Joseph was the sinner for being a liar.

I was fine with our both being sinners. As a convert-in-progress, I did not have the classic born-again desire to be washed free of sin. I was possessive of my sins. I had suffered for my sins but also had learned the most important things in my life through my worst sins. I could see sometimes praying to do God's will, but not always. I reserved the right to make up my own mind about whether I would commit what others considered a sin. I'd known transforming love by sinning. Actually, at the time, this love had seemed like the sort of conversion that can happen only once in a lifetime.

I could appreciate Joseph's struggle with his double life. I'd grown up in my father's. At first, when it turned out he worked for the CIA and not the State Department, his actual job just seemed like part of his godlike progress through the nation's seats of saving grace. America was a beacon to the world because the CIA kept it strong. I didn't know there was another way to see my father's work until after Brigade 2506 landed at the Bay of Pigs. It took less than three days for Castro's militia to defeat the small army of Cuban rebels. Soon after their surrender, my political science professor at Sarah Lawrence interrupted his scheduled lecture on NATO to denounce the invasion. He told us that the brigade had been trained by the CIA, and he described the venture as a shameful blunder on the part of "arrogant, misinformed" men. I realized I did not know my father at all. I began my life of spying on the spy.

As the sixties heated up, my father came to be my generation's enemy: CIA, secret user of American power, impervious authority figure. I read the books that described his work serving the interests of United Fruit, overthrowing Arbenz in Guatemala, moving onto postwar Germany, and then returning to Cuba and the plots to assassinate Castro. These weren't things we brought up at the dinner table. I developed habits of keeping my own counsel. I assumed everyone else was an underground person, too, that being a subversive person just went with civilization. I let the authorities think I was cooperating when I really wasn't. My cooperative behavior was based on being cowed and not, as I think people thought, because I was friendly, adaptable, and interested in others. These qualities arose as much out of distrust as the good animal spirits I really did have. As time passed, and I graduated from college, married, and had children of my own, being divided was just my modus operandi. I had my secret thoughts, and then I had my spoken ones. I'd learned it from my relationship to my father, but even after he died, I felt like a spy in the world, a double agent.

As alienated as I was, I needed access to the inner worlds of those around me in the social life I enjoyed through my husband's job in academia. If there was another way to live, I wanted to find out what it was. I hated the view I had of reality as an often beautifully disguised prison camp in which the weak were at the mercy of the strong, always having to hide their vulnerability. I *wanted* fresh information from those who seemed less despairing than I. But I also wanted intelligence for its own sake, so I could keep track of the sources of potential danger I felt in my surroundings. There was pleasure in gathering drawing-room intelligence in a town where most people lived through books; pleasure in thinking I knew more than some others who in many ways were so much more brilliant than I; pleasure in having crushes on people who did not know that I carried things they said and ways they looked back into my cave strewn with bones of bygone imaginary love affairs.

I'd been married for ten-plus years when my mind was flooded with terrifying, unbidden fantasies. If you were interested in your own personal safety, you did not then have these fantasies. I was a constant fantasist; I was familiar with what might be considered the ordinary shocking fantasy. These were of another order. They were urgent, unrelenting, powerful visions. And like murder in Shakespeare, they really wanted out. I had two young daughters I adored and believed my husband did, too. I wasn't that happy, but I was puritan enough to feel you counted your blessings in terms of what hadn't happened yet. I'd flirted with crazy, had been attracted to other men, was an armchair Marxist, but mainly I was a total clock puncher when it came to the daily schedule of accomplishment. I had to be up with the children; they had to be out so I could work on fiction, which was then my focus; I had to be finished in time to exercise, buy groceries, pick up the children at school; they had their play dates; we all had dinner and so to baths, books, and bed.

My fantasies of women came like gushers. There was nudity but not really sex. My fantasies about men had an organization I knew well from the bedroom. These fantasies of women were more like explosions of emotion, riots of unbelievably beautiful feeling. Yes! to embraces, to a sincerity that was overpowering, otherworldly, and sacred always. If I once walked down the street thinking about which word would best describe a character's nose or whether to put half a teaspoon of sesame oil in my hot and sour soup, I now was without measure. I was the exact opposite of J. Alfred Prufrock, who wondered if he dared to eat a peach. I'd never liked him, though I'd sort of identified with him at the same time. Now I saw I was from New Guinea, and he was Kensington Court Gardens.

I was swamped with tender feelings for these imaginary women. *And blown away by the tender feelings they had for me!* I'd never known such exquisite love; and after some reconfiguring the switchboard, the sex didn't seem that hard to get on with, either. I was starved for this. The darling love I shared with my children was a pulse in a vast arterial system of love. I hadn't known grown-ups could feel this way about one another. I couldn't believe I was being allowed to experience this love even in fantasy. It wasn't life as it was led on earth or in my neighborhood or my family. The power of these feelings was exalted to the point of exhaustion. If, by my sheer inability to continuously envision this incredible love, I had to take a rest, I was desperately bereft and quickly bored in the harsh reality I'd constructed for myself.

I can see enough time has passed for me to sound like I channeled these insane feelings easily. That was not the case. I was alarmed and terrified by the hurricane sweeping my basic assumptions out the French doors into the garden. I was petrified this was lesbianism and had to admit that it was. The fort I'd lived in was being blown up at its foundations. My spying was just detachment, not a universal law. The raging child was going to get what she needed. She'd had it with being dutiful, controlled, and self-sacrificing, as I thought I'd been. The full transcript could easily show that I'd been otherwise, but it no longer mattered. The rule of law was over and the reign of love had been inaugurated by a tribe of unclad Amazons.

I developed "worms in my eyes," tiny little wiggly things that turned counterclockwise inside my pupils. These really freaked me out. I could not write. I had dizzy spells and finally went to a doctor. I was so dizzy while I was lying on his table, I told him I was having a stroke. He told me there was nothing wrong with me, that I was having an anxiety attack. I could have killed him for reminding me of my unacceptable secret life. I loved my Amazon thoughts, but I hated having them. I hated the total contradiction in which I was living. The total cognitive dissonance. I wanted my world to know my mind, but what could I reveal? How? Maybe I could introduce these thoughts drop by drop, preparing my husband, who definitely was not going to like this. I couldn't blame him, but if I could slowly educate him to the new New Guinea culture, maybe he would have an insight that could get the reign of love back on the right track. He already felt very beleaguered by feminists, whom he suspected of being behind my attempts to get him to vacuum more. I knew there was a connection between the feminists and the unclad Amazons, but I wasn't sure what it was until an old friend of ours, an unhappy, raucous Irish writer, opened Gilbert and Gubar's epochal *Madwoman in the Attic* and read the first sentence aloud for our amusement: "Is the pen a metaphorical penis?"

He roared with laughter as he read it. Then he read it again and roared again. He acted as if it were the stupidest thing he'd ever heard. I thought I was having another stroke. Of course, the pen was a metaphor for the penis. How much more solemn could a truth be? How much more obvious? Did the names of Hemingway, Mailer, and Roth mean anything to him? Did they not mean, among other things, to be sure, that their pens spoke for their penises? And, furthermore, that anyone who did not have a penis would never truly be able to wield a pen? Our old friend is gone now, otherwise I would call him up and ask him if he realized he fired a shot heard round the world? Well, my world anyway.

I was so furious so fast I almost choked to death. I believed I'd been very timid in the things I said out loud about feminism in those days. It was a very touchy subject, an amazingly touchy subject given how laid-back both men and women are about much of it today. But when our unhappy Irish friend mocked what to me was the most obvious statement of fact, I realized the intellectual, literary men in my circle, all guys who loved to collect arguments, just had no interest in the one about how women were second-class citizens. The depth of their obtuseness went all the way through the globe to China, where they could bask in the attentions of women whose language, mercifully, they literally did not speak. Neither side had to pretend to understand the other.

I began wandering around in a perpetual state of self-strangulation. Too mad to say what I felt calmly, the love that dared not say its name kept saying mine to me instead. Finally, weirdly, my thoughts burst out through no effort of my own. My former husband and I were having a dinner party. The company was all friends we saw frequently, so it wasn't surprising that there were jokes about who did the housework, who pretended to do it, who had cooked, who hadn't. Honestly, if Waterloo was won on the playing fields of Eton, feminism was won at summer camp, where girls had their household tasks written into the weekly schedule. Anything less clear-cut wasn't fair. If only the boys had been willing to budge about doing their share! The joking got sort of edgy at the dinner, and a woman must have made a crack about men being afraid to vacuum because they feared they would be taken for homosexuals. Whatever led us there, something in the conversation inspired two men to jump up, announcing they weren't scared of homosexuality. Then they gave each other a big, fat, hard kiss on the lips.

This was a sign to me, yet, amazingly, also to everyone else as well. Though we hadn't finished eating dinner, we all leapt up from the table, and seemed with uncanny accord to swap clothes, put on rock 'n' roll, and dance with women if you were a woman and a man if you were a man. At some point, two gay men arrived, remarkable for that long-ago time, an out couple in respectable university life, and they looked like they had walked into paradise. They danced with both boys and girls, and there was some wrestling among women, which was perhaps bizarre, but to me part of my private gusher had come into the world. I felt as if the top of my head had come off, releasing my desire or part of it, and instead of the end of everything, we were all being lifted up by the universal exuberance underlying our regimented days. Everyone left early like square dancers after a harvest celebration.

I couldn't believe how much fun it had been! How much fun and how innocent it all felt. Well, maybe not so innocent after all. As days passed and memory couldn't keep the sensations fresh, gloom began to fall on me and uncharacteristic depression. I wondered once again if I should send myself to a therapist. But what would I say? "Dr. SaveMe, my imagination came to life, and people were unharmed"? Other guests would bring the party up and laugh amiably about being "teens for a day." They did have innocent fun. It had come and gone and that was that. I felt as if I was going into mourning. Then a woman who had been at the party told me she wished it hadn't happened. She'd been so happy in its midst that she saw how unhappy she was in her actual life. I remember exactly where we were, standing in the driveway at my old house. I had no idea what to say, but I felt we'd dropped into a secret glowing corridor that tunneled along under the rest of the world. I was panic-stricken.

We had a new awareness of each other. Even if we were just trading recipes, the ingredients glowed in an alluring light. I found it hard to talk at first, but always studied every word afterward. We talked about where we came from, what our parents were like, how we'd fared in school and college, what we'd felt about the world as adolescents, our ambitions. There was a deliberate unfolding to our talks, almost as if we were workshopping novels-in-progress and getting the classiest, most sympathetic critiques. The degree of our feminism, its impact on us, what it meant, how we regarded men was a grave and constantly evolving discussion.

It felt as if talking to another serious, intelligent woman about feminism was really dangerous. That may have been why we began writing letters—to create some distance as we engaged these inflammatory truths. Though our upbringings were very different, we both had been raised to view men as faulty creatures whom a woman had to manage (not quite to say manipulate) to get anything done. We shared a sort of Jane Austen sense that our repression was key to social life and civilization. But playing the repressee hadn't played well with either of us.

After a while, none of that mattered. Drop by drop, letter by letter, a new knowledge came into my heart. Love was real. I worshipped her letters. This was just before e-mail, when the effort connected to writing letters had almost consigned the genre to the dustbin. Her letters revived my faith in writing; they gave meaning to words like "trust" and "imagine" and "love," actually the whole vocabulary of feeling. When I saw her handwritten name at the bottom of a page, I believed that she cared. She said she did and then signed her name to it. We might have been developing the ultimate prenup, a soulful contract in the sky composed of sentence after pithy sentence outlining what we were to each other. Worlds of sympathy and forgiveness opened in me. I could love and be loved by another grown-up human being. I always wanted her to explain how this could happen between us, how had we been so lucky? Her answer was grace, God's grace. Conversion was involved, transformation through a scary crisis. I had been lost and now was found. I was washed in beauty and truth every time she started a letter with the words "My Jane." I felt like I had never belonged to anyone before. Sometimes after I'd flown up to heaven on the wings of one of her letters, I couldn't have expressed my appreciation more except by eating it. This was my communion wafer! Our kisses were my wine. Our embraces might as well be God-given; they called up powers that were way beyond the sum of our parts.

Still, though it had now became possible for me to use the word "God" as shorthand for the intervention of the ineffable in my life, I worshipped our love, our passion. I'd had a conversion to be sure, but I didn't feel we were an example of grace so much as grace was a metaphor for us.

That conversion was a scary crisis, then a wonderful one, and finally an arduous course in suffering for everyone involved— even those who were innocent. I had to face the implications for my marriage, as my lover did for her relationship. When I told my sister what was going on, she looked as if she was reassessing her moral ABCs. She finally said, "Your *feelings* weren't wrong." I felt it was a kind way to comment on what the world would consider sinful. I could see why the world thought the sex was wrong; but I would always, in whatever parallel universe I might find myself, do it again. There was no way I could have argued for this passion rationally. Some purity burned in the experience, some integrity so terrible that only God, if He existed, could observe it. Even if He didn't exist, I felt He'd ordered it (and because of that I would have my own particular sympathy for Joseph's polygamy later on). God did not judge. Others did, and they should have. I could see the pain I'd caused. While our lives unraveled, the pain to my husband, the pain I would have rather died from than inflict on my children, clouded everything. There was light behind the fog, though who knew from day to day whether it was enough to see everyone through the long haul.

My turning toward human love, toward being found, was followed by an apprenticeship in confusion, a long shouldering of responsibility as our lives were dismantled. It began when I was separated with joint custody of the kids, who now went back and forth between the parts of their broken home. It was terrible for them. It may still be. The only redemption was to be accountable, and there was no telling how that could be fully achieved.

FIVE

Joseph Smith Couldn't Have
Written the Book of Mormon

God's authority was not absolute in Smith's time. Much is made of the revivals in the early 1800s, public displays of religiosity and the proliferation of new cults, sects, and prophets. But these might also have expressed anxiety about religion. Not only were many of the revival conversions rescinded, but those that stuck were not necessarily the beginning of a generous new life. Joseph was deeply bothered by the petty partisanship he often noticed between converts and their preachers. As he wrote in *The History of the Church*, "Yet when the converts began to file off, some to one party and some to another, it was seen that the seemingly good feelings of both the priests and the converts were more pretended than real; for a scene of great confusion and bad feeling ensued; priest contending against priest, and convert against convert; so that all their good feelings one for another, if they ever had any, were entirely lost in a strife of words and a contest about opinions."

As the nineteenth century progressed, God's shifting place

was reflected in the arts. Painters who'd been trained in Christian iconography like Goya said, "There are no rules," and didactic traditions about how the Christian story should be told began to be challenged. Joseph seems sensitive to this, or if not sensitive in an educated way to the Enlightenment and its consequences, he seems to intuit how being Christian was fraught in new ways. Religion was losing its dignity. Science was coming on.

Joseph's first great trauma at eight was a showdown between the two. His whole family had fallen ill with typhoid during the early months of 1812. His older sister, Sophronia, almost died. Joseph seemed to recover, but after several weeks, he developed painful infections, first in his armpit and then in his shinbone. Doctors wanted to amputate, but Lucy fought it. The surgeons explained the only alternative was risky surgery, which might result in Joseph's death. Lucy's determination held steady.

When the surgeon arrived on the morning of the operation, Joseph climbed into his father's lap on the bed. His swollen leg was propped up by folded sheets. The doctor was going to cut out the infected bone in three sections. He would do this first by boring through Joseph's shin from one side and then the other. Everyone understood the operation would be excruciatingly painful: there was no anesthetic. But there wasn't any prayer, either. Joseph was offered brandy first, wine second, and restraining ropes third. Yet he was part of a household that prayed regularly and where the parents had just tearfully petitioned God on their knees to save Sophronia, their young daughter, in the darkest hour of her typhoid fever. Sophronia lived. Before Joseph's operation, God did not come into the conversation until after the boy had rejected alcohol and restraints and urged his mother to leave the room because his suffering would be too much for her. Finally the boy said as the last thing he could think of, "The Lord will help me, and I shall get through with it." That brandy should be offered under the circumstances before God was only realistic. But that realism spoke volumes. The Smiths knew they lived in a world where medications could reach physical pain that God could not.

Joseph was born after the Enlightenment. He was born after the American Revolution, which guaranteed religious freedom. It was the first time the state and the Christian religion had been set apart since Constantine the Great made Christianity the established religion of the Roman Empire. Joseph was familiar with family members who'd turned their backs on evangelic religion. Once, when Lucy started attending Methodist services, her father-in-law threw Thomas Paine's *Age of Reason* through the doorway of the Smiths' home. Jesse Smith, an uncle on Joseph's father's side, was an outspoken critic of conversion. He dismissed his young relative's prophetic revelations from the start. When Joseph confided his vision of God and Jesus in the grove to a Methodist minister—who had taken part in the wildly expressive revivals around Palmyra—the man said such visions had "ended with the Apostles."

Joseph's "fertile imagination" inspired worldly doubt in his friends. They weren't critical of his treasure digging, but when

Joseph began to blur gold in caves with gold plates and God in heaven, several felt he was stretching the truth. Joseph himself wasn't totally convinced of his visions. Some claimed that on several emotional occasions, Joseph admitted he had never seen anything with his peep stone. In Fawn Brodie's telling phrase, there is a "savagely cynical account" by one of Joseph's early confidants, Peter Ingersoll, about the origins of the Book of Mormon. According to Ingersoll, Joseph told him he'd brought home some fine white sand wrapped in his shirt, and his family wanted to know what it was. Joseph said, "I happened to think of what I had heard about a history found in Canada, called the golden Bible; so I very gravely told them I had received a commandment to let no one see it, for says I, no man can see it with the naked eye and live. However, I offered to take out the book and show it to them, but they refused to see it, and left the room. Now, I have got the damned fools fixed, and will carry out the fun."

These all make me feel that Joseph swung in and out of belief and nothingness as he zigzagged between the moment Moroni appeared to him in 1823, when he was seventeen, and the time when he dug up the plates in 1827 at the age of twenty-one. From the time Moroni told Joseph he had been chosen to deliver a book containing "the fullness of the everlasting Gospel," he must have constantly meditated on what was being asked of him. His family had every confidence he was wonderful, but Joseph was terribly alone in conceiving and pursuing his religious destiny. There were no AP courses for a religiously gifted teenager. He had no experience of "translating" and no idea he was getting on a career track as a prophet until 1830, when he received a revelation to that effect. No grown person around him had a whisker of the kind of originality that he would display as God's vehicle for the Book of Mormon. His learning curve was going to be incredibly steep and challenging.

In many ways, he was like a devotional painter trying to work after God had been declared to be dying. His story was filled with angelic visits, a familiar part of the folk worship around him, but his strong, untutored intelligence also "got" the contemporary anxiety about God's authority. Joseph had that anxiety himself. He understood the implications. Joseph was always extremely alone as he chose the next rung in the climb to prophethood and was probably frightened by his despair when it came on. Yet he was inspired by Moroni to the most daring self-invention. The angel helped Joseph sense his own powers in relation to the Force who scared Tom and Huck out of their skulls. It may have even been the angel who helped Joseph understand how undermined Jesus was, and how it might take some sort of hyperrealism to restore him. Fortunately, Joseph was a quick study in the uses of magic. I believe that under the twin pressures of his faith and his despair, he created a model of the gold plates as a finishing touch to the authority he wanted.

Moroni had clearly laid out the standard of behavior he expected from Joseph: "He must not lie, nor swear, nor steal." Somehow, Joseph had to make it all up as he went along and also become worthy of being the guardian of the gold plates. He was supposed to visit the plates every September until he was ready.

Describing himself in retrospect, he wrote, "I frequently fell into many foolish errors, and displayed the weakness of youth, and the foibles of human nature; which, I am sorry to say, led me into divers temptations, offensive in the sight of God." He once again criticized his "levity," love of "jovial company," and the shallow tendencies of his "cheery temperament." He might lack seriousness and integrity, yet now realized he was called to have an eye "single to the glory of God." He understood the overlap between make-believe and religious belief. When the moment was right, if it became necessary, he could make a model.

According to his friend Oliver Cowdery, the first time Joseph went and looked at the gold plates in 1824, "he could not stop thinking about how to add to his store of wealth . . . without once thinking of the solemn instruction of the heavenly messenger, that all must be done with the express view of glorifying God." On another visit, Joseph could not resist temptation and tried to dig up the plates. That was when he got knocked over by the towering toad that whacked him with a rusty sword. In *Rough Stone Rolling*, Richard Bushman says there were "three other attempts" whose failure made Joseph cry out to the Lord "in the agony of his soul." Every time, he was chastened by Moroni, saying the temptation for gold was from the Devil.

Apart from his own desire for success and money, Joseph's family had other serious needs for cash. In this same period, the Smiths were desperate because they had built a house on rented land, property carrying a debt of long standing. But just then, "the angel told him he must quit the company of the money-diggers. There were wicked men among them. He must have no more to do with them." Joseph had no other means of making an income *except* for treasure digging. He had never made much from it, but his professional reputation had spread so that he was getting better offers. In Harmony, Pennsylvania, Josiah Stowel, a prosperous, respectable landowner, had heard of Joseph and believed the reports about the boy with a gift for seeing what others could not see with the natural eye. Stowel offered good wages in return for Joseph's help searching for a lost silver mine. Joseph couldn't turn the work away because of the family's pressing debts, but his sense of conflict grew.

Joseph and his father found lodging with Isaac Hale, a settler and legendary hunter. At the start, Hale invested in Stowel's project. Gradually, though, he came to feel the whole enterprise of money digging was a delusion when Joseph turned up neither silver nor gold after weeks of effort. Hale's opinion of Joseph followed the same trajectory. To begin, he had some interest in Joseph, but by the end Hale saw him as nothing but trouble. In between, the tall, fair, blue-eyed youth had fallen in love with Hale's daughter Emma, a remarkable young woman who returned his feelings. She was a brunette with deep, brown eyes, a spirited and witty person with some education. She was seen as a good judge of character by her family and friends, also "fine looking, smart, (and) a good singer" who "often got the power." When she was a child, her prayers for her father's return to orthodox Christianity persuaded him to do so. While Joseph and Emma were living under the same roof, their relationship developed quickly and soon reached a point where they wanted to marry. Isaac Hale was furious. He wouldn't hear of his daughter marrying "a stranger" whose only means of support was to dig for treasure.

Soon after, in March 1826, Joseph was arrested and taken for trial in South Bainbridge, some miles away in New York. Though Josiah Stowel still believed in Joseph's gifts, his nephew had charged him with being a "disorderly person and an imposter," a legal term of art really aimed at curbing magic practices. Whether the nephew felt some part of his own property was threatened isn't clear, but Joseph, who was already on trial within, now had to go on the stand publicly to answer charges of seeking to defraud his employer. Just when he was most conflicted about money digging, most intent on becoming worthy to marry the woman he needed, most striving to be worthy to receive the plates, Joseph stood accused of *pretending*. What, if anything, was real in him?

According to the 1813 New York statute by which he'd been charged, "All jugglers, and all persons pretending to have skill in physiognomy, palmistry, or like crafty science, or pretending to tell fortunes, or to discover where lost goods may be found . . . shall be deemed and adjudged disorderly persons." Once the statute had been passed, it might as well have stood as an unofficial boundary between the Age of Magic and the Age of Science. It was certainly a moment that raised the question of what would be left of religion when magic was gone. Religion and magic were still floating around in the culture in a pool with "superstition," "witchcraft," and "lying." Visions were part of daily life and language, although losing respectability, and many people who believed in them didn't like to admit they did. Joseph had them and wasn't afraid to say so. His boon companions admired his boldness, but didn't stand by him when it counted.

Again and again in the court record witnesses say Joseph "pretended" to be able to find treasure in the earth; that he "pretended" that he could see precious things at a distance by holding a white stone to the sun; that he looked into a hat "pretending" to find a chest of dollars. Some of these witnesses had been in a position to see Joseph "pretend" to do these things because they were with him, hoping that the pretense would pan out. Two of the witnesses called to testify about Joseph's activities, Peter Ingersoll and Willard Chase, were annoyed with his inflated claims about an angel, gold plates, a new Bible. Only two men, including Josiah Stowel, vouched for Joseph's "professed skill" and gave examples of his finding gold with a white stone.

Joseph was found guilty and fined, which seemed to focus his energy. He was "mortified" that people would think he had dedicated his God-given power to the pursuit of "filthy lucre." Even before the trial ended, he began to distance himself from peep stones, saying he had used them only "on a few occasions." The gold plates, however, were different from the stones. After the trial, he went back to Harmony and again asked Isaac Hale for Emma's hand. Her father was even less interested in having Joseph as a son-in-law. When Joseph returned home and told his parents he was determined to marry Emma, they gave him their blessing.

On his annual trip to the plates on Hill Cumorah, the angel told him he must come back with the right person. Joseph was sure that person was Emma. Not only did she believe in his First Vision, Moroni's visit, and the gold plates, he confessed to his parents that she filled his terrible loneliness. This connection between Emma and his prophetic mission had become so crucial that Joseph went back to Harmony once more and persuaded Emma to elope. They were married on January 18, 1827. Emma was the first significant intimate from outside his family in a long list who helped Joseph complete his unfinished self. He had an instinct for these collaborators, and Emma, with her sure, steady intelligence, was an irreplaceable long-term fit for his work in progress.

After their marriage, they stayed with the Smiths for eight months before her father would let Emma and Joseph pick up her belongings. Isaac wept when he saw the couple. He accused Joseph of "stealing" Emma, and then extracted a promise from Joseph never to engage in money digging again. Now, according to Peter Ingersoll's recollection, Joseph cried in his turn as he promised and "acknowledged he could not see in a stone, nor never could; and that his former pretensions in that respect, were all false." His tears were real and pathetic as he gave up this important part of himself. The stones had had their place in the story, but now there would only be the plates. The plates could stay. They were what the stones had never quite fully been: symbols.

Everything was now in place for Joseph to act. It didn't take long to make his model. He had wooden frames, tin. He'd heard the preachers talk about the symbols of the church. Now there was going to be another one. Still, I am sure it took a last visit from the angel before he created his model. As Joseph passed the brushy place where the plates were on Hill Cumorah, Moroni stopped him and delivered "the severest chastisement" of his life. The angel told the faltering prophet apprentice, "I had not been engaged enough in the work of the Lord; that the time had come for the record to be brought forth; and that I must be up and doing and set myself about the things God commanded me to do. . . . I know the course that I am to pursue, so all will be well." When Joseph finished making the model of the plates, he had a crucial clue in the modern scavenger hunt for God. Then he took his model and buried it in its appointed place on Hill Cumorah.

I am not the first follower of Joseph to say he made the plates. In *Joseph Smith: The Making of a Prophet*, Dan Vogel, a former Mormon, imagines the scene when Joseph cuts out the plates from tin and crafts them into a loosely fashioned book. He does not say when in his prophetic journey Joseph made the plates; he never speculates on how making the Book of Mormon plates might have played in and out of Joseph's conscience over time, Vogel believes Joseph is a "pious fraud," a prophet who created a prop for the sake of giving his religion reality for the many who needed an outward sign.

In a phone interview, Richard Bushman, another Joseph biographer and a faithful Mormon, told me, "The gold plates are the hinge between different views of Joseph. If he just had visions of God, it would be one thing. But once Joseph dug the plates up, there are no categories except fraud—or miracle. Our doubts about his sincerity hinge on that claim. In an effort to prove their authenticity, he shows the plates to other people and publishes a kind of deposition over their names. The plates and the witnesses then force people to a stark decision: Is he a fraud or did he actually find plates?" Richard Bushman believes completely that Joseph found gold plates. So do many other faithful Mormons.

I believe Joseph created a model of the gold plates shortly after his encounter with the angry angel Moroni. I don't think it makes him a fraud—unless you think the Book of Mormon is a fraud. To me, the Book of Mormon is a strange work of God's genius. There were four years between Moroni's first visit and the night Joseph finally took the plates. All that time, at some level of his imagination, he'd been preparing to fulfill the truly unbelievable task of translating a work of new scripture. Daring to think he could do this took incredible belief on his part. I would describe him in some sort of collaboration with God as he moves toward the hour when he has to deliver. God is doing His part in calling Joseph to a dramatic role so far beyond himself. Joseph does his part by setting the stage: by making the plates and burying them. The angel's impatience and fury is his cue to finally act.

A few days later, Joseph and Emma, dressed all in black, went to Hill Cumorah in a carriage. His wife waited for him while Joseph dug up the plates, then brought them back wrapped in cloth. Within hours of their coming home, the neighborhood was buzzing with rumors that Joseph had the "Gold Bible" at home. Men who had hunted treasure with Joseph felt he owed them a share of his good fortune. Willard Chase hired a conjurer to help a posse of disgruntled locals discover where Joseph had hidden the plates. A crowd pounded on the Smiths' door, and the Smiths rushed out roaring to scare them away. The plates (which had been put into a chest and stored under the hearthstone) were now moved to the cooper's shop in the yard. After the plates were taken out of the box in their wrapping, the empty box was put under a floorboard; the plates themselves were hidden anew in a huge heap of flax. Willard Chase and his sister, Sally, returned that night to find the plates with her peep stone. They tore up the floorboards and when they didn't find the plates, smashed the empty box in their fury. These kind of skirmishes went on until December. By then Joseph was so frustrated by interruptions, he took his wife to her parents' house in a horse-drawn carriage, with the gold plates submerged in a barrel of beans.

Isaac Hale, who felt his son-in-law was off on another tear, nonetheless put the couple up in a small house of their own.

Joseph now found the peace and quiet he needed to learn how to translate the plates. How he found the learning to create a work of world-renowned scripture remains a subject of study. Joseph had a total of three years of school, broken into several months here and there. Before scribes began writing down his every word when he was twenty-seven, Smith recalled that he had been "mearly instructed in reading, writing, and the ground rules of Arithmatic which const[it]uted my whole literary acquirements." Still, he had insatiable curiosity and soaked up much more than is generally allowed. His parents took a newspaper. Joseph read it. His parents gave him a foundation in the King James Bible; and though his mother reported that he never read the Bible through, Joseph searched the scriptures on his own from the time he was twelve. In his coming and going to different churches, at a certain point, he said he became "somewhat partial to the Methodist sect." He felt "awakened" by Reverend George Lane's discourses. He developed into a "very passable exhorter" and helped his friends "solve some portentous questions of moral or political ethics, in our juvenile debating club." These debates could have contributed to Joseph's considerable knowledge of the religious issues of his own day. Given his fascination with American Indians, he probably adopted ideas about the Indians being of Israelite origin from Reverend Ethan Smith's widely read *View of the Hebrews: Tribes of Israel in America.*

Yet knowing Joseph had some intellectual background doesn't

explain much about his part in the Book of Mormon. To begin with, Joseph described himself as its "translator" and not its author. Once he began working with his hat, he adapted the methods he used for earthly treasure digging to search in the dark for the words that deconstructed God's sentences. To start, he wore the Urim and Thummim—the special "interpreting spectacles" that came with the plates—or used his peep stone. He had sworn off the stone, but began his translating work by putting it into the brim of his hat. Perhaps he depended on the stone to reconnect him to the tradition he'd called on in his earlier searching for treasure. The gold plates were his own contribution. Like Magritte's pipe, under which the artist playfully wrote, *"Ceci n'est pas une pipe,"* Joseph's plates were both symbol and antisymbol, a way of saying that he used a prop and that props were illusions, too. No one part of his process was uniquely powerful. It was the whole mix that was sacred.

Once he put his face into the hat, "Reformed Egyptian," a language Joseph had discovered, crossed the darkness inside. A piece of "parchment" with sentences in Reformed Egyptian would move from side to side. The writing came one character at a time with an "interpretation" in English below. Joseph read it off to the person taking down his words. From this time on, Joseph dictated his written work. This process seems to have freed him from any inhibition his limited writing skills might have imposed on his visionary imagination. Over time, once he started dictating, his writing grew in literary appeal, power, and persuasion. Though he had many scribes, Joseph's older style has a consistent breadth that argues for his having developed a voice of his own. Meanwhile, those who worked with him on the Book of Mormon had the extraordinary experience of working with him through the sudden eruption of gifts beyond anyone's dreams, including possibly his own.

The entire translation of the Book of Mormon took place between December 1827, when Joseph and Emma moved into the house on her father's land, and June 29, 1829, when Joseph registered his title page to secure a copyright. The process involved two distinct phases. Between April and June 1828, Martin Harris was Joseph's scribe for translating and recording the first 116 pages. Harris was a devout, wealthy farmer who lived in Palmyra. He was susceptible; his wife was suspicious. From the start, he and his wife, especially his wife, wanted to see the plates, as did most of Joseph's family and friends. Joseph had already told them they might touch the plates through the linen in which he'd wrapped the gold leaves. But his instructions were then not to show anyone the plates themselves *under pain of death*. Before the two men began to work together, Joseph allowed Martin, but not his wife, to feel the plates through the cloth. Mrs. Harris would not let her husband hear the end of this.

Martin came and went to Harmony several times before he and Joseph began seriously working on the translation in April. During that gap, Emma transcribed for her husband, who experimented with various strategies for handling the plates during the translating process. Sometimes they were in another room, sometimes hidden outside. With Emma and then Harris, Joseph hung a blanket in the middle of the room to hide the plates while he had them on his lap. Harris worked hard for two months, but was increasingly tormented by his wife. She told Martin that Joseph owed him "a further witness." She had already come to Joseph and Emma's house once and searched unsuccessfully for the plates. Finally, Martin asked Joseph to let him take the 116 pages they'd completed with him when he went home to visit. Three times Joseph asked God through the Urim and Thummim if he should agree. Twice the answer was no. When Martin begged for a third time, Joseph asked and the Lord consented, providing Martin showed the manuscript to only five people, one of them Mrs. Harris.

Soon after Martin left, Emma was confined for the birth of her first child, a son, who died the day he was born. Emma herself hovered near death for two weeks. Then it was Joseph's turn to die a hundred deaths for having let the manuscript out of his hands. He had heard nothing about it from Harris. Joseph finally returned to Palmyra to find out what had happened. He watched with his parents as Harris trudged dejectedly along the road. Martin paused at the gate, then got up on the fence and pulled his hat down over his face. Joseph already knew his worst fears had been realized. The pages were gone! Everyone believed Harris's wife had stolen the 116 pages, but she admitted nothing. "All is lost," Joseph cried over and over when Martin confessed.

"All is lost!" He spent the day pacing the rooms of his parents' house, blaming himself for letting Martin have his way, raging against Mrs. Harris, protesting, protesting that after all Emma had been through, now he was piling the devastation of their sacred mission on top of that.

Joseph returned home in misery. He would never translate with Harris again. Because of his personal weakness, the powers of the Urim and Thummim were withdrawn. He was punished by a series of scathing revelations about his shallow amiability and dependence on other men's opinions. "For behold, you should not have feared man more than God, although men set at nought the counsels of God, and despise his words, yet you should have been faithful." Richard Bushman points to this period as the beginning of Joseph's prophetic voice. "The speaker stands above and outside Joseph, sharply separated emotionally and intellectually. . . . By this time, the treasure-seeking language has disappeared. . . . The language was biblical rather than occult." As Joseph works through his despair, his revelations come more quickly; Bushman observes that "his prophetic identity was gelling."

It took about a year for Joseph to recover. The angel restored the interpreters in September 1828. The next winter, Joseph started translating again with Emma. Along with his family and a few close friends, she was among the small group of ardent converts who believed the Book of Mormon would be "a marvelous work and a wonder." In that spring of 1829, Oliver Cowdery arrived at the Smiths' house with one of Joseph's brothers. Oliver was intrigued by the story of the plates and wanted to know more. He was twenty-two, a year younger than Joseph; he was a warm, informal person. Like Joseph, he had a sense of humor. Their religious sensibilities were also kindred. Cowdery had a treasure-seeking background, but aspired to the world of purer revelation associated with the gold plates. One night he and Joseph stayed up late, bonding with such speed Joseph asked him to stay on as his scribe.

He engaged with Joseph as the latter's religious gifts caught fire, giving him the confidence to just let the lost 116 pages go. Joseph had to start all over from the beginning again, but now his new thoughts came at the rate of about eight pages a day. Oliver kept pace both mentally and physically as he wrote line after line, page after page of Joseph's dictation with a quill pen. They were so complementary, they shared visions of figures from the Bible. Once they were prompted to leave off translating and go to the Susquehanna River, where they were baptized together by John the Baptist and received the authority conferred by the priesthood of Aaron. Within three blazing months, with Oliver's help, Joseph had translated the 275,000-word Book of Mormon. In years afterward, Cowdery always looked back at their experience with wonder. "These days were never to be forgotten—to sit under the sound of a voice dictated by the *inspiration* of heaven, awakened the utmost gratitude of this bosom! Day after day, I continued, uninterrupted, to write from his mouth, as he translated."

Once they found a willing printer, Martin Harris redeemed

himself by raising $3,000 on his farm as security. (When his wife would not lend her name to the mortgage, their marriage finally ended.) Books arrived in March 1830, and in April, Joseph baptized the first members of his church. Joseph's passage from near-illiterate to scriptural genius and prophet is wildly improbable. His transformation from farm boy to prophet is absurd. But try this: Under the intense inner pressure we associate with budding artists, improvising recklessly and freely, Joseph parlayed a real but evolving experience of God into an original act of religious performance art. He seems most like a modern artist to me in his intuitive leaps and openness to lightning. But it may also be that modern prophets are more like modern artists because both are struggling with forms of realism that have been undermined.

The Book of Mormon was instantly attacked as blasphemy. It was called a fraud by a liar who pretended to find gold plates. But Joseph's symbol had served God's cause. People like Emma who knew Joseph and believed in his book were sure his scripture wasn't a fraud. They'd watched the whole process, knew his gifts *and* his enormous limitations. They saw the paraphrases from the Bible, maybe Emma—who was so perceptive—saw where Joseph had used things from his family's life and father's dreams. It didn't matter. The book was leaps and bounds beyond the sum of his parts. His intimates' rallying cry became, "Joseph Smith couldn't have written the Book of Mormon!"

As Emma once said, "He could not pronounce the word Sariah," the name of a central Book of Mormon's patriarch's wife.

Joseph was unsure of biblical history, yet wrote in detail of things and places he had never been. He once stopped in the middle of translating to ask if Jerusalem had walls around it. When Emma, the better scholar, confirmed that had been the case, he breathed a sigh of relief. He'd already written the walls into the text. Could he have "been deceived"? Not according to his wife, who said, "Joseph Smith could neither write nor dictate a coherent and well-worded letter; let alone dictating a book like the Book of Mormon. . . . It would have been improbable that a learned man could do this; and for one so ignorant and unlearned as he was, it was simply impossible."

SIX

Back to the Future

I had my encounter with God on the road to Richmond long after my divorce was over, after my children were grown, after the many years during which my life-shattering love ran its course. While I was divorcing and the years afterward when my children were growing up, it felt like all particle accelerator all the time. I was being shattered on a daily basis. The deep habits of thinking about myself as a woman in a male-and-female world didn't just go away. I stayed in Charlottesville, where my children could be near their father. He lived in the house where they had grown up and our marriage had gone through its seasons. Those were powerful reminders of a woman I had been, a woman whose pieces circulated in me still, barely on speaking terms with the pieces of another person who had no idea what she was doing.

The pull to loving the woman who had changed my life was terribly strong. She had taken a job at a midwestern university. I felt my children shouldn't have more controversy added to the upheaval they were living through, so my friend and I saw each other at intervals, usually in the distant town where she lived.

We wrote letters in between, and they were still so powerful, one sheet of her closely scripted handwriting could hold me together for days. They were an otherworldly transfusion that made it possible to handle the shattered world without anger or pride or any other self-dramatizing emotion. At times like these, I felt like an incommunicable truth, like a digest of all the lines of poetry I memorized when I was young.

When we were together, I marveled at her actually existing. I remember watching her take her evening run in snowfall along the street of homey, homely Germanic houses where she had her apartment. Her feet rose and fell with a hypnotizing and regular rhythm; each time she lifted her foot and set it down, she seemed to be inscribing the slightly dusted pavement with the secret marks of self-possession. I watched her make the trail until she disappeared around the corner into the dark beyond the street lamp, but her image stayed with me.

It was always restoring to live in such companionship, then not always easy to bring it back to the world of young children becoming teenagers and my daily work. I moved from writing fiction to working on films with Helen. My friend moved from teaching to administration and from one midwestern university to another. Yet despite the very different demands in our lives, our relationship was allowed to unfold. It grew possible to spend more time together, be more open, travel, live together, even finally for our relationship to run its course. When it ended, I didn't feel the possibility of love had ended. But I wasn't sure what love I wanted.

As much love as I'd been given—and as real as I experienced myself when I gave it—when I was alone again, my jumpy thoughts were chaotic and contradictory, brimming with my anxieties, my fleeting ideas, self-told jokes, and transient joys. I knew death in my insubstantiality; death was already a dreadful part of me. I wanted some other experience in death's place, but how to find it? I found my mind going back to a boyfriend of my teenage years: Tovi. In a way, his nickname with its broad-shouldered T and soulful V said it all. He was a man of strength and sensitivity held together by Openness and Imagination. He and I were raised in a similar 1950s WASP world of manners and symbols. When we met I was fifteen and he was seventeen. I was wandering around in the dark like a firefly waving a flag that said, "Am girl, need boy." I was a rebellious, ambitious person who didn't relish being in the role of need. Tovi was the kind of teenage firefly who flew a flag saying, "Am boy, *love* girl!" He was a tall, blond, broad-shouldered Tovi, with dancing blue eyes.

When he was a freshman at Williams College, I was a junior at Concord Academy, a boarding school in the same New England environs. I used to fill the margins of my notebooks with caricatures of his profile; it was an easy line to draw because his large, downward-curving nose and big, upward-tilting chin made him look like a jester. Thanks to Tovi's open-hearted enthusiasm, I'd had my first orgasms necking fully clothed with him on the long sofa in my parents' living room. I thought they were great, but mysterious—like going over a bump too quickly in the car. He was a gentleman who never took advantage. But then he wrote a letter asking me to marry him. I was shocked. I had dreams, places to go! I wrote back saying that we had to break up immediately. We went our separate ways for forty years.

It was not until my late fifties that I really thought about him again and wondered if there was any way to explore our missed opportunity. Thanks to the Internet, I was able to find him in Brooklyn, New York. I sent him an e-mail asking how he was. He wrote back saying that he'd been a Marine captain in Vietnam. He'd gone on to become a partner in a prestigious New York law firm. He'd enjoyed "three decades of the same job, same wife and same apartment." But then he parted ways with his firm; divorce laid hands on him; there followed disastrous alimony payments, some poor investments, and a recent diagnosis of Parkinson's.

He didn't act like someone who'd been crushed. His e-mails were alive and witty. He answered his phone cheerfully, "Hello, my blue-eyed, philanthropic entity." When we finally met again, Tovi was beautifully dressed in a cashmere coat and silk tie. He looked like a million bucks, was still playing squash and looking fit. He still had a jester's face, and his flag still endearingly said, "Am boy, *love* girl!" He pitched woo with words like "pulchritudinous" and "callipygian," and talked about himself as Hairy Breekniks, a Viking warrior deserted by history.

I wasn't sure how he would respond to my having been married to a man, then in a long relationship with a woman, and now headed in his direction. When I put my history to him, he gave it some thought before quoting his hero Churchill, "Anyone can rat, but it takes a certain ingenuity to rerat." That he had that quote on tap was just too wonderful. I had never heard it, and there was such politically incorrect truth in it. Soon we were paddling a course through pan-seared foie gras and excitement about finding each other again. *Casablanca* for seniors! Why shouldn't we have a big romance? I was scared of becoming a nurse, but so far there had been no pressure on me to be one—even after he grew determined to move to Charlottesville. When I protested that he needed some medical game plan before he went anywhere, Tovi kept saying his Parkinson's could be stabilized as it was by new medicines for years.

He laughed off my reservations, but it wasn't all that funny when he drove his U-Haul into town. It was so unfunny that I signed on as Helen's cowriter for *The Mormons* not long after he arrived. Swapping red suspenders and blue jeans for his cashmere coat, Tovi settled into his new apartment over a BBQ restaurant called Hog Heaven. I began to come and go to New York as I worked on the treatment with Helen. Then as we began filming, I came and went to Utah as well. Despite my prickliness about need and being needed, Tovi seemed like a messenger. I knew something about the power of youth. But what about the poetry of ruin? I was touched by his uncomplaining grace, and I was learning from it. I just couldn't get him to plan for the future of his illness. Because I couldn't (though it felt like a hard stand to take, and not that he ever asked), I was always clear that we couldn't live together.

Along with not planning for the future, the other thing we

didn't have in common was religion, but more especially, church.
He was a boarding-school Episcopalian, meaning he loved the
days he'd spent in church as a boy at St. Paul's. To some extent
he also felt those days excused him from ever having to go again.
That plus the fact he was in deep mourning for the loss of
the King James translation of the Bible. Furthermore, in case
he needed to strengthen his defense against attending church, he
had once written a college paper about the Mormons' abandon-
ment of original sin. Tovi was fascinated by that, perhaps because he had a sort of William Blake child of God innocence to
him. He was also the sort of reader who knew that Mark Twain
had famously characterized the Book of Mormon's style as "chlo-
roform in print." Though I often heard him extolling the Mormons' disregard for original sin to friends and strangers, Tovi also
loved to glory in Twain's witticism.

The fact he did not share my passion for Joseph Smith was
never an impediment to my working on the film; it was never a
barrier after I started wondering if I might convert to Mormonism. Though I thought of myself as having "fallen in love with
Joseph," and Tovi and I said "I love you" to each other frequently,
I didn't feel there was any conflict. I could have used more company in my study, but then in many ways my study was so quirky
I don't know how he could have been my companion in it. And
then, very unexpectedly, he helped me toward a turning point in
my reading of the Book of Mormon, one that moved me beyond
a huge obstacle in myself.

While we were working on the film, I had thrown myself into

the Book of Mormon many times, and it had thrown me right out. First off there was the problem of its style. Impatient outsiders always complain about it. But the style was a real problem. There were a number of phrases that Smith repeated and repeated, though as Twain observed, "'It came to pass' was his pet. If he had left that out, his Bible would have been only a pamphlet." A close second among belabored phrases was "thus saith the Lord." The repetitions might have helped Joseph in his inspired way of dictating the text. They could have been devices to kick-start the flow of revelation or to make a quick transition. They may have saved time and driven Joseph on, but they now drove readers like me away.

During research for the PBS film, after I stalled again and again in my reading of Joseph's scripture, I started asking people I was interviewing to give me their summary of the Book of Mormon. Most LDS readers made the Book of Mormon sound like the Bible. Generally, they agreed that the story was composed of big characters, family sagas and conflicts, historical cycles, and moral precepts. Joseph's scripture opened in 600 BC Jerusalem as God commanded the patriarch Lehi to leave the city, which would be destroyed, and go to the Americas. Once there, Lehi's sons divided into the Nephites and Lamanites, who started the quarrels that developed into endless war in the centuries to come. Sometime during Christ's Resurrection, the savior visited the New World and his good influence brought three hundred years of increasingly uneasy peace. In AD 400, there was a final, bloody struggle in which almost all the Nephites except Moroni, an ancient prophet and historian, were killed. Moroni preserved the gold plates on which the story of these first Americans had been written and buried the record in the Hill Cumorah, where Joseph would find it almost fifteen hundred years later.

As soon as the Book of Mormon was published on March 26, 1830, part of the world was instantly ready to malign it. The Palmyra newspapers had printed rumors about Joseph Smith "pretending" he was going to publish a Gold Bible. Then those papers covered the book's actual publication as a local scandal. Some orthodox Christians who'd heard dark rumors of Joseph Smith and his Gold Bible were gunning for it. *The Rochester Daily Advertiser* cried "Blasphemy" in its front-page headline. In Virginia, Alexander Campbell, a nationally known theologian and preacher, tore into the Book of Mormon in language that would dominate the discussion for decades to come. He called Smith "ignorant and impudent", "a liar"; he lumped him in with "the Barkers, Jumpers and Mutterers of the present age," as well as "Miss Campbell, who in Good Old Scotland a year or two since came back from the dead and had the gift of tongues." Alexander Campbell attacked Smith's "plagiarisms" (borrowings from Shakespeare and the Bible, among other places), his anachronisms, and Smith himself for being the author and not God, as Joseph claimed. These dismissals are still heard around the non-Mormon water cooler.

Secular people are also amused and/or outraged by the fact that horses—to which Joseph made many references—weren't in the Western Hemisphere during the pre-Columbian era of the Book of Mormon. An academic archaeologist actually hung up on me when I called to ask him questions about the evidence for Nephites in Central America. He wouldn't even address the question of objective proofs for the Book of Mormon. Everybody knew there weren't any! True, there was no shard of pottery, no bit of text supporting the historical world Joseph claimed for his scripture. Still, I didn't think the good professor had to be so rude. It was not new news that there was nothing to corroborate Joseph's claim that he'd received a history of ancient Israelites bringing their religion to the New World. New DNA testing even showed the people in Central America trace their ancestry back to Asia. Nonetheless the anti–Book of Mormon huffs and jokes were slowly growing irrelevant as progressive Mormon and non-Mormon scholars increasingly focused on the Book of Mormon as religious scripture.

In its own time, the Book of Mormon was not that much read among Smith's followers—not even by those converts who received a free copy from the missionaries when they were baptized. Not until 1986, when President Ezra Taft Benson ordered his people to read the Book of Mormon, did it become such a constant focus of Mormon study. In his own era, when Joseph preached about his scripture, he focused on it as carrying several key signs of the times. The Book of Mormon was a supernatural affirmation of his own prophetic calling; and it pointed to the restoration of Christ and his return at the end of the world. While his preaching spoke in this way to some of the most important concerns of his time, it makes Joseph a stranger to me in my own. I couldn't relate to the Joseph who believed he lived in a millennial hour. But once I was exploring conversion, I had to read the Book of Mormon and decide what I thought for myself. It might be a deal breaker. What if it never spoke to me? What if I never got over feeling it was horribly written? What if I didn't respect it? What if I believed it was a hoax?

Could Joseph's scripture have been the basis for a dramatic, no-holds-barred, death-defying, world-winning, long-running charade? The Mormons themselves have gone to the mat from the start. The apostle Orson Pratt spoke for other early Mormons when he said the Book of Mormon "must either be true or false." If it was true, then no person could be saved and reject it. "If False, it is one of the most cunning, wicked, bold, deep-laid impositions ever palmed upon the world, calculated to deceive and ruin millions." I loved Joseph, but I did not respect him in the way that Apostle Pratt wanted me to. He raised the same either/or challenge that many Mormon presidents and leaders have raised since. I would have to find a way to respect Joseph more than I did if I were really converting. My love for his colorful story about Moroni and the plates wouldn't be enough.

Finally, I began losing respect for myself for trying and failing to get through the Book of Mormon. I went at it in earnest. Every hurdle I got over was followed by a new one. I got acclimated to the style and peculiar genre, but then could not make it past Nephi's confusing murder of Laban in the early pages of the first book—the First Book of Nephi. I had to read it all from the beginning several times until I understood that Nephi, the author, was referring to himself as the author and the actor (murderer), as well as commenting on how he was writing his book and what will go in it. Beneath the deceptive biblical façade, we have a modern self-referencing narrator. The first topic of the first chapter of the first book in the Book of Mormon was not God, but the *role* of writing about God. Everything was set in motion on page two, when an angel brought a book to Lehi that prophesied the downfall of Jerusalem. This was the event that started the action that drove Nephi to kill Laban for the plates on which were written the history of the Jews and the genealogy of Lehi's forefathers. The real story of these religious seekers was so important that possession of the record justified murder.

In some ways this sounds like the Old Testament. However, although the Book of Mormon is set in the same time period—600 years BC—it is not the Old Testament redux. From the first pages, the Book of Mormon prophets already know about Christ and are constantly foretelling his coming. Not only do they continuously prepare us for Christ's arrival, we are told from the very beginning that his special prophet will be Joseph Smith. Since that Joseph will be a descendant of the line of Joseph of Egypt, I gradually understood that the story of the Book of Mormon was meant to be a continuation of the Bible. It would take me a while to see the continuation was much more sophisticated than I'd been led to understand. It's not just like the Bible, not just a Bible knockoff. The Book of Mormon is a self-conscious meditation on what had become of the Christian saga eighteen hundred years after Christ's death.

Lehi's pseudo–Old Testament world is drenched in Christ-consciousness; yet the Spirit tells Nephi he must go through with the murder because the Lord requires it. There's a whiff of God's commanding Abraham to sacrifice his son here, but only a whiff. The murder is bafflingly unrighteous, strangely ambiguous, as if God had read Dostoyevsky and Camus and now was sending his man to kill for possession of the text. I was seriously, deeply unprepared to consider Laban's murder as part of a modern parable about religious truth and the power of texts. There was nothing anyone had ever said to make me expect that Joseph had framed his "Bible" stories in a modern literary echo chamber. I felt hopelessly disoriented and wanted to stop reading again.

But I still had seven-eighths of the Book of Mormon ahead of me. I tried a new approach, the one where people seek an answer by opening scripture anywhere and reading the first verse their eyes fall on. Saint Augustine's conversion began that way. I was not too proud to try. I opened the Book of Mormon at random to see if things picked up in a way I could follow with more pleasure. I turned to Mosiah 21: 26–27. My eyes fell on some people getting to "a land covered with dry bones." And they've got "a record with them, even a record of the people whose bones they had found." That did not do the trick. I was not hooked.

Now I'm in Helaman 14. In the little summary at the front

of the chapter, it says there will be signs when Christ is born: light during the night and a new star. The signs at his death will include "three days of darkness, the rending of rocks, and great upheavals of nature." I start looking for Christ's birth. I turn pages, no birth. Then I turn pages and there are the signs—light during the night and a new star—but the birth takes place off-stage. The same is true for his death. Christ's crucifixion also takes place offstage. The missing dramas are, well, missing. There's no here here, no retelling of the key stories of the manger or arduous ones from the crucifixion. We keep hearing about Christ coming and then his going through his known story off-stage. The endless prophetic run-up to Christ's saga—with no appearance of Christ himself—made it feel as if he was being walled off. The more Christ's truths were mentioned in his ab-sence, the more abstract and disembodied they seemed. Then, just when Christ's life as we know it from the Bible is over, he came into the narrative in the New World. What was going on here?

It's as if Thomas Pynchon had fabulated a work about the direction of modern religious literature by writing in the style of Milton's *Paradise Lost*. Hold that thought. Breathe on that thought. Stay in your discomfort. Then imagine buckets of words about Christ being poured over your head, familiar words, yet not the exact words you've always known. For pages and pages, buckets and buckets, the savior is just offstage; people are show-ing themselves worthy or not worthy of him. History is flowing by in a waterfall of words about an offstage Christ. Experience the subtle squirming feeling of dissonance between the Christ you know and the Christ you're being blanketed by in Joseph's scripture. It's like having a piece of aluminum resonate against a silver filling in your mouth. Joseph mixes his imitation of the style of the King James Bible with actual passages, particularly some long and famous ones from Isaiah. They don't quite fit; we don't at first know why. Along with the moralizing characteristic of the genre, nineteenth-century religious issues like infant baptism are mixed in with unorthodox ideas about reopening the closed canon of the Bible. For a non-Mormon outsider picking up the scripture for the first, second, and third time, the text is mind-boggling and crazy-making on an unconscious level.

At least it was for me. This now-you-see-him, now-you-don't Christ, this constantly predicted but never-arriving Christ, also pushed some savage button in me. It was like reliving and reliving my recurring disappointment in the Christian churches I'd gone back and back to without ever finding nourishment. I was never moved by the promises that Christ really was the Son of God; that Christ could save us, could forgive our sins; or that Christ gave us eternal life through his death on the cross. I'd never found a way into this vision. It was terrible to suffer crucifixion, but I'd never had the slightest inkling of what it meant. How could his suffering save our sins? How could his sacrifice give us eternal life? As I tried to read my way into the Book of Mormon again and again, it brought up my boiling rage at these claims. How had I sat for so many hours trying to figure out what they were supposed to mean? Their only connection to reality was the ghostly tether tying them to Christ's return! But if he was coming back, he should have done it long ago. If he was just, if he was loving, if he was sane in any recognizable way, he should have returned to a generation for whom he was a real and palpable figure. It was criminal to think of the hundreds of years when his promise floated in incense-filled cathedral spaces with ethereal song, causing endless bloodshed and death, death, death that Christ did not exist to redeem.

My fury against God and son boiled over in conversations with Tovi. He was shocked by my fire-breathing rejection of the Christian "psychosis." I railed unforgivingly against the crime of Christianity, the immorality of promising and not delivering, of forcing billions of sincere people to hang their hopes on an untrue story. Tovi looked more and more upset. Finally, he said shyly, "This is your father." I was momentarily fifty times more furious. I hated the cliché of God reflecting our idea of an actual parent. If God was made only in such predictable human form, seeking Him really was just hogwash.

Yet as I screamed at the ceiling, I could see the *tiny* touch of truth in what Tovi suggested. And the fact that it was Tovi, who had met my actual father, who made me feel he could see a truth I was overlooking. Why else would I be so insanely mad at Christ, except that he was standing in for some person in my life? I slowly had to admit I was not raging at my relationship to God's son. Christ and I had long since parted ways. I was amazed to find I still had any fury at Daddy. I felt I'd spent it long ago. But here my anger was again, chastising the towering prince of Christianity with my charges against my father: for being so compelling and so unavailable, so not what he seemed, a father you wanted to have, but not one who wanted you to have him as he really was.

"Why do you keep reading the book if it makes you so mad?" Tovi asked next.

That was a good question. A very good question. I wanted to understand the Book of Mormon, but couldn't. I couldn't finally dismiss it, either. After all, I who felt primitive anger against Christ for not fulfilling his promise to return, I of all people should be interested in a modern work in which he breaks the rules and does come back. Once I calmed down, I asked myself: How had I gotten on this path in the first place? I'd been drawn to Joseph's irreverence. It had struck a new note for me in the search for God. Now when I went back to his scripture, I tried to keep that in mind. The Book of Mormon must also reflect at least some of Joseph's irreverence. Soon enough, I had to allow that framing the Book of Mormon in a sense of Christ's shifting place in history was at the very least irreverent. It certainly showed God changing his mind about the Christian story and possibly admitting that His authority was not the absolute kind He'd enjoyed when He wrote the Bible. Joseph, prophet to this new incarnation of God, had an intuition of God's weaker authority. He had given God a necessary prop. As a prophet, Joseph interpreted Him with the Urim and Thummim, spectacles called "Interpreters." No wonder Joseph called himself a "translator." It was all anyone could do under the circumstances. Joseph was not acting as God's scribe. He was interpreting God in translation.

Now, for the first time, the things which had been off-putting about the Book of Mormon were intriguing. Because it starts with Lehi killing Laban for a record, I knew texts were important in this scripture; and I knew there was constant prophecy of Christ's life and death, but his only appearance was in the New World after his crucifixion. I was excited, hopeful, and had a focus to guide my reading. I went through the Book of Mormon, underlining the commentary about texts in black ink and highlighting the prophecies of Christ's coming with a green soft-tipped Sharpie. Once I didn't have to deal with the battles between Nephites and Lamanites, the moralizing about the battles, and all the reversals of fortune that resulted from the battles, I felt I had the necessary key.

The gold plates are the record of four sets of other plates, told by three different narrators who are compiling and editing the work of many other writers. The three different narrators—Nephi, Mormon, and Moroni—are also characters in the drama. Though they live at different times and each is very individual, they agree on the prophetic essentials of Christ's coming. His familiar story is kept offstage, and when he does enter the narrative, he seems at first to behave like the Christ we know. He gives the Sermon on the Mount to Americans who otherwise would never have heard it. He lets the people touch his wounds, so they will know he is still the suffering Christ. Yet he is not *necessarily* this Christ. By breaking open the closed canon, Joseph put Christian tradition itself into the particle accelerator. Christ may have emerged from a continuous tradition, but Joseph's Jesus is a revolutionary new character, a Christ who is no longer restricted by a closed canon. He dramatically expresses his difference by appearing on a stage outside biblical time and place. This new Christ will be subject to interpretation as now God his Father also is. The tradition is shattered. If we have been reading the scripture as a narrative about narrative, we are ready for the new Christ. It is just not clear who the new Christ is or will be. When Joseph opened the canon, he started a new tradition of continuing revelation. The Book of Mormon has carefully, constantly, subtly been revising the Christian tradition in a sort of *Back to the Future* move that prepares readers for an entirely new outcome to history. Joseph has not gone back to preserve the present; he changed the past so the present could also be different. Theoretically, the Mormon prophet would be the sole authority over which revelations counted, but in the years after the Book of Mormon, Joseph's ideas were more and more empowering of man as himself a god.

The whole Book of Mormon is surprisingly the Declaration of Independence for scripture. Not only does it break Christ out of the Bible, a scary and liberating act for the living God, but it also understands the consequences. If the Bible needs to be supported by further scripture, then all sorts of prophets, all sorts of individuals will claim their scripture is the holy one.

Joseph's scripture sees to the bottom of this crisis. Christ must be made anew in a world where his reign will be decided by the battle of the books. The Book of Mormon opens with a writer killing for the materials that make up truth. Nephi murders Laban for the plates with the canonical history leading up to Christ's life. The right people must be in charge, though as we will come to realize, the Nephites are only human, too. The Book of Mormon is here to tell us that in the future religious truth will only get more and more controversial.

I felt as if the top of my skull had come off. I felt that I knew what was in the Mormon scripture and that Joseph could not have written it. He might have intuited the need to give Christ new life. But by giving Christ as much new life as he did, he put the traditional savior in a position where I personally could see him as an idea whose time had passed. Joseph wasn't capable of being that irreverent. He couldn't have foreseen that his liberated Christ could be so different to such different people, the Jesus of the atonement in today's Mormon Church *and* the Jesus of being born again to Bob Dylan: the one Dylan met in his Tucson hotel room in 1979. Once Christ was out of the Bible, he was given over to the democracy of inquiring minds. As Dylan told Karen Hughes in 1980, "Christ is not some figure down the road. We serve the living God, not dead monuments, dead ideas, dead philosophies. If he had been a dead God, you'd be carrying a corpse around inside you." Joseph had envisioned a Christ who could as easily be the Jesus in Martin Scorsese's *Last Temptation of Christ* as a teacher in the Unitarian Church.

Joseph could not have come up with the intellectual structure of the Book of Mormon. It is inconceivable that he understood writing and narrative the way we do. Yet his book is written as though he did. Once I understood this about the Book of Mormon, I couldn't understand how earlier readers had found anything for themselves. We'd only recently ripened to the point where the fatwa against Salman Rushdie's *Satanic Verses* gave us a clue to what the Book of Mormon was saying about religion in our time. I was ecstatic to know what I now knew. I felt tremendous respect for Joseph. God had spoken through his prophet, Joseph. He had spoken through his prophet to *me*! I had my own testimony! I felt intellectual respect for the Book of Mormon and for Joseph Smith, who was its vehicle. It was . . . it was, well, mind-blowing.

SEVEN

Past-Life Digression

Sometime in 2009, I started going to my local Mormon Church in Charlottesville, Virginia. My first visit was not to the Sunday service, but to the Family History Center. I'd been wondering about my family history ever since I began interviewing Mormons for the PBS documentary. At the start of my questions, I'd ask, "How far back does your family go?"

I meant how far back in Mormonism. I meant to be cozy in a slightly unearned way: to show that I understood how deep their family roots went. Soon, though, I began to hear the following answer, "We go back to the *Mayflower*." At first, I thought the person was putting on airs. I thought, *No, no, no, no, no, your family does not go back to the* Mayflower. *Maybe my family goes back to the* Mayflower, *but not yours.* I kept hearing the same answer from one Mormon after another: "We go back to the *Mayflower.* . . . My fifteenth great-grandfather sailed on the *Mayflower.* . . ." *Mayflower, Mayflower, Mayflower!* I got generational rundowns from one family member to the next, hearing about one begetting after another until we'd crossed the ocean to Plymouth and gotten all the way to Utah. These could have been fantasies for all I knew, yet I was not quite moved to check it out with the Utah chapter of the General Society of Mayflower Descendants, about which I was also learning for the first time. After all, though I thought of myself as more *Mayflower* material than were the Mormons I was talking to, it was part of my eastern WASPhood to stand on ceremony and to make fun of standing on ceremony at the same time. We were born ironists.

I was not that impressed by the *Mayflower* tales until I started hearing again and again that Joseph Smith had a direct ancestor, John Howland, who'd come on the Mayflower: and that John Howland begat Joseph Howland, begat Hannah Howland, begat Hannah Crocker, begat Lydia Fuller, begat Lydia Gates, begat Lucy Mack, who was Joseph Smith's mother. This made a dent, since Joseph's ancestors could claim to have produced a character with a big impact on what, in my family, was always referred to portentously (with our own crown grant to the Royal Capital) as "the Nation." When I was growing up, though having ancestors on the *Mayflower* was a fake big deal, it was some kind of deal, and it would have followed a person from dinner party to dinner party like a faux halo. By the time I got to the Family History Center, I'd been forced to admit to myself that I was the one putting on airs about the *Mayflower*, not the Mormons. No one in my family had ever said we'd come on the *Mayflower*. But somehow, deep down and out of sight, I'd gotten the notion that if the *Mayflower* was an important feather in the patriotic hat, our family must have some relation to it. But who did I secretly think we were?

Well . . . well . . . well . . . we were WASPs. Our importance was just in the air I breathed as a child in Providence, Rhode Island. My father had come home from World War II as a hero. He'd won a Silver Star; my mother was beautiful; we had servants; we belonged to country clubs. I was four. My father was handsome and terrifying. The air he breathed seemed important by going up his nose. Lucky to get inside his head and see what he was thinking, feeling. He'd gone to Groton, Yale, and Harvard Law School. He was the only person who talked when he was in the room. He said disturbing things about men named Hitler and Stalin. He tapped his finger on the table and said that we were in the top one percent of the top ten percent of privileged Americans and must someday give back to the country that had given so much to us. In his spare time he made swinging a golf club look like a mythological act. The next thing we knew, he was leaving his law practice in Providence to work in Washington, D.C. He called us into the dining room and made a point of explaining that he was taking a cut in pay because he felt it was so important to fight Communism.

WASPs were public-spirited, but they were also snobs. Though I worshipped my parents, I sometimes felt more like a guest than their child. They had an assumptive way of talking about their dogs, parties, appointments, plans, politics, and America itself, which made them seem like gods. They knew important people whose names appeared in the newspapers; my father gave my mother giant pieces of jewelry from Tiffany; my mother had gone dancing at the White House with her mother and stepfather, a congressman. She and my father had fancy friends we never met. Something about the way they talked about their friends the Whitneys or Barneys or Aldriches, those strangers seemed to have an especially important claim on my mother and father. Once I was really put off by the snooty way my mother told Daddy, "The Whitneys are coming through town when they leave Fishers Island next week." Later my mother tried to teach me to curtsy when I shook their hands. I cried and refused to do it. I was not going to act snooty for some dumb person I didn't know. Even if the Whitneys were our distant cousins.

As I grew up, my WASPy friends tended to be like me: unconventional, antiauthoritarian, reverse snobs. We were fodder for the social upheavals of the sixties. We marched on Washington, protested at draft centers, and took over buildings. Some of my friends put trust funds on the line. No one I knew went to jail, but friends of friends did. I met a woman whose cousin had left the country. We wanted to be writers, social workers, professors, artists, wilderness explorers, therapists, reformers. The sixties were a huge mess in many ways, but they powered the revolution in new civil rights for blacks, women, American Indians, and, more recently, gays. Things changed for these groups, but one thing that was always disappearing in one place had a way of popping up in another: snobbery.

Socially, I found that falling in love with Joseph Smith was some kind of cousin to falling in love with a woman. Today, I'd say gay manners are better than most people's Mormon manners. At the time that I sidestepped from the straight dimension to the gay one, however, the manners for dealing with a gay brother or sister weren't that much more advanced than Mormon manners are today. Having been in the straight pride parade and then gone to the rally on the other side of the street, I may have put a special strain on drawing-room encounters. I saw embarrassment and censure in people's eyes. I saw people excuse themselves to go to the bar for another drink.

The world feels entitled to know whether you are married and if not, why not, but there's some tacit agreement not to mention church. If you do have a religion and it's not the right one, watch out! I was stunned that some people felt they could laugh in my face when I said I'd flipped for Joseph Smith. I wondered if they reacted that way to Mormons and felt they probably didn't. These scoffers usually thought they knew enough of me to assume I couldn't have anything positive to say about Joseph. When I finally got my enthusiasm across to them, they simmered down, followed by an unspoken vow to never mention the subject again.

I didn't like being seen as a fool or an idiot for being attracted to Mormonism. It made me want to duck. I hated my lack of bravery—just as I was offended by my snobby dismissal of the Mormons who told me their families went back to the *Mayflower*. I already took Joseph seriously when I responded condescendingly, *"No, no, no, no, my family may go back to the* Mayflower, *but not yours."* So much for having rooted the snobbery out of myself. At least having seen this new form of it put me on guard. After that, when I encountered snobbery against the Mormons while we were working on the film, I tried to stand up to it. My younger brother and I fought for the first time since middle school. When he teasingly asked if Joseph Smith was the prophet who had the vision in a cow pie in Pennsylvania, I said he sounded like a Boston grande dame, shocked to learn how flimsy and odd religion was when you got beyond the stained-glass windows.

I felt my brother's prejudice was a form of aesthetic snobbery. It was as if Joseph Smith had washed God's dirty laundry in public by creating such an uproar about His real existence. Religion should be seen and not heard. A lot of my friends and acquaintances responded the way my brother did. I saw something more threatening in some of the producers at *Frontline*. They felt our portrait of Joseph wasn't critical enough, and when our producer, Helen Whitney, argued against their negative changes about Joseph (as trite and overdone), the team at *Frontline* joked about her having "drunk the Kool-Aid." *Frontline* had a documentary about Jim Jones scheduled to air three weeks before *The Mormons*, so the reference was fresh in their minds. I couldn't believe that these men felt nothing about conflating Jim Jones and Joseph Smith. There were other PBS executives who didn't have that issue; they loved the film not least because it brought a fresh appreciation of Joseph to a national audience. But those supporters wouldn't be drawn into the fray. I also felt then, and feel now, how wrong it was for any producers to mock Helen's superior work so crudely. Their breezy disrespect helped poison the working atmosphere for me.

Some months before the series aired, WGBH began giving out reels for the media to screen. Alex Beam, a columnist at *The Boston Globe*, got one. He staged his response as a damning-with-faint-praise review of Part One. Actually, his piece was called "A Mormon President? I Don't Think So," and it moved quickly from our documentary to a campaign memo, which had been leaked from Romney's camp. The memo acknowledged "Mormonism as weird," and portrayed Romney's staffers kicking around strategies for how that weirdness should be handled. Beam hammered all the ways Mormonism was a lost, "weird" cause: crazy ideas about Independence, Missouri, as the Garden of Eden; policies toward blacks and gays; and yes, polygamy: the sin America loves to hate. Beam ended his piece by saying that even if only a twentieth of the PBS weekly audience watched, "that's four million men and women who will know more about the Mormon faith than Romney might wish them to know. It's bad math for the Mittster."

Times may have changed. The Mormon unease has only begun to be articulated in early 2012. It may get worse. In 2007, I found it disturbing that an exemplar of the liberal media—the few from whom we still expect objectivity and fair play—thought nothing of using his position to give the Mormon *religion* the back of his hand. It is one thing to argue with the church's politics, another to slam the faith. When I went to the LDS Family History Center, I was on a penitential errand. I was going to deal once and for all with whatever snobbery I had toward the Mormons. I felt that even just the faintest hint of superiority here was on the same continuum with the bullying we'd encountered at PBS. Since I'd harbored pretensions about my family coming over on the *Mayflower*, I'd committed myself to track my ancestors back to the seventeenth century and see what was real and what wasn't. It wasn't impossible that we had some relative who'd come on the *Mayflower*. I wouldn't care if we didn't, but for the record, just so no pretentions could ever grow up again in the dark, I wanted to nail this down if I could.

A cousin who'd gotten into Barnes genealogy gave me a list of my paternal forefathers and told me about FamilySearch.org, the free Mormon online genealogy database. You start by putting in a forefather's name with birth and death dates and the places where those events happened. The software gives you a "pedigree chart," with backward-trending ancestors whose names have been officially recorded and collected in the huge Family History archives. The Mormons have gathered records from all over the world, and, according to the Family History Library website, as I write, "approximately 200 (LDS) cameras are currently digitizing records in over 45 countries. Records have been filmed in over 110 countries, territories, and possessions." Both Mormon and non-Mormon have been integrated into LDS databases (not all free to the public). I had a passenger list for the *Mayflower*, and though no Barnes was on it, I figured I could just go back one Barnes at a time until I found a relative—if I did— who'd married a Bradford or a Latham, names of actual *Mayflower* passengers.

I had just gotten into the nineteenth century when I saw that information for some of my Barnes relations had been submitted by members of the LDS Church. I discovered that Julius H. Pratt and his wife, Adeline F. Barnes (married in 1843 in New Haven, Connecticut), had been sealed to their children for all eternity in the Salt Lake Temple sometime between 1943 and 1970. I wasn't sure what it meant (or why it was done so late). Then bells really went off when I got to Eli Barnes (1775–1812) of Hartford, Connecticut. He was Adeline's father (my third great-grandfather). He'd had the ritual baptism for the dead done for him in the Mesa Temple in Arizona sometime between 1927 and 1974.

Baptism for the dead is when a Mormon in this world under-goes a watery immersion in an LDS temple for a person who's deceased. It's not a kidnapping as is generally thought. Accord-ing to Mormon belief, only those baptized in Joseph's restored Christianity can go to heaven. Thus Mormons here are baptized for people who died without knowing about Joseph's restoration. Spirit missionaries on the other side tell the deceased person that he or she has been given the opportunity to join the Mor-mon Church. The deceased spirit may accept or decline. If the spirit accepts, the acceptance has the same weight it would have on earth.

I may not have found any Barneses on the *Mayflower*, but now I was seeing there might be Barneses—my Barneses—who converted to Mormonism long before I thought of it. How else would my third great-grandfather have had a baptism for the dead done for him except by one of our ancestors who had converted? *Ker-thunk*. My heart went *ker-thunk*. Could this really be? There was something almost ominous about the *ker-thunk*. When I showed my research to the woman at the Family History Center, she looked over my printouts quickly and got on her computer. Her hands danced back and forth on the keyboard, her fingers flying over the letters as if they were piano keys. "I don't have time to track the suspect down now," she said, smiling, "but there's a Mormon in here somewhere." She directed my attention to the name of one of the submitters, a man named Willard Ames Barnes IV, with an address in Georgia. My new Mormon guide at FHC told me there was enough information to get his phone number, which I should do, and call and find out what he knew about the Mormon side of the Barnes family.

I called Mr. Willard Ames Barnes IV, a friendly, dedicated member of the growing army of Americans researching their family trees. He was not Mormon, but he had found Anna Barnes, who was a convert to the first generation of the early church. Willard and I were related through Julius Pratt, and Willard had figured out how he was kin to Anna, so I was related to her, too. Anna had converted to Mormonism in 1833. Her husband, Jesse Harmon, and their four children followed her into the church in 1838. *Ker-thunk*: the sound a baseball makes when it hits the hollow of the catcher's mitt. The more I found out about Anna, the more completely I felt I'd met a rebel's fate. It was one thing to tell Ma I wasn't going to curtsy. But now God was demanding that I bend my knee. I might never stand upright again.

Anna and her husband were pillars of the early church. They popped up in all sorts of digitized materials in online LDS archives. Though she was my eighth cousin once removed, her intense ties to major Mormon figures brought the early church close to me. Her husband became Joseph Smith's bodyguard and went to jail with him at the end; Anna would become a plural wife before they left Nauvoo; and her daughter and sister would both marry H. C. Kimball, one of the early Apostles, shortly before leaving Illinois for Utah. Anna was born in Windham, Massachusetts, in 1798, the first child of ten born to Abijah Barnes and Abi Bradford. Records show the family moving from Windham to Cayuga County, New York, and then, in 1818, to Springfield, Pennsylvania, where many poor people moved as land became available after Erie became a county in 1800. Jesse Harmon was born in 1795 in Rupert, Vermont, and joined the U.S. Army in time to fight in the War of 1812. A man of legendary courage, he'd ducked flying tomahawks. He had lived through an explosion that dismembered many of his friends, and he had held his dying brother in his arms at the Battle of Lacolle Mills.

Jesse received his honorable discharge from the U.S. Army in 1815 and followed the country west, looking for opportunity. He ended up in Conneaut Township, Pennsylvania, where he met Anna Barnes. They were married in 1819 and settled in a log cabin Jesse built for his growing family: Milo, born 1820, Sophronia, born 1824, Amos, born 1827, and Ansel Perse, born 1832. If they weren't too busy, they probably read the weekly newspaper. Anna and Jesse might have followed Joseph Smith's arrival in nearby Kirtland, Ohio, and read the notices of when the Mormon missionaries would be speaking in their town.

We know from the historical record that Joseph galloped into Kirtland in January 1831 in the back of Sidney Rigdon's sleigh. Rigdon was a well-read and powerful speaker who'd developed his own brand of restoring the Christian Church to its original purity. He'd gathered a substantial following in Ohio when one of his followers gave him a Book of Mormon. At thirty-seven, Rigdon could not believe a twenty-four-year-old had written it. This young, new prophet stirred the depths of his God-haunted soul, roiled his unsatisfied longing for the new gathering of Israel and the return of Christ. Rigdon went to New York to meet the prodigy. The men connected instantly, bringing youthful fire together with seasoned smoldering, and, as often was the case, their collaboration came just in the nick of time, at a moment when Joseph had to leap an abyss if he was going to survive. When he met Emma, he needed to spring for serious new maturity; when Oliver Cowdery turned up, Joseph was straining toward a new creative process. Rigdon arrived just as the Mormon Seer, Translator, Prophet, and Apostle of Jesus Christ was desperate for a stable place to build his church. Joseph's welcome in upstate New York was grinding to a halt. The law was after him on new charges of pretending; his followers were growing rapidly and in annoying numbers; his enemies were sending him death threats. At this point, when Rigdon—now a convert—invited him to lead his church community in Kirtland, Joseph had the new fresh start he desperately needed.

As they galloped into Kirtland, Rigdon stopped the sleigh at Newel K. Whitney's general store, the center of useful information for the town. Joseph found Whitney behind the counter and introduced himself exuberantly, "I am Joseph the prophet!" Then he added a clairvoyant hunch. "You've prayed me here, now what do you want of me?" Whitney was astonished; a few days before, he and his wife had seen a cloud of glory resting on their house. Now this shining son of the New World was here. He must be the fulfillment of their vision. Newel invited Joseph and his family to stay in his house while they got settled.

Soon enough Joseph was hard at work on fifteen different tracks simultaneously: receiving revelations for a book of commandments, organizing the priestly structures for his new church, wrestling with finances. At the same time, Joseph grew more systematic about deploying missionaries around the countryside. He soon had them covering Erie County, Pennsylvania, where they held meetings in schoolhouses and sometimes sold the Book of Mormon afterward. The missionaries also went door to door. A few of them carried the prophet's revelations, which had been written out on scraps of paper and were shown around as tangible pieces of God's word. The missionaries won so many converts in the county it was called Mormon Run. A few Baptists were even redipped, in spite of the enmity between their church and the Mormons. By 1833, Joseph's missionaries had gained 121 converts, among them Anna's parents and her sister, Hulda, probably "under the hand of Elder D. Philastus Hurlbut." If this elder's name sounds like one of W. C. Fields's characters, it's because he should have been. Of the scandalous Elder Hurlbut, more later. In May 1833, Orson Hyde, an early Mormon leader, knocked at Anna's door. First he asked for a "cooling" drink, and then he taught her the restored gospel of Jesus Christ.

After the first lesson, Anna expressed her readiness to investigate the teachings of the church. She was soon converted and baptized on May 29, 1833. Jesse did not convert right away, nor did Anna's children, who were in their early teens and younger. But Appleton Milo Harmon, their oldest son, left a colorful journal of his family's gradual conversion to Mormonism. He describes how "twas in our humble cottage" that a "pilgrim of God arrived . . . on his holy errand." Elder Hyde "imparted to us the word of the eternal life that was like a well of living water springing up into everlasting life. . . . It worked upon us. It would not let us linger." They thought about what Hyde had said for weeks and months to come. They talked about it at dinner. Appleton Milo never mentions whether the family had to make their terms with the rumbling of anti-Mormon controversy. Grandfather and Grandmother Barnes apparently never looked back. Aunt Hulda, because she lived alone, would have to make peace with rumors of spiritual wifery that trailed Joseph Smith's missionaries to her very door. She never complained.

Ker-thunk. I wasn't just a twenty-first-century woman studying Joseph and his religion. Part of me had been a nineteenth-century woman in the thick of the contagion at Mormon Run! As Elder Hyde's words worked on him, Milo felt something similar happening to his father and siblings. Anna's example, he wrote in his journal, helped bring the "wonderful change in our family." Mormonism was in my blood. *Ker-thunk.* Anna Barnes was an eye-opener, though I was surprised to find her on my father's side. My mother's family had been in New England since the seventeenth century, and they were WASPy, but not as snobby as my father's family. It seemed very possible that some of her hardworking, land-clearing relatives might have gravitated toward a radical new church. I sent both my parents' genealogical information to a Mormon genealogist in Utah.

There were a few hits on my mother's side. Among them, most dramatically, I was related to Caleb Baldwin, who converted in 1830 in Ohio. Through his experience, I found I wasn't the first member of my family who'd been bound to Joseph and refused to give him up when the outside world protested. Caleb was sent to Liberty Jail with Joseph at the end of the Missouri War. He was interrogated while he and the prophet were chained together. Though offered his freedom if he would renounce the Book of Mormon and Joseph Smith's religion, Caleb refused. He is a distant cousin of mine, but even distant cousins share a drop of blood; and where there's a drop of blood, there is, as my genealogist has often said, *consanguinity.* Without that, our encounter might seem only as real as sharing an umbrella with a stranger at a bus stop. Or being temporarily stuck in a broken elevator together. But consanguinity is full of the poetry of affiliation and sympathy. Caleb's intense feelings and dander in his own defense were qualities I knew in my mother and her side of the family. I could see myself in him.

My fishing on my father's side continued to fill the nets. It turned out that my father's Whitney cousin, Jock Whitney, WASP, and Newel K. Whitney, Mormon, both sprang from different branches of a family tree originating in one John Whitney, who emigrated from England to Watertown, Massachusetts, in 1635. Most sensationally, I was related to the grand pioneer Royal Barney, whose daughter, Harriet Emeline Barney, became Brigham Young's forty-ninth wife. I personally was related to Brigham Young through matrimony, a marriage Harriet entered when she was twenty-five and Brigham fifty-four. This was incredible, but not as meaningful to me as the fact that Anna Barnes's mother, Abi Bradford, was a direct descendant of William Bradford, renowned governor of Plymouth Colony and author of the enduring history *Of Plymouth Plantation*. I did have connections to the *Mayflower* after all, and they were Mormon!

While these kinds of coincidences were often codified as religious signs, I found myself going in the other direction. The more Mormon connections I found in my family past, the less I had the *ker-thunk* reflex. There were too many coincidences for this to be all about me. There must be some larger pattern at work. Once I found Professor Val Rust's very interesting book *Radical Origins*, the obvious fact came forward. Any American with ancestors in New England even by the late eighteenth century would be likely to have Mormon relatives starting from 1830, when Joseph founded the church. The whole population of the time was small; people were very religious; Mormonism was an exciting refiguring of Christian themes. Joseph Smith was from New England. Though his church ultimately spread west, the word first spread from Palmyra into Vermont, Connecticut, Massachusetts, and Rhode Island.

Still, no one in my family knew we had Mormons among our forefathers. I never heard people out in the world talking about having Mormon ancestors the way they mentioned that their families originally came from Ireland or Czechoslovakia or wherever. The Mormons' separateness often made it seem that they'd sprung fully formed from Joseph's head. But people with no connection to him had been moved by his words out of the mouths of strange missionaries. One day Anna Barnes had been a housewife whose brothers and sisters had all the family things in common; the next, she converted to Mormonism. What had Anna thirsted for that her eight siblings hadn't? Only one sentence of written description about her character has survived, and it follows her wherever she goes: "Anna was a kind and loving wife and mother, very sweet and gentle and strongly spiritual." There's nothing in that sentence to indicate a restless spirit seeking something more than her comfortable Congregationalist faith.

What did Anna and I have in common? How would I ever find out? As far as I knew there were no letters between Anna's side of the family and her Barnes siblings who, as one of our family genealogists has written, "kept the ruts deep." In the absence of family correspondence, *Radical Origins* gave me something pretty rich to go on. Val Rust, too, began by wondering what kind of people were attracted to a new religion that "provided little more than a promise of some future paradise on earth." Drawing on the Mormons' impeccable genealogical data, Professor Rust was able to track the families of forty percent of the earliest converts back to their early American origins. A disproportionate number of these earliest converts were Pilgrim Separatists, many of whom first landed at Plymouth.

Radical Origins was extremely circumspect in its arguments and conclusions. But I fell in love with Rust's discovery. I stayed up all night admiring its suggestiveness and drawing out his fabulous implications, saying, Wow! Wow! Wow! The Mormons morphed out of the Pilgrims! They were working people without a gentleman among them. Religion was first, second, and third in their lives. The Pilgrims wanted to withdraw from the Church of England. The Puritans wanted to reform it. The Puritans were men of property, men like John Winthrop, the first governor of Massachusetts, who was a trained lawyer. Whereas Pilgrims were said "to be careless of fame," the Puritans had, as Edmund Morgan put it so trenchantly, "that unabashed assumption of superiority which was to carry English rule around the world."

The Mormons and Puritan America were fraternal twins separated at birth! Consider how many early Mormon names are also among the Puritans: Abbott, Adams, Bundy, Lowell, Norton, Parker, Pierce. On and on. The Mormons' religion and our Puritan capitalism had been incubated in the same womb. And when they went their separate ways, they dramatized the split between perfect good and perfect gain in our national character. It explained why, as different as we were, we also resembled each other in many of our basic characteristics: practicality, orderliness, the obsession of each with its own righteousness. I found our deep prenatal bond one of the most unheralded facts of the Anglo immigration, which founded our country. It shed new light on the fate of the WASPs, whose rhetoric "originated in the European pulpit, was transformed in both form and content by the New England Puritans, persisted through the eighteenth century, and helped sustain a national dream through two hundred years of turbulence and change."

Who knows how the fateful destinies of the twins and their interplay will ultimately unfold in our country? As related communities, we have shared territory on several levels, yet have also fought to the point of bloodshed in the past. Now, though, the Puritan WASPs seem spent. Perhaps we'll watch the flowering of the Mormons in American public life together. After so many decades of continuing stability in their own world and growing participation in ours, the Mormons seem to be finally coming into their own at the start of the twenty-first century.

The ideal WASP combined public service, stiff upper lip, noblesse oblige, and a lightness of touch. I had accumulated these assumptions drop by drop as I was growing up. Even the newly arrived pretender President Jack Kennedy was a WASP protégé; he was a master of grace as he sent our first troops into Southeast Asia. But then the Vietnam War turned out to be a long unmasking of our ruling-class code. The WASPs' grim re-alpolitik on behalf of keeping power was exposed. Their primacy was badly wounded. I finally touched down on the hollowness of everything around the time the newspapers were reporting my father's involvement in assassination attempts on Castro. He was long dead and couldn't speak for himself. Drop by drop I cleansed myself (or tried to) of my own coldness and secret desire for advantage. I was hungry for truth and filled with questions about my new place in the universe. When we were making the film, I was amazed to hear answers coming out of President Gordon Hinckley's mouth. They were the very questions, he said, that Mormonism answered: Who am I? Where did I come from? Where am I going? At some level, that's what I'd been asking myself when I had my near-conversion on the road to Richmond. Maybe that's what Anna Barnes had been asking, when she converted in 1833. Maybe the desire for that knowledge was what we had in common across time.

EIGHT

Joseph Through the Particle Accelerator

The Joseph Smith who settles in Kirtland, Ohio, in 1831 is a fabulous, new creature. The Book of Mormon came through him in a flash. The first half of his life has been a pastoral shepherd's tale compared with what is going to come. The Book of Mormon shatters the theological mold. Joseph's creative act is more like James Joyce writing *Ulysses* than Martin Luther's posting his theses on the church door. Not only was he presenting a new vision of the old Christianity, he was a complete outsider, as big a nobody as van Gogh. In the years after the Book of Mormon, Joseph strained at every limitation in himself; he lived by the seat of his pants, exploding conventions both social and religious, pushing, pushing the envelope of common sense, dread; reaching, reaching for "the character, perfection, and attributes of God." He used life like an Action Painter prophet, hurling it in combinations that were holy, deep, and contradictory.

He was a different person in the wake of the Book of Mormon. He had ridden round in the atom smasher. When he began the Book of Mormon, Joseph was a boy calling on the powers of the universe with a peep stone and a hat. As God's fire poured through him, it took that boy apart; it flayed him, it released hidden powers and energies. He'd been a confident boy without much to be confident about. Now he knew he was some sort of genius chosen by God to change Christ's place in history.

When Joseph arrived in Kirtland at twenty-five, people remarked on his "intelligence" as often as on his "benevolence." He was informal, quick with a joke, loved to wrestle. John D. Lee, one of Joseph's early bodyguards, said that he had an "eagle-eye," and that "there was something in his manner and appearance that was bewitching and winning; his countenance was that of a plain, honest man . . . and void of deceit or hypocrisy." Yet Thomas Ford, an Illinois governor and former judge, said of Joseph: "It must not be supposed that the pretended Prophet practiced the tricks of a common imposter. . . . He could, as occasion required, be exceedingly meek in deportment; and then rough and boisterous as a highway robber; being always able to satisfy his followers of the propriety of his conduct."

If he had not been able "to float like a butterfly, sting like a bee," Joseph could not have survived, especially in these years when ideas and themes and revelations were erupting from him. His sudden abilities in unlikely areas were astonishing. As boys, Joseph and Tom Sawyer spent about the same amount of time in pews on Sunday, but Joseph now unveiled the radical structure for the new church through revelation. It would be staffed by its own untrained laity. Men were called to positions of authority by other men. Its flexible but structured model adapted brilliantly as the church grew over time, community by community. As time passed and church authority needed to expand, Joseph revelated other innovative levels of bureaucracy.

Yet for as long as he lived, his open, experimental personality tossed procedure into a cocked hat when he was inspired. Richard Bushman describes the young Joseph as having "outrageous confidence" at this point in his life. He was too spontaneous, too responsive to be a true authoritarian. As he became a worldly leader, he was the player carrying the football. He was constantly buried under piles of flying tacklers. The historical record of what he did and thought, whom he was close to, and how he changed got more and more hectic from this point on. Who he became, whether he fell apart or grew corrupt, remained important to me. I wanted to know whether he taught me what keeping faith means when you are living in the particle accelerator. Or whether he was another romantic American figure who was somehow undone by his tremendous gifts. Or an extraordinary youth who couldn't fully mature. Joseph, the son of the frontier, gradually became the prophet of America the Dissonant, holding his proliferating parts together through prayer and revelation.

In early July 1831, even before his lay structure for his church was in place, Joseph received revelations about the site for Zion. It would be in Missouri. Joseph and his men must go there to sacralize the space. This fulfillment of ancient Bible prophecy would not have been surprising in a conventional Christian from an earlier century. Or even a radical American preacher in Joseph's own time. It was amazing in a youth who only five years before was living by the seat of his pants, expressing no particular commitment to the fate of the ancient Israelites. Suddenly, his people had to bring the distant biblical past into the present world. Only then would the Mormons—like early Puritan settlers—also be "exiles from the Old World, figurative Israelites who were guided to this Promised Land to establish a spiritual Zion." The phrases and allegory were in the air of his youth, but not everyone who picks up a jazz trumpet is Louis Armstrong. Joseph Smith was. Just like that: he could play like a master and administer to beat the band.

Joseph attracted men and women whose minds were bursting with visions, prayers, and revelations. They were living in the red-hot core of their religious passion. His followers spoke in tongues, fell into raptures, healed with sensitive hands and enthusiastic cries. These were people who craved stronger spiritual nourishment, who wanted fiery preaching and miracles. Joseph had them to give, but then converts who "could not sleep for joy" were moved to give wilder and wilder testimony of their revelations. It was not uncommon for angels with horns to be seen in the streets or for men who weren't prophets to feel their revelations were equal to those of the prophet himself.

The author of the Declaration of Independence for scripture began to realize the confusion of unsettled authority by which he was surrounded. It was not long before Jesus Christ began dictating the Doctrine and Covenants to the prophet, who was referred to as Joseph Smith Jun. throughout its pages. The D&C

was the new rule book from the new living Christ. It made clear that not just anyone's revelations will matter. The revelator must have "authority" and "be regularly ordained by the heads of the church." Though every man must experience the living Christ for himself, the hierarchy of the church would decide what would be taught and who would teach. The prophet and his revelations would be the most important. Yet now, as Joseph asserted his authority, there were the first notes of irony.

They may have begun in the inadvertent, endearing campiness of Christ dictating the rules through the young prophet, described with his proper generational title, to his scribe. "Wherefore, I the Lord, knowing the calamity which should come upon the inhabitants of the earth, called upon my servant Joseph Smith Jun., and spake unto him from heaven, and gave him commandment." According to the Book of Mormon, Joseph, the new Prophet of Christ, must identify himself as the son of Joseph in the correct patriarchal line. Prophecy had already made known that Joseph Smith, the modern prophet, would be such a son, and that the filial relation would establish his descent from the biblical Egyptian Joseph. But when I see "Joseph Smith Jun.," erupt in the midst of the pious compendium of rules and regulations, I think, *David and Goliath meet Wonder Boy.* Every now and then I also catch a whiff of camp in the Book of Mormon (as when "eat, drink and be merry" leaps off the page). There was more campiness to come in Joseph's proclaiming that the Garden of Eden was actually in Independence, Missouri, in a place he said was called Adam-ondi-Ahman. Adam himself came here in exile, it seems, and its designated name is given in Adamic, a language Adam supposedly spoke and apparently Joseph did, too. It's not a mocking campiness (though all campiness is distancing). Joseph's campiness seems like the unavoidable result of a fresh son of the New World swinging an ancient tradition by the tail. The clash of cultures is a sacred form of Americana, one filled with Joseph's egalitarian panache. He's a free man saying his approach to God is just as good as any King James.

In the early years as a leader of the church, he threw himself into his work and gloried in his connection to God whatever form it took. But he was also growing aware of the difference between his limitations as a man and his calling as a prophet. Converts came to Kirtland to meet "God's mouthpiece." There were those who found that in Joseph. Others who traveled to meet him often said he didn't act the way a prophet should. He was informal, had a big temper, was contradictory. In Kirtland, his sexual energy was also beginning to boil to the surface. Joseph must have been aware of the incongruities between those unruly impulses and the decorum he was supposed to maintain as a prophet.

It was probably easy for him to be honest about things like the smoking and spitting that led to the Word of Wisdom in 1833. Under pressure from Emma to keep his officers from making a mess when they met at her house, Joseph had a revelation, saying it would be better for the men's health (and his) if they restrained from smoking and drinking so much. This was a feel-good opportunity to admit his flaws and pronounce against them. But there were darker things about himself he didn't mention. It would have been hard to do and chaotic if he had. Instead, he routinely emphasized that his followers should know he was a prophet only when he spoke as one. Joseph was adored when he claimed he was a prophet, but he could get in trouble for saying he was also only a man. After one occasion when he insisted he, too, was human, members of the church were so upset he had to apologize. In his sermon "It Has Gone Abroad That I Was No Longer a Prophet," Joseph confessed, "I said it Ironically. I thought you would all understand."

Joseph could step back to comment on his being both prophet and man. He never commented on his prophetic gift for revelation. He gloried in his gift: he developed it. His revelations were sometimes moralizing, sometimes mystical, often visual. He saw heaven with casts of characters ranging from the angelic hosts to members of his family. He had intimate meetings with Christ on earth. He was never detached about his revelations as he was about himself. Usually, his revelations flowed, especially in his late twenties and early thirties. As he got older and more conflicted as a prophet and a man, his revelations sometimes came at a cost. As a child, Adaline Knight saw Joseph's limp figure carried into the house while he was having a revelation. "The children all sprang to their feet for Bro. Joseph lay helpless in their arms, his head resting on his brother's shoulder, his face as pale as death, but his eyes were open, though he seemed not to see earthly things."

His prophetic gift for revelation made it difficult for people to assess the man. His followers were awed by the fact that he could have revelations in the middle of a meeting. As a thirteen-year-old teenager, Mary Rollins watched as Joseph had a revelation while the service was going on. "He was looking ahead and his face outshone the candle which was on a shelf behind him. . . . He looked as though a searchlight was inside his face and shining through every pore." The men who led the church with him were also reverent toward his gift. Parley P. Pratt, one of the early leaders of the church, remembered Joseph dictating a revelation after prayers in his Translating Room. "Each sentence was uttered slowly and very distinctly, and with a pause between each, sufficiently long for it to be recorded by an ordinary writer, in long hand." William McLellin, someone who was a longtime scribe of Joseph's, praised him for being able "without premeditation, to thus deliver in broken sentences some of the most sublime pieces of composition which I ever perused in any book."

Some of the men around Joseph in Kirtland were not admirers; they were interested, but had not yet made up their minds. Some were intelligent, educated men with a testing attitude like Ezra Booth, a Methodist clergyman, who was an early convert. He and his wife came to Kirtland to investigate in the spring of 1831. After witnessing an extraordinary healing by Joseph, Booth joined in the belief that the prophet and his church were blessed by the "signs and wonders" known to the early Christians. Booth soon regretted his conversion, because when Joseph "speaks by the Spirit, or says he knows a thing by the communication of the Spirit, it is received as coming directly from the mouth of the Lord." When Joseph's revelations superseded the Bible, the prophet's attitude was: So be it. But this rubbed Booth the wrong way. If "placing the Bible under circumstances which render it entirely useless, is infidelity, Mormonism is infidelity."

Booth went with Smith and his company on the first trip to Zion. While they traveled together, Booth speculated whether Joseph's revelations weren't suspiciously convenient. First, through God's instruction, Joseph said the men would canoe the Missouri River. When he found its "rough and angry" current too risky, too uncomfortable, the prophet counteracted the first revelation that had put them all in boats. "A new commandment was issued, in which a great curse was pronounced against the waters: navigating them was to be attended with extreme danger; and all the saints, in general, were prohibited in journeying upon them, to the promised land." For its sins, Joseph renamed the Missouri River "the river of Destruction." The company was rerouted to go by land, with the encouragement to preach as they went. If Booth had not been so furious, he could have been Mark Twain, recording tongue-in-cheek how they all "violated" the commandment by never preaching. Next Joseph got word that there were "plots for their destruction" awaiting them on steamboats. Booth noted dryly, "This too we proved to be false."

It's easy for me to imagine how a wet holy man, one who might not have enjoyed riding the rapids, and not necessarily a great wilderness scout, would adjust the comfort level of his revelations. Joseph often said he was fallible, and Booth struck me as quite humorless. But when he left the church, Booth drew attention to an edge in the prophet he had studied to his own disillusion. In his published letters about Joseph, Booth asked his fellow apostates for whom he was writing: "Have you not frequently observed in Joseph, a want of the sobriety, prudence and stability, which are some of the most prominent traits in the christen character? Have you not often discovered in him, a spirit of lightness and levity, a temper easily irritated, and an habitual proneness to jesting and joking?"

From now on, Joseph's edgy self was part of the mix. It was not just that he has a sense of fun, nor that he could be funny, Joseph's irony began to deepen. Perhaps it was because the conflict between the man and the prophet deepened, too. There were rumors that he'd been forced to leave Palmyra because of his womanizing. Rumors of this kind arose again quickly in Kirtland. As demands on the prophet intensified, these murmurings were oil to the flaming disappointment some new arrivals felt as Joseph led the young church through its early stages. After a year and a half in Kirtland, Joseph wrote a friend that he felt the pressures could "destroy" his mind. These pressures would only get worse. Ezra Booth's condemnatory letters and rumors of the prophet's wayward sexuality excited such rage that a mob of discontents broke into Joseph's house in the middle of the night. They dragged him out into the cold and tied him naked to a board. Once they'd tarred and feathered him, the crowd shouted as they pushed a doctor, a real one, to the fore. He had a knife.

But when he saw how Joseph's front teeth had been pushed down his throat, how he was bleeding and badly beaten, the doctor could not go through with the castration he was supposed to perform.

Joseph preached the next day with a swollen face, tar stuck in his hair. He "preached as usual," making no mention of his beating the night before. His sense that he was not seen for all that he was may have been strengthened by resentment for being punished beyond any wrongs he might have committed. Around this time, Joseph started attracting unsavory admirers along with the many able men and talented collaborators he continued to draw into his church. D. P. Hurlbut was among the first; Porter Rockwell, John C. Bennett, and Joseph Jackson would follow. Sometimes they mirrored him in such a distorted glass we can't be sure if Smith was being defamed or whether, by having something in common with these rogues, Joseph was much worse than we ever imagined. The Elder D. Philastus Hurlbut, the Mormon missionary who converted Hulda Barnes, my eighth cousin on my father's side, was an early example of one of these unsavory admirers. Hulda was very small in Joseph's biography, but Hurlbut was quite big; the tiny part my cousin played in Mormon history helped catapult Hurlbut deep into Joseph's vulnerabilities. I believe the relationship is fair to study here, especially for its glimpse into Smith's ambivalent relation to his doppelgangers.

In 1818, a twelve-year-old Hulda Barnes moved to Erie County with her parents; Anna was six years older. The record has been good to Anna, but not to Hulda, her sister, who at the very least was an odd duck. She seems to have converted at the same time her parents joined the Mormon Church in May 1833. Hulda was then living alone, showing an independence that historians have now agreed did not do much good for a woman's reputation in those days. If she'd tried it in Salem in the seventeenth century, she would have been called a "witch" in a moment. But trying it in Conneaut Township, Pennsylvania, in 1833 earned her the title of "the Mormon woman of very bad character." She'd had help gaining this reputation from the infamous Dr. Philastus Hurlbut, a preacher who "could win his way into the churches, but could not make good."

Dr. Hurlbut did sometimes practice medicine, but he was a doctor only in the W. C. Fields sense. That is, he was nicknamed "Doctor" by his mother since he was her seventh son: it was a convention of the time to call that child, if a boy, "Doctor." There was no framed degree on his wall, and history can at least be grateful that he never pretended to be a surgeon. A native of Vermont, he made his way to Ohio in 1832 and settled in Geauga County. His activities before he arrived in Ohio, along with his activities through 1852, follow a pattern that would finally be summed up by one observer of his time: "In regard to D. P. Hurlbut . . . He was excommunicated from the Methodist Episcopal Church for improprieties with the opposite sex and lying. . . . He was excommunicated from the Church of Jesus Christ of Latter-Day Saints for improprieties with the opposite sex and lying. . . . [He later] wormed himself into the 'Church of the United Brethren of Christ' and was ordained an Elder." But after a trial in 1852, Elder Hurlbut was once more excommunicated from that church for "improprieties with the opposite sex, lying," and this time, in addition, "intemperance."

Ordained an elder in Kirtland, Hurlbut was sent into the Conneaut Township mission field with John F. Boynton in April 1833. "Whether or not Elder Hurlbut was meeting the local Mormon girls this early, he must have known most of the LDS converts in southwestern Erie County by the first week in April, simply by attending meetings of the LDS Elk Creek branch." Notes from a special, closed April 5 meeting show that Elder Hurlbut attended. It had been called by Elder Hyrum Smith, Joseph's broad-shouldered older brother, "to root out cases of 'fornication' among the Saints." It seems reasonable to conclude the Mormon Church leaders had gotten wind of Hurlbut's reputation. But it also seems reasonable to wonder if they were afraid that Hurlbut's womanizing would enhance rumors about Joseph's.

Emotion was running high in the barely fledged Mormon community because of Joseph's tar and feathering, arguments within the church, and constant apostatizing by discontents. Elder Hyrum Smith called for more self-control among the missionaries at the meeting of the LDS Elk Creek branch. The record shows he took action by separating Hurlbut from Elder Copley, with whom he'd first been paired. Elder Hurlbut was sent on with Orson Hyde, a Mormon leader known to be upright. However, once the two men set out on their own, it did not take long for the bracing influence of Hyrum's words and Hyde's example to evaporate from Hurlbut's memory. When he knocked at Hulda's door, he was the same D. P. Hurlbut who'd gotten in trouble with the Methodist Episcopalians for improprieties with the opposite sex.

Elder Hurlbut converted Hulda Barnes. He also seduced her. Soon after Orson Hyde baptized Hulda's sister, Anna, his sixtieth and last convert of that missionary tour, he hurried back to Kirtland, where he brought seduction charges against Hurlbut. Page 12 of the Kirtland Council Minute Book, June 3, 1833, says "a conference of high priests convened" at the Translating Room. They decided Hurlbut must marry Hulda. But he refused. He was disfellowshipped and his Elder's license confiscated.

Yet word also went out that Hurlbut, who was absent during his trial, could be reinstated if he would only return and make a public confession. Despite the fact that he was described as a man with "a big I, and a little u," Hurlbut came back and submitted to this public humiliation and reconciliation on June 21 in a meeting presided over by Joseph Smith, Jr. The record reads: "He wept like a child and prayed and begged to be forgiven." Dale R. Broadhurst, a historian who has laid out Hurlbut's Mormon chronology online, believes that Hurlbut would not have gotten a second hearing unless he held some secret threat over Joseph. Broadhurst wonders whether this secret threat might have been polygamy.

Though Hurlbut would not walk Hulda down the aisle, he

was rumored to have taken her as a spiritual wife. "Spiritual wifery" was a sort of folk form of what would later be outright polygamy. It was a religious concept, one that mainly hallowed a widower's marriage to a new wife, though he still expected to meet his deceased one in heaven. It could also apply to the consummation of certain exalted relationships between an unmarried man and woman. Joseph's first official spiritual wife dates back to 1835, but his preoccupation with plural marriage began much earlier. He began to pray about it in 1831 while he was working on a translation of the Bible. There was plenty of gossip about Joseph's worldly womanizing and also about his having taken his first unofficial plural wife in 1832. Hurlbut was known to be courting other women besides Hulda, and apparently telling them that he'd had "revelations" about their predestined appointment with shared passion. Whether Hurlbut pressured the prophet with exposure of spiritual wifery not long after Joseph had been publicly punished for his sexual waywardness is not clear. This is: At the end of the June 21 council, Hurlbut was rebaptized into the church and his license was restored.

Did Joseph harbor resentment toward Hurlbut? Why else did he have him followed after he went back on the road as a missionary? Does it not take a certain kind of thief to catch a certain kind of thief? Before he got very far, Brother D. P. Hurlbut was boasting to friends that he "only confessed to see whether the Council had power to discern his spirit." Not only that, he also claimed he had "deceived Joseph Smith[s] God, or the Spirit by which he is actuated." For his boasting, Hurlbut was back in the Translating Room on June 23, 1833, being deciphered within an inch of his life. At least as far as we can tell, he was.

The Kirtland Council Minute Book for these days when Hurlbut was in and out of court was in disarray. His full testimony on June 23 was nowhere to be found. Other papers except one amount to marginalia. That one was an undated document in Joseph Smith's hand, though written as if by Hurlbut himself on June 21: "I, Doct. P. Hurlbut, having been tried before the Bishops Council of High Priests in a charge of unchristian like conduct with the female sex . . . do by (these present) most solemnly enter my appeal . . . for a rehearing." Had Joseph seen enough of himself in Hurlbut to write the man's own appeal for forgiveness? This cannot be determined. But Hurlbut was forgiven, broke the council's trust once more, and was excommunicated.

Hurlbut returned to Erie County, where he stayed with Hulda while he plotted how best to get his revenge. He heard of a manuscript written by Solomon Spaulding from which Joseph might have forged the Book of Mormon. It turned out to be a false lead. There was a manuscript, but there was no resemblance to Joseph's scripture. Nonetheless, it muddied the water of the Book of Mormon authorship for a century to come. It's not known if Hurlbut got the pleasure of leaving Joseph with this black eye. He soon moved on to a cache of slanderous stories about Joseph from his Palmyra days. He spent two months in the fall of 1833 with Joseph's former neighbors, collecting affidavits of their memories of the Smith family and the treasure-digging boy and his father.

I found them rather fun reading. Though the affidavits have been used as evidence of Joseph's scandalous boyhood, they don't seem that derogatory to me. They often portray a more innocent time and place, a time when a man (Peter Ingersoll) who having a free moment after his lunch, while his oxen were taken up with eating grass, could join Joseph Smith, Sr., to learn how to use a mineral rod. Joseph Sr. told him to say "Work to the money" to his stick. Peter made several tries before he got his whisper right. The affidavits belong to an era when people took time to make lists of all the sorts of gold Joseph Jr. claimed to see under the ground: barrels and hogsheads of gold coins, bars of gold, golden images, brass kettles filled with gold, gold candlesticks, gold swords, gold buttons and pins. People weren't ashamed of facts about buried gold or peep stones or the different kinds of adventures Joseph Jr. had while getting the plates. There was, of course, the toad with the rusty sword. Things young people in the country invented when there was no television, movies, Facebook, and so on. I would have loved fooling around in search of gold. I'd have seen the holiness in it. The men who were so outraged by Joseph's treasure digging had themselves gone looking for money with him. All of them showed a passion for storytelling, which their former friend, the prophet, ultimately laid at the service of divinity itself.

Hurlbut sold these affidavits to Eber D. Howe, editor of *The Painesville Telegraph*. In 1834, Howe published them with his own critical history in a volume called *Mormonism Unvailed* [*sic*]. It caused an uproar in Kirtland, where anxious members of the new church were horrified by the accusations against the Smith family for being intemperate, lazy, and worthless. Joseph Sr.'s drinking was cited, but Joseph Jr. was also reported as staggering around after too much cider and molasses. Men who were disappointed when they didn't get rich with Joseph said he was a liar. They claimed he could never tell a story the same twice in a row. When he couldn't find gold, he thought up the plates and started looking for a Gold Bible. He and his family tried to drum up business by starting the "Gold Bible Company."

Joseph accused Hurlbut of being a liar, of trying to destroy Mormonism. Hurlbut read his affidavits in the churches of Erie County. The battle of insults escalated until Hurlbut swore he would kill Smith. Now Joseph, who'd read and disputed his old neighbors' accounts to his congregation, filed a complaint against Hurlbut in the Kirtland courts. The justice of the peace at first did not act because, he said, he got so many complaints against the Mormons, he ignored them. Finally, Joseph succeeded in getting a court order against Hurlbut. His hold over Joseph was broken. In May 1834, Joseph went to Missouri, where violence had broken out against Mormons in Jackson County. Hurlbut left town, headed for the United Brethren. Hulda, my poor distant cousin, was on her own again.

NINE

Contradiction Is Not a Sign of Falsity

During the Ohio years, the demand for Joseph's leadership was constantly intensifying. He lacked many qualifications. Once the Book of Mormon reinterpreted Christianity, he was under pressure to run a small but growing organization. He had new ideas for structure; he had the drive to implement them, but he was often more sociable than systematic. As a quintessentially gregarious person, Joseph said he "would rather go to hell with his friends than go to heaven alone." He had the heart and mind for leadership, but not necessarily the savvy calculation or steel. He had vision. In the way his visions came and developed, he seemed more like a modern artist or a novelist than a traditional prophet. His imagination was richly visual and often dramatic; his visualizing and his theology formed an ongoing narrative about the salvation of people who were close to him. He could vividly draw his disciples into his intimacy with the other world.

But in May 1834, Joseph had spread his vision too thin. Both Kirtland and Jackson County were in crisis. Both of these communities were made up of new members whose conversion had required complete relocation. Following Joseph meant leaving everything behind. We can hardly imagine their experience. They were closer to heroic immigrants—literally, boat people—rather than middle-class professionals of our day who suddenly attach themselves to a guru and his ashram. Many of the new Mormons were rich in God, but had lived itinerant lives of poverty. In Kirtland, the church gave every man a responsible role and supported him through storehouses with surplus food, clothes, seeds, basics. Yet as involved as these new Mormons were, their salvation depended on the mercurial prophet in their midst. Joseph was charismatic, but also always at the center of argument and controversy. He loved all sorts of different types of men and women, many who loved him, but hated each other. Allegiances shifted chaotically. Membership rose and fell in the Ohio outpost, reaching about five hundred in 1834, when Hurlbut's affidavits caused an uproar. Many new converts were so shaken they began looking around for proof the gold plates were real.

Joseph Smith had shown eleven witnesses the gold plates. Their signed testimonies were published in the Book of Mormon. Oliver Cowdery, David Whitmer, and Martin Harris, the first Three Witnesses, as they were called, had come to early Kirtland with Joseph. By the time Hurlbut's affidavits were published, Cowdery and Whitmer were in and out of town on different missions, but Harris could be seen on the streets every day. He was often surrounded by pilgrims who had driven in wagons for hundreds of miles on word that Joseph had seen God and that he could show them papers signed by Christ person-ally. Though Harris was also becoming one of Joseph's most unstable admirers, the easygoing prophet let him handle public relations here.

Unlike Joseph, whose visions were convincing, Martin Har-ris was a visionary lite, someone who saw so many angels and ghosts a friend described him as "a great one for seeing spooks." His mind could also "darken," causing him to say wounding things about his brethren, even Joseph. But unlike Hurlbut, who wanted to undo the prophet, Harris was more a bumbling loose cannon. He'd had the generosity to take the first 116 pages of the Book of Mormon home to his wife; she was the one with the force to get rid of them. Joseph later so completely forgave Har-ris for his part that he asked Harris to stand with Cowdery and Whitmer while he showed them the gold plates. Their signed statement as witnesses was published in the final text of Joseph's world-shattering text. In Kirtland, when frightened converts turned to him for assurances the plates were real, Harris held steady. He and two others had indeed seen them, as had eight other witnesses. Would Joseph also show the plates to those who'd come from across the country and now depended on the prophet for everything? No, the plates would never be seen again. According to Moroni's instructions, Cowdery and Joseph had taken them back to a secret cave in Hill Cumorah, where they were locked up again with hundreds of other stored plates of sacred history.

While the Ohio town simmered nervously, the Missouri

church of three hundred members seemed to be stabilizing and succeeding in ways Kirtland couldn't. Joseph had designated Independence as the center of church publications, another example of his preternatural grasp of what was necessary to start a world church. It had not occurred to the prophets in bear suits to set up presses in the middle of nowhere. But newspapers and books were crucial to forming this new people called the Mormons, and both were being produced in Independence.

The Evening and the Morning Star, the early church newspaper, was part of the Missouri success story. Then, not quite without warning, Independence became a nightmare, and the newspaper itself was part of the cause. In Missouri, a state with an instant antipathy to the Mormons' sense of being God's chosen people, *The Evening and the Morning Star* printed Joseph's holiest revelations and his most millennial letters. In a state that bridled at Indian resettlement, *The Evening and the Morning Star* celebrated the gathering of Israel as the tribes trekked across Missouri before the eyes of one resentful farmer after another. Tensions exploded when *The Evening and the Morning Star* published what was seen as an antislavery editorial in support of some free blacks who, having joined the church, were forbidden entry in Missouri.

More than one-fifth of Missouri's population was made up of slaves. None of the owners wanted to lose this property, which seemed threatened by the encouragement to the free blacks. Overnight the resentment that had been simmering against the

Mormons was channeled into massive resistance. Five hundred settlers met together in Independence; in a single meeting they decided to expel the Mormons from Jackson County and to forbid any more from coming. All Mormon businesses, including *The Evening and the Morning Star*, would be closed. Going straight from their insurrectionary meeting, the enraged Missouri mob descended on the newspaper's office. They destroyed the press and demolished the two-story brick building in which it was housed. They found the bishop and tarred and feathered him. They were ready to burn the Mormons' crops and houses if the entire colony did not leave. The leaders reluctantly agreed they would get out by January 1, giving others time to organize their families for a spring departure.

Oliver Cowdery brought news of the Missouri debacle to Kirtland in August 1833. Joseph was stunned. So far there had been no deaths, but death was in the air. The Missouri Mormons had been stripped of everything. By the terms of their "agreement," the Mormons could not own property, vote, print a newspaper, or work in the county. Citizens of Zion had been forbidden to obtain any redress by petitioning the state government. When the Mormons successfully petitioned Missouri governor Daniel Dunklin for protection and hired four non-Mormon lawyers, the citizens of Jackson County were enraged. Fifty men rode into a Mormon colony near the Big Blue River. They smashed windows and furniture; tied single ropes around roofs, which one man could then pull off suddenly as he galloped away on his horse. Mormon men were whipped, women and children driven into the woods. Violence begat violence. The Mormons organized to defend themselves and fought back.

Joseph was himself not a violent person. He had lived through intense, two-fisted controversy, but had nonetheless remained sanguine, almost happy-go-lucky. He was twenty-eight when he heard about Mormons being jailed and killed in Missouri. He was old perhaps not to have prepared himself for the suffering of his people; but he was devastated as they were ordered to surrender their arms, and then, after they did, were systematically attacked by a mob. In a raid on one settlement, the Missourians dragged a Mormon out of his bed and beat him to death with his own gun. Twelve hundred Mormons were hounded out of their homes for Joseph's beliefs. Some people were able to get over the border into Clay County, Missouri. Families stayed together, crawling into trenches or covering themselves with bark. Joseph, who still slept in a bed and prayed in safety, was responsible for what they were enduring.

Knowing his people were being harmed drove him, he said, almost to "madness and desperation." Yet Joseph did nothing active on their behalf. He went on a preaching tour to Canada. For several months, Joseph drifted and waffled, offering little leadership. He told the Saints not to sell their lands, but also not to tell anyone they weren't going to cooperate. He promised the men of Kirtland he would defend Zion with swords if that was what God commanded. But revelations on Zion weren't very forthcoming.

Following Joseph's process as he decided what to do means hopscotching among his letters, revelations, journals, *The History of the Church*. There were large gaps. The spaces here while he absorbed the Missouri violence were telling just by being left unfilled. Once he was the leader of the church, his life was jam-packed with action, preaching, revelations, and constantly writing it down, writing it all down. Joseph left a mountain of personal materials that hid as much as they revealed.

Once he kept a personal record, the spaces were as noteworthy as the pages that were written over. For an illiterate boy who grew up on the frontier, freedom rang in the wild: in the places beyond words. For the prophet whose work depended on words, the empty page would be a wild space, a return to wholeness. His journal was full of spaces in 1833–1834 as he tried to come to terms with the threat to his people in Missouri. Maybe in those spaces, Joseph remembered the days when his powers were given to him. He had known then that he needed prayer as much as he needed necromancy. He had prayed, and the magic plates had materialized. Joseph knew the converts were begging Harris for confirmation that the plates were real.

For years Joseph had acted as a prophet without having the slightest idea how a modern prophet would operate. In 1834, in the thick of the actual experience, did he distance himself from the flawed boy he'd been? While Joseph drifted, Harris seems to have started to doubt his prophet. He doubted the foundations! He went around telling people that Joseph "drank too much liquor" while he translated the Book of Mormon! Even

worse, he put himself above Joseph by claiming that he—
Martin—knew the contents of the Book of Mormon before it
was translated. Joseph found the contents out only as he translated. For these errors, Martin was called before Kirtland High
Council with the prophet himself present. He listened to Martin
protest that he never said Joseph took a drink while translating,
no, never. This drinking happened before Joseph ever even got
involved in the translating. Then Martin, overcoming his rival-
rous feelings, apologized for claiming he had been ahead of the
prophet. The claim had come out of the darkness in him. The
council forgave Harris.

Joseph didn't shut Martin down. A more fearful prophet
might have sent him off on a distant mission. Joseph let him go
on telling the story of the gold plates. Let him be the keeper of
their legend. Let him shoulder the responsibility of their reality:
Martin, who sometimes said he saw the plates with his natural
eyes and sometimes said he saw them with his spiritual eyes.
Martin had grown worried about whether they were real or not,
but he was too inconsistent, too wavering to ever really make a
decision. Joseph meanwhile had resolved the fragile basis on
which his authority rests. He was able to move forward again. At
last, on February 24, 1834, he had a revelation in which God
commanded him to lead an army into Missouri.

For the rest of the winter and spring, acting as "Commander
in Chief of the Armies of Israel," Joseph tried to recruit five
hundred men—as he'd been instructed to do in the February
revelation. In early May, he set out with the one hundred who'd

responded to his call. Armed with knives, swords, rakes, pitchforks, pistols, rifles, and axes, the ragtag brigade gave their detractors new amusement. In *The Painesville Telegraph*, Eber D. Howe likened Joseph to "Peter, the Hermit, in the days of the crusades." But for the men in the group, the nine-hundred-mile march from Kirtland, Ohio, to Clay County, Missouri, was a transforming experience.

Many of the men in Zion's Camp would go on to serve as officers of the church; virtually all of the First Quorum of the Seventy went through Zion's Camp, among them Anna Barnes's husband, Jesse Harmon. Unlike a lot of his comrades, Jesse was already a military man. When he signed on to Zion's Camp, he brought with him years of battle experience from the War of 1812, when his brother died in his arms. He had seen so much action that he could refer to a certain sortie as a "military chef doeuvre." He would have been a tough judge of Joseph's idea of battle strategy or soldierly discipline. Jesse was a man to whom no adjectives attach. In his biography by Raymond W. Madsen, he is "born," "fights," "marries." Without any adjectives, he was rather wooden. Though Madsen wrote that "his destiny would lye [*sic*] with the Mormons," in May 1834, a year had passed since his wife converted. Jesse still had not made up his mind. Nor had his children joined the church. Perhaps he held back permission for them to do so. Maybe Jesse saw the long march to Missouri as an opportunity to take the measure of the prophet whose religion had caused his wife such happiness and her sister such misery.

As new converts, Anna and Hulda probably saw each other at the Elk Creek Meeting on Mormon Run. There were also reports that the Harmon family moved in early 1834 to Ashtabula, Ohio, to be closer to Kirtland, and that Hulda moved there at the same time. She appeared in Milo Harmon's journal, treated like a loved member of her family. As her eighth cousin, I hope she found a haven somewhere. Her relations with Hurlbut had been public enough and sufficiently disgraceful that the world freely commented on her weight. History has preserved the arguments over whether she was too "obese" for Hurlbut to have ever taken as a wife, let alone a spiritual one; or whether because she was "robust," Hurlbut as "a large man" would have found her attractive. In the midst of this gossip, the enthusiasm that drew Hulda to the church may have turned to a loneliness and desperation that kept her there. Anna heard her sister's story, and so did Jesse.

Anna had found what she wanted in the Mormon Church. Four of Jesse's siblings had also converted. Almost all the "troops" in Zion's Camp were members, and Jesse's long gestation as an investigator was unusual. In many ways, the peculiar circumstances of the march were an ideal showcase for Joseph's gifts. It was a time-out-of-time moment for him. He could act younger than he felt. As he led his men across country, they had to be careful; but they weren't in terrible danger. The conflict in Missouri was still in the legal stages. Claims by Jackson County Mormons were going through the courts. Joseph had corresponded with Governor Dunklin and actually worked out the defensive terms on which his men would be allowed on Missouri soil.

The prophet's band of brothers started at a hundred, but gained numbers as they went until they were about a hundred eighty-five strong. Hyrum had come, as had their temperamental younger brother, William Smith. George A. Smith, Joseph's younger cousin, marched in pantaloons made of striped bed ticking. Many of Joseph's companions had marched with him for years: Parley P. Pratt, Orson Hyde, Heber C. Kimball, Martin Harris, Wilford Woodruff, Brigham Young. The physical challenge of walking twenty-five miles a day brought the soldiers closer. In one of his few military revelations, Joseph organized the men into companies of twelve. Each was allowed to elect its own captain. Every man had a post and a duty. Joseph gave instruction as they marched. He commanded the beginning and end of each day with ritual. "Every night before retiring to rest, at the sound of the trumpet, we bowed before the Lord in the several tents, and presented our thank-offerings with prayer and supplication; and at the sound of the morning trumpet, about four o'clock, every man was again on his knees before the Lord, imploring His blessing for the day." Brigham Young later said he learned how to lead the church by watching Joseph of Zion's Camp.

All this Jesse saw and took part in. He saw Joseph suffer along with the men. Once the prophet was given sweet bread when the rank and file got bread that was sour. Joseph returned the sweet and took the sour. He bore the heats of May and June, shared mosquitoes, mud, and rain. His feet bled from blisters. Jesse must have witnessed or even perhaps experienced, as many men reported they did, the times when Joseph's buoyant spirit helped cheer others on. He might have admired Joseph's handling of the discontents among them, including Martin Harris, who boasted that he could handle a black snake and then got bitten by it. Something in Joseph's leadership carried Jesse through the anticlimax in Missouri, where there was an impasse in the courts. Fearing that a Mormon army would arouse public alarm, lawyers for the church urged Joseph to lead his soldiers home. As they turned around and started back, the disappointed troops were hit by a serious outbreak of cholera. Fourteen men died. In the aftermath of Zion's Camp, one of its most outspoken discontents brought Joseph before a high council on charges of criminal conduct. Whether this provoked a special display of loyalty is not known, but Jesse was finally moved to become a full Mormon convert at just this moment.

Though Zion's Camp was seen as a failure, Fawn Brodie and Richard Bushman see the next few years as the happiest in Joseph's life. I would say his parts are circulating in relative calm, but the center will not hold for long. His parts don't harmonize. At the same time that he works on completing the extraordinary Kirtland Temple, he translates ancient papyri, which he claims are written in Abraham's actual hand. (A century will pass, but his overconfidence here will catch up with him when these papyri are found in the Metropolitan Museum of Art in 1967.

Scholars judged them to be ordinary funeral documents and not cosmological writings by Abraham.) As Joseph completes his revelations for the Mormons' unique priesthood and church government, he has an affair with Fanny Alger, a young woman working in the home he shared with Emma. This may have been his first polygamous marriage; certainly it was the first in which there was documentation to show that both Joseph and Fanny Alger regarded it as such. To many people it seemed like simple adultery. After the triumphant dedication of the temple in 1836, a peak moment for Joseph the prophet, he overreached himself in the Kirtland Safety Society Bank scandal. When the impoverished community failed to get its charter, the bank collapsed within weeks.

The Kirtland period ended in apostasy and disaster. For the most part, Joseph must be held responsible. Fawn Brodie believes he has been exposed as a dark and empty character. Richard Bushman extends all the mediating justifications for the prophet's overextending himself as a translator, married man, revelator, inexperienced financier, leader of the church, but admits Joseph's life in this period "descended into a tangle of intrigue and conflict." I see him as battling through his own contradictions: between religious idealism and worldly maneuver, artistic vision and artistic license, morality and experiment. Contradiction is not good or bad. "Contradiction is not a sense of falsity," Pascal says, "nor the lack of contradiction a sign of the truth." Contradiction is struggle.

The old school of critics, and Brodie is among them, seemed to feel that Joseph was too divided and insincere to really be a man of God. She believes he probably falls under a diagnosis of "Imposter," men who "struggle between two dominant identities in the individual; the temporarily focused and strongly assertive imposturous one, and the frequently amazingly crude and poorly knit one from which the imposter has emerged." Brodie does not really believe in Joseph as a religious person. I don't see how Joseph can't be seen as religious. Once he starts writing the Book of Mormon, he is entirely focused on God. The question is whether Joseph is a coherent man of God. He certainly tries to work God into what might be seen as sin: translating the Book of Abraham under false pretenses or introducing plural marriage without any group consent from his community. These are the provisional moralities, the ends-justify-means ethical strategies that radicals have often turned to as they break through the status quo. This is religion in the midst of our sort of change, when our morality is so often a postage stamp on our best guess about God, a letter that will be delivered probably after that guess has given way to a new one.

As a dynamic theologian, one who had liberated Christ from his constraints, Joseph's ideas were more and more like those circulating now about personal growth. He started finding new, godlike potential in his intuitions, his sexuality, and his intelligence. From the Kirtland years on, Joseph expressed these views in what would become his canonized scriptures, which, with the Book of Mormon, include the Doctrine and Covenants and the

Pearl of Great Price. But I think they are nowhere more clearly put than in a sermon Joseph preached at the funeral of his friend King Follett. Joseph delivered the sermon to a huge gathering in April 1844, two and a half months before his death. He urged his followers to become all they could be "by going from a small capacity to a great capacity"; by enjoying their own divine "glory, powers, and exaltation"; by climbing the ladder "until you have learned the last principle of the Gospel." Here he speaks to my own aspiration, a quality I associate first with freedom—with the chance for self-fulfillment—but also with the worst risks in freedom: self-delusion, self-aggrandizement, selfishness. Working with human beings as I know them, he said, "you have got to learn to make yourselves Gods." He was saying we can parlay our little selves into that which transcends them. The important question is not so much whether Joseph was conventionally "good." He was clearly much more. At his best, he wanted to transform morality itself, and knowing that he was taking moral risks, we have to ask whether he took responsibility for his actions.

As Richard Bushman says, "It depends on who speaks." Faithful Mormons believe that his actions were good and that he was responsible. They accept Joseph's translation of the Egyptian papyri as the Pearl of Great Price, one of four new scriptures that the prophet gave the church. Those who had been transported during the dedication of the Kirtland Temple were convinced by Joseph's transcendent powers as a prophet. Fanny Alger never went on record. (Her relatives provided the documentation.) Oliver Cowdery called Joseph's relation to her a "dirty, nasty, filthy affair." Emma Smith "saw the transaction" when she spied on Joseph and Fanny in the barn. She was furious and kicked the girl out of the house. After the failure of the bank, Heber C. Kimball said, "there were not twenty persons on earth that would declare that Joseph Smith was a prophet of God."

During these distresses, Jesse Harmon remained committed to Joseph, as did his wife and their newly converted children. Jesse left no spoken words about his experiences in Kirtland. We know he was woven into the fabric of the society. His brothers, Alpheus and Nehemiah, are listed among those who assisted in building the Kirtland Temple. In 1835 Jesse was ordained a Seventy, and called to serve in its First Quorum. In the aftermath of the bank scandal, when hundreds of Mormons lost all their money, the congregation was torn between feeling that the church had grown proud and that Joseph Smith had been deluded. Jesse stood by the prophet.

The upheaval intensified into what has been called the Great Apostasy, a time when the early church almost collapsed completely. There were assassination plots on Joseph's life. His most passionate enemies entered the Kirtland Temple during a Sunday service armed with knives. Joseph Smith, Sr., was one of the people forced to jump out of windows as the rebels took over the sacred building. While his parents and Emma packed up their houses, Joseph and Sidney Rigdon escaped to Missouri by horseback at night. As splinter groups began to form, Jesse Harmon helped organize more than five hundred Kirtland Mormons who wanted to join Joseph in Far West, Missouri. He added his name to the Kirtland Camp Constitution, a document signed by those he accompanied across Missouri, binding them to the prophet.

Research shows that men like Jesse, salts of the earth—the average member—were less inclined to leave Joseph's church during the apostasy. One-third of the General Authorities, among them three Apostles, as well as all of the Three Witnesses and three of the Eight Witnesses left the church in 1837 and 1838. Two other Apostles who were critical of Joseph Smith were almost excommunicated. Brigham Young was one of the top leaders who remained faithful. He attended endless meetings where people complained about Joseph, and he argued force-fully on Joseph's behalf. When he could take no more, Brigham finally told an unruly crowd, "They might rail and slander him as much as they pleased, they could not destroy the appointment of the Prophet of God, they could only destroy their own author-ity, cut the thread that bound them to the Prophet and to God and sink themselves to hell." Soon after, feeling he was not safe in Kirtland, Brigham left town, too.

Martin Harris was among the close associates who turned on Joseph in 1838. He had turned on Joseph before, but the Prophet had never turned on him. As Joseph lost support after the bank scandal, Harris sided with the apostates. He began to deny that any of the Witnesses to the Book of Mormon had seen or handled the gold plates. Harris went so far as to join Warren Parrish's ascendant splinter group. Joseph may have considered excommunicating Harris, but before he could, he himself was excommunicated by the apostates Harris had joined. Joseph also chastised Oliver Cowdery during this time and gave a warning to David Whitmer. In time they would both be excommunicated. Neither of them ever recanted their witness of the gold plates. Martin recanted and then renewed his claim that he had seen them. But when he once more testified to their existence, he began to say that he'd held the plates on his lap and they weighed between thirty and sixty pounds. As a mirror of the sacred originating relics, Harris was an ongoing study in instability.

TEN

The Pure Products of America

Joseph took two months to reach the town of Far West in the cold January of 1838. Sidney Rigdon rode beside Joseph on horseback. Emma and her three children followed in a creaky lumber wagon. As relieved as Joseph was to reach Far West, it was no oasis. The Missouri Saints had been expelled from Jackson County, and then again from Clay County for the "eccentricity of their religious beliefs." Finally, the Mormons had settled in a part of Caldwell County, which was especially carved out for them by the Missouri legislature. These tireless settlers met Joseph with a brass band eight miles out of town. They marched noisily alongside the prophet into Far West, already a small city of a hundred buildings built around a central square.

Missouri had been treating the Mormons like wartime enemies since driving them out of Jackson County. The governor had gone so far as to tell the church that "neither the courts nor the state militia could give assistance to such a hated people." Once Joseph arrived, Missouri expected every Mormon problem to multiply. Tensions did increase. Finally, on Election Day, August 6, 1838, fearing their voting bloc, the old settlers tried to stop the Mormons from casting ballots at the Gallatin polls. Missourian and Mormon, were soon engaged in the brawl that started the Missouri War. After the fight in Gallatin, rumors flew. Aggression escalated. Then Missouri vigilantes burned a Mormon house in De Witt, laying siege to the town. Saints there were allowed to leave only if they sold their property. The Mormons soon had five hundred men in arms. When some of these forces marched on Adam-ondi-Ahman, the Missourians marched on Daviess County. The throb of violence could not be contained. The governor sent out the order to "exterminate or expel" the Mormons from the state. October 30: A militia entered Haun's Mill, a small settlement of Mormons, and killed seventeen people, including children. The horrible massacre sickened both sides and brought the war to a swift close.

The Missourians' frustration with the Mormons, a case of opposites repelling, now turned on Joseph. An army of more than two thousand men gathered to the south of Far West. Joseph must surrender or they would raze the town. If he did "not beg like a dog," the Missouri militia would also carry out the governor's order to exterminate the Mormons. Joseph's aged parents watched in horror from their front door as the prophet walked the six hundred yards between Mormon Far West and their enemies' newly conquered piece of it. As Joseph was swallowed up in the double lines of soldiers, his parents heard screaming and gunshots. "Had the army been composed of so many blood-hounds, wolves and panthers, they could not have made a sound so terrible." Joseph Sr. was sure his son was murdered and then he must die, too, because, the father wept, "I cannot live without him."

Within a few hours, the Missouri governor sent an order to execute Joseph, but General Alexander Doniphan was in charge of the prisoners. He had long been a Mormon ally, a lawyer with a sense of fairness and a strong character who'd stood up for Joseph in dire circumstances before. Though Joseph was taken into the marketplace to be shot, Doniphan refused to do it, saying it would be outright murder. Joseph and five others were packed into a wagon and covered with canvas tied down so that the cloth outlined the top of their heads. The journey ended in Liberty Jail, in a damp, smelly cell that was fourteen by fourteen feet.

While his fellow leaders moldered in the damp prison, Brigham Young planned and oversaw the exodus of the ten thousand Mormons who'd been ordered to leave the state under penalty of death. Emma got to Illinois with a group led by one of Brigham's lieutenants. She crossed the frozen Mississippi on foot with an eight-month-old baby in her arms, holding her two-and-a-half-year-old by the hand, trailed by two small sons on a wagon. Handbags of Joseph's heavy papers were wrapped around her waist, her eight-year-old daughter and six-year-old son clinging to either side of her wide skirt.

The prophet sank into himself in his prison cell. Death was a shattering new reality for him. His people had been killed, and he had almost been executed. He wrote his wife letters filled with longing for their dear "prattlers," asking for her assurances of affection and loyalty. Joseph could have spent the rest of his life brooding on the confusing experience he'd had and mopping up after his own theological contradictions. Instead, after the terrible defeat in Missouri, he found the materials of godhood in the affirmation of his own sexuality. As Joseph dwelled on death in jail, his sense of personal potential became his salvation.

Polygamy may seem alien, and it is always a stretch to explain to outsiders why it's religious, yet Joseph's plural marriage—like other aspects of his theology—reflects many of the concerns of modern literature and art. We have only to reach over Norman Mailer's shoulder to Hemingway's and then to D. H. Lawrence's to connect with what the latter called "man-life and woman-life, man-knowledge and woman-knowledge, man-being and woman-being." We may be living toward the end of this article of gender faith, but Joseph was in the thick of it. He breathed the same air as his contemporary Walt Whitman, who might have spoken for them both when he wrote in *Leaves of Grass*:

> *Sex contains all, bodies, souls,*
> *Meanings, proofs, purities, delicacies, results, promulgations,*
> *Songs, commands, health, pride,*
> *the maternal mystery, the seminal milk,*
> *All hopes, benefactions, bestowals, all the passions,*
> *loves, beauties, delights of the earth,*
> *All the governments, judges, gods . . .*

As both Lawrence and Whitman are religious poets in their ways, so Joseph was a poetic religious in his.

In his polygamy Joseph showed how he shared our contemporary preoccupation with personal relationships. His religious experiment turned every personal connection into a window on God, an opening through which He can be experienced and His desires made known. Joseph's life also ranged beyond personal relationships and he knew God in many settings, but as Joseph headed for Nauvoo, he entered the phase of his life when he was most intent on making connections between personal growth, love affairs, domestic relationships, theocracy, church ritual, the design of the afterlife, and the nature of God. It was a time when his mind frantically wove these elements into a first-draft blueprint for the next stage of Mormonism. Christ became more like a brother and God more like a man. Inevitably, as God became more of a man, Joseph became more like a God. For Joseph, intelligence began to run neck and neck with love in God's priorities. Love was still there, but intelligence and continual growth began to take over as Joseph broke out of his cell, not just the anticlimactic Liberty Jail from which he was allowed to escape, but the bars of death, which were pressing in on his mind and slowly making him lose his bearings.

Joseph was freed in April 1839 and made his way to Illinois. Anna Barnes arrived there with Jesse Harmon and their children a little more than a year later. The family had left Ashtabula County, Ohio, for Caldwell County, Missouri, in 1838. The

Saints were then being driven out of Missouri, so the Harmons retreated and settled temporarily in Springfield, Illinois. When Jesse was baptized, his children were also. Milo, the oldest son, wrote in his journal that the words of the Gospel had moved them ever "toward Zion." In Nauvoo, he recorded the thrill of enjoying "refreshing teachings from the lips of Prest. Joseph Smith." Having already been elected to the First Quorum of the Seventy, Jesse quickly moved into the prophet's inner circle in other positions: as an ordained Priest and a Major of the Second Battalion, 4th Regiment, 2nd Cohort of the Nauvoo Legion. Jesse often went along as Joseph's bodyguard when the prophet went on ordinary errands like visiting his boot maker.

Though he visited President Van Buren in the White House, Joseph was never able to recover Mormon losses of land and personal property in Missouri. When he returned from Washington, D.C., Joseph's description of his meeting with the president was filled with remnants of the humor that had been the glory of his youth, but was fast becoming a symptom of his growing anger. According to a reporter for the New York *Journal of Commerce,* who was at Joseph's late-March speech in Montrose, Iowa, when he got off the boat, the prophet said the president had treated him with disrespect. Joseph decided to tell Van Buren he was getting fat. "The president replied that he was aware of the fact; that he had to go every few days to the tailor's to get his clothes let out, or purchase a new coat. The 'prophet' here added, at the top of his voice,—'*he hoped he would continue to grow fat, and swell, and, before the next election, burst!*'"

Joseph may have soothed his own sense of injury by telling the president his clothes didn't fit, but probably drew more substantial comfort from the triumphs of his new city. In Nauvoo, everything was on a grander scale than ever before: the number of Mormons, the size, luxurious accommodations, care for the needy, Joseph's ambitions. In 1843, when Nauvoo was nearing completion, Josiah Quincy observed, "The river enclosed a position lovely enough to furnish a site for the Utopian communities of Plato or Sir Thomas More; and here was an orderly city, magnificently laid out, and teeming with activity and enterprise." By the time they arrived in Illinois, the Mormons were experienced community organizers. As penniless converts streamed in, skilled craftsmen were put to work on the temple in return for food and clothing. Impoverished farmers from England were given plots in the communal farmland outside Nauvoo. Industry came: two big sawmills, a steam flour mill, a tool factory, a foundry. There were plans for another temple and a spacious hotel with rooms set aside for the prophet and his family, a brick building that housed a store and Joseph's office upstairs. Joseph was married to many of his plural wives in this office, and he would ultimately dictate the polygamy revelation there.

According to Fawn Brodie, Joseph's polygamy really began in Liberty Jail, where he had time to dwell on his injuries and dream of women who could reward him for all he had been through. There is probably truth here, but Joseph's celestial marriage was not only selfish. Richard Bushman cites Joseph's early interest in Old Testament patriarchal polygamists as the beginning of his working out a religious precedent. I believe Joseph's polygamy was religious, but that his references to Abraham and his concubines were window dressing. They were superficial compared with the divine decree Joseph received personally. Between 1834 and 1842, an angel appeared to Joseph three times with a drawn sword and threatened him with death if he did not obey the commandment to practice plural marriage. The call from his fundamental connection to God was very deep.

Joseph often said that "a prophet was only a prophet when he was acting as such." This was truthful and modest and may have been the prophet himself speaking. The man was never more tempted as when the prophet challenged him to be a celestial groom to so many wives. He apparently had already taken two plural wives between Kirtland and Missouri, and then he married three wives in 1841, eleven in 1842, and seventeen in 1843. Todd Compton, author of *In Sacred Loneliness*, the scholar whose research is most recent and thorough, adds eight more "possible wives" to the list of thirty-three "sure" plural wives.

During these years he persuaded men like Brigham Young, Heber C. Kimball, Newel Whitney, and others of his inside circle to enter celestial marriages of their own. Brigham would end his life married to sixty-five women, Heber, forty-three. There was genuine theology involved. Joseph's visions of godhood and exaltation depended on polygamy, on man and woman married eternally and procreating as spirits throughout all time.

In his understanding, the more wives a man had, the higher his level of exaltation. A woman could never progress in the afterlife if she had married only "for time"—married, that is, monogamously according to social convention and worldly law. She must have a celestial marriage, too, or be excluded from the greatest blessings of heaven.

There are theories about male bonding and Mormon polygamy. Sometimes Joseph and his comrades married one another's plural wives, sometimes their daughters. There's evidence that older women, especially widows, were taken in plural marriages to protect them or so that they could be sealed in a family for eternity. But Joseph often married women whose husbands he knew; sometimes it was okay with the men, sometimes not. Occasionally, Joseph sent a man off on a mission so he could take his wife in plural marriage. These marriages were shrouded in secrecy and surrounded by gossip. The community that "knew" was intensely divided between those who accepted and those who repudiated spiritual wifery.

I feel Joseph's polygamy was a mixture of true religious idealism, genuine reaching for group solidarity, real personal experiment, risky behavior, and defiant letting the chips fall where they may. Part of it seems like an admirable religious experiment with the possibilities in personal freedom. Part of it seems like an intense, modern attempt to overcome death. Part of it seems like chaos that Joseph pushed much too far, destabilizing everyone in his community as he did. Increasingly, from 1841 on,

Nauvoo was a hotbed of small-town speculation, overstimulated by excitement as often as by anger, buzzing with the latest about who said what about whom.

Amid this instability we now meet Joseph's most unsavory admirer, John C. Bennett. He was a prominent, natty physician and instructor of midwifery, the Illinois quartermaster general, and one among several wealthy and influential converts to the church in this period. Joseph's usual intuition for the best collaborator he needed in a turning point went awry with Bennett. His choice was telling nonetheless. The doctor's diplomas, training, and familiarity with government and social life in the state capital all recommended him to Joseph when they met in the summer of 1840. The prophet was working on a charter for Nauvoo, and Bennett helped Joseph craft a document that guaranteed the city virtual autonomy, including the power of habeas corpus. Later as Joseph was pursued justly and unjustly by outside authorities, he was able to seek protection under this writ. It probably would not have passed the Illinois legislature without Bennett's persuasive lobbying, which assured members there was nothing they need fear in the charter.

Though the charter also authorized the Nauvoo Legion, an autonomous militia, Bennett got it passed by a voice vote. Back home again, he was made the major general of the legion and Joseph became the lieutenant general, and soon they would have handsome uniforms as befit the commanders of the largest body of armed men in Illinois. They would ride fine horses in parades through town to review the troops, also now in uniform, in the central square. Bennett became the Assistant President of the Church, and he and Joseph often went to inspect the work under way at the temple. In early 1841, Bennett was elected mayor of Nauvoo, Joseph the "sole" Trustee of the Church. He was also still its President, Prophet, Seer, and Revelator, and he was well on his way to having established his own theocracy near Tom and Huck's old stomping ground: the banks of the Mississippi.

In the early period of Nauvoo polygamy, the Mormon records are so richly varied we can lay out parallel strips of Joseph's life ranging from his most public to his most private actions. Moving through the *History of the Church*, personal diaries, affidavits, John Bennett's *History of the Saints*, Richard Van Wagoner's *Mormon Polygamy*, articles in *Dialogue*, and Linda King Newell and Valeen Tippetts Avery's *Mormon Enigma: Emma Hale Smith*, we can compare and contrast what he's saying in his sermons to what he's whispering to his plural wives; what he's saying to Emma to what he's sharing with Bennett.

My sympathy survived the painful contrast between Joseph in his divided worlds. It wasn't good in any conventional sense for him to be going forward on two fronts: willful honesty and willful lying. But I understood that here, as Joseph went forward on the cutting edge of the acceptable, he sought transforming knowledge. I'd done it myself. I don't know how any modern person worth his or her salt could turn away from the call to transformation. Even if you don't believe in God, isn't transformation our highest ideal? If you do believe in God, isn't the call undeniable? Don't we seek transformation to become larger, truer, holier people? Aren't the sorts of wrong Joseph committed in polygamy the sins of a free person negotiating boundaries that had never been tested before? Maybe he is the pioneer American sinner who teaches our freedom-seeking country to judge not, lest we be judged.

For a long time, while Joseph was lying to his wife, to people who questioned him, and to his church, his unsavory admirer, Bennett, was lying to him. The prophet was getting religious support from a very weak reed. Bennett was happily committing adultery under the cover of celestial marriage and telling people it was fine with Joseph if he did so. Early on, Joseph learned that Bennett's wife had left him and taken their children, because of the doctor's repeated infidelities. When Joseph confronted him with these facts and asked why the doctor had kept them hidden, Bennett tried (feebly) to kill himself. He begged to be forgiven and given a second chance. The men were very thick politically at that point. They were confidants and rivals in their pursuit of women. Though Joseph's diary was mute, Bennett mentioned Joseph going off to meet this or that particular woman. Bennett also let history know that he was already wooing a young woman Joseph unknowingly approached, that she resisted Joseph because she was already negotiating with Bennett.

Though the prophet taught other men they should consult their first wives when taking a second, he did not fly that one by Emma. Joseph's honesty with her was very slow in coming. She was a formidable brain in her own right, and a warm, generous, devoted wife. She had borne his children, eased his suffering, opened her house to the world, shared his religious destiny. The biggest difference between Emma and Joseph might have been humor. She would never have made jokes about President Van Buren being fat, either in his office or afterward as Joseph did. A friend once asked Emma if she felt that Joseph was a prophet. "Yes," Emma answered, "but I wish to God I did not know it."

Emma had suspicions about polygamy, and they were confirmed by women in the Relief Society. She was devastated. At home, she confronted Joseph. It wasn't good that he hadn't told her himself. He had probably feared it would be unpopular with Emma, but it was probably much, much worse because she had heard it from other women. There were terrible quarrels between the prophet and his wife. Not surprisingly, Emma showed herself to be an incorruptible pillar for the principle of monogamy. She believed in *Joseph*. *He* was that transforming love that had pushed her beyond her more conventional self. She did not need polygamy to stretch her love for God by loving Joseph in a new exalted way.

The blowups with Emma came in 1842, about the same time that new rumors of Bennett's past and his actual behavior in Nauvoo were circulating in church councils. They were also making the rounds of the women's Relief Society, of which Emma was president. Though Joseph had written up papers excommunicating Bennett in May, he was slow to deliver them. Whether he delayed because of sympathy, guilt, or denial is not known. In June 1842, Joseph married Eliza Snow, a poet, a noble, distinguished woman as Emma was, and a single teacher who lodged with the Smiths. In the same month he married Elizabeth Davis and Sarah Kingsley, and not long after, the controversies around Bennett came to a head. There were so many shocking rumors about Bennett's affairs and abortions, the outraged High Council investigated. The council grilled two other men who confirmed Bennett's immoralities, admitted their own, and said they were only following the prophet's teachings. Bennett now wept crocodile tears in a huge public meeting, but Joseph finally saw the handwriting on the wall. He had to repudiate his sleazy doppelganger or go down to the same fate. He gave Bennett the bull of excommunication on June 23, three weeks after he had written it.

Now the particle accelerator really began to fly. Everything sped up. Emma realized that Eliza Snow was married to Joseph while living under her roof. There was a huge public showdown and Emma may have pushed Eliza down stairs. Eliza Snow moved out. Emily and Eliza Partridge, both daughters of Bishop Edward Partridge, then moved into the Smiths' house. After some persuasion from Joseph, Emily married the prophet on March 4, 1843. Eliza married him on March 8, 1843. Emma still opposed plural marriage. She did not know the two girls were married to her husband. At the same time Joseph was teaching that unless wives accepted polygamy they could not be sealed to their husbands for all eternity. Other women were accepting polygamy, but not Emma. The prophet wondered why his wife refused to do what was necessary for eternal life with him.

Emma finally relented; she agreed to plural marriage as long as she could choose the women. Her first choices were the Partridge girls to whom he was already married. Emily, Eliza, and Joseph all agreed to the charade (for the sake of Emma's feelings). Emma attended the pretend wedding of both Emily and Eliza to Joseph in the Smiths' home. Emma was then sealed to Joseph for all eternity. Nonetheless, she soon despaired when she started coming home and finding her husband in Eliza's bedroom. Her depression deepened as her bargain with Joseph meant consenting to his marrying two more women: "By later summer 1843 most of Emma's friends had either married Joseph or had given their daughters to him."

Emma and Joseph again began to argue bitterly about polygamy. Joseph's older brother Hyrum said that if the prophet would write his revelation on celestial marriage, he would take it to Emma and convince her of "its truth, purity and heavenly origin." She tore the piece of paper up. The next day, Joseph and Emma quarreled all day and finally called Joseph's scribe into the room with them. Speaking their misery and shedding their tears before a witness did not help. Some days later Joseph received a new revelation saying Emma must obey as a wife. He had his scribe write it down. When he gave it to her, she used tongs to put the piece of paper in the fireplace. Joseph next received a revelation that those practicing celestial marriage would have unusual endowments in a new holy order. Emma did not receive her endowments. The elect wore special garments. Not Emma. Joseph blessed his oldest son, Joseph III, and ordained him as his successor. That was the end for Emma. She had to put an end to polygamy lest her own son grow up to practice it. She ripped into Joseph in their bedroom, then called in the Partridge girls and said that Joseph must give them up. Emma said she would "rather her blood . . . run pure than be polluted in this manner."

The Partridge girls were angry, but they departed. So did two other young women living with the Smiths. There was a dreary honor in all this. The prophet did not take another plural wife for the last eight months of his life. Our own contemporary literature describes similar domestic drama that was just as dreary, and ended with less honor. John Updike's stories of the suburban Maples come to mind. In *Separating*, a book of stories about serial polygamy (as the modern Utah polygamists call our secular adultery), Mrs. Maple went to the women her husband has slept with and cannot face to explain that their adulterous relationship must stop. The Maples end up divorcing after Richard Maple's long, drawn-out season of infidelities during which Mrs. Maple was sort of his PR rep. Joseph and Emma did not divorce. It showed something about Joseph's integrity that he fought the polygamy issue through with his strong-willed wife. Emma may have threatened him with divorce, but after he had blazed through seventeen wives in 1843, it said something about his respect for her that he stopped—or paused his headlong rush into marrying.

As males, Mr. Maple and Mr. Smith may have both wrestled

with their pride. Updike's hero was annoyed by being weak while his wife was strong, but he didn't try to hide it. He didn't punish himself particularly. His infidelity was a way of pressuring his wife for a divorce, and when she agreed, he was free to finally marry the woman he had been in love with. Once he stopped taking plural wives, Joseph's conflicting assertions demonstrated both remarkable humility and remarkable pride. In private, he told William Marks that the Mormons were "a ruined people. . . . This doctrine of polygamy, or Spiritual-wife system, that has been taught and practiced among us, will prove our destruction and overthrow. I have been deceived in reference to its practice; it is wrong; it is a curse to mankind." In public, Joseph raved against his accusers. He threw down extravagant denials that he had ever had plural wives. "Come on! Ye prosecutors! Ye false swearers! . . . I will always come out on top. . . . I am the only man that has ever been able to keep a whole church together since the days of Adam. . . . I boast that no man ever did such a work as I. The followers of Jesus ran away from Him; but the Latter-day Saints never ran away from me yet. . . . How I do love to hear the wolves howl!"

At the end of his life, Joseph went from one extreme to the next. He celebrated his last Christmas by hosting a dinner for fifty couples. He was dressed in his Legion uniform with all its gleaming brass. Emma had a new red velvet dress. There was a band for dancing. In January he declared himself a candidate for the president of the United States. He excommunicated dissidents, among them important men, close friends who had begun to organize a reformed church in Nauvoo. He believed his enemies were plotting to kill him. They believed Joseph was plotting to kill them. In April 1844, the Council of Fifty elected the prophet the King of the Kingdom of God "who would rule over the house of Israel forever."

In one of his most famous poems, "To Elsie," William Carlos Williams wrote: "The pure products of America / go crazy." He was talking about wrecked men and women who strive after some sorry chimera in the world we've destroyed. In his final days, Joseph seems in danger of becoming one of these desperate characters, fleeing "gauds / from imaginations which have no peasant traditions to give them / character." It seems like his originality has devoured him; that though his life began at sunup in the great American morning, it ends in our day of exhausted self-betrayals.

ELEVEN

Faith and Irony

This maddened Joseph was the Joseph whom Hon. Charles Francis Adams and Josiah Quincy, Jr., came to meet in Nauvoo on May 14, 1844. The New Englanders were graduates of Harvard, cousins and players in the Eastern establishment. Both men took good notes and Quincy used his as the basis of his later memoir. Charles was the grandson of President John Adams and son of ex-President John Quincy Adams (still living at the time of the Nauvoo visit). Josiah's grandfather had helped win acquittal for Captain Prescott after the Boston Massacre; his father had been president of Harvard and then mayor of Boston. Adams had the more formidable national pedigree; and he was indelibly marked with class snobbery. As his diary showed, meeting the unorthodox Mormon prophet gave him the heebie-jeebies at being pushed so far outside his comfort zone. Though Quincy's fascinating account was critical, it also showed that Joseph Smith's powers forced him beyond his mandarin shortcomings.

On a whim, Adams and Quincy altered their western itinerary to include a meeting with the prophet. Though both untitled aristocrats had been to Europe, they had never crossed their own country. Lest they ever have to get too far from home, they started with a visit to Quincy, Illinois, in Adams County (named, of course, after John Quincy). From the start, their adventure was strewn with unacknowledged literary symbols. The men started down the sparkling waters of the upper Mississippi on the *Amaranth*, a small steamship named after a flower the Greeks believed was a symbol of immortality. Quite by accident, they met Dr. Goforth, "a chivalric, yet simple" person, whose name said so much about the spirit these men needed to explore.

Dr. Goforth urged them to stop at Nauvoo and meet General Joseph Smith, a rather good friend of his. The doctor's gentility led them to expect something more civilized than what they found. They were promised a "good bed," which turned out to be one covered with cockroaches in an Irish shanty. They awoke to pouring rain, and they could see through the window that the roads were knee-deep in mud. Word had somehow already gone ahead that ex-President John Quincy Adams himself had come to visit. To save everyone any disappointment, Dr. Goforth rode into Nauvoo on his own to explain who the guests actually were. If his expectations had ever been disappointed, the prophet had adjusted them by the time the men arrived at the door of the Nauvoo Hotel. Joseph showed a confident and finely calibrated sense of the pecking order. This was not wasted on Quincy. He noted that Joseph blessed Adams with an official familiarity, "such as a crowned head might adopt on receiving the heir presumptive of a friendly court." Meanwhile, he showed Quincy a cordiality "with which the president of a college might welcome a deserving janitor."

Joseph had forty-three days to live. He knew how tense his situation was. The elephant in the room was polygamy. No mention was made of it ever during his day with the cosmopolitan outsiders. From the moment when Quincy picked the prophet out from "the stragglers" at the tavern door until the moment of departure when Joseph showed his moral edge, he said nothing about the controversy seething around him. Quincy and Adams had never met a living prophet before. The encounter between the arch-mandarins and the Mormon prophet was an educative glimpse of their clashing cultures. Joseph's belief in the supernatural put both Quincy's and Adams's teeth on edge. The New Englanders were the sort of rational Unitarians who'd stepped back even from Emerson's transcendentalism. They came from a status quo that wasn't budging; Joseph's was in constant disintegration. In their own ways, Adams and Quincy applied exquisite manners to what was nothing if not the Bostonians' once-in-a-lifetime trip to New Guinea as embodied by Joseph. Most of the visit, he behaved like a gallivanting monkey of world-class irreverence.

Adams and Quincy might have been better prepared if they'd hung out with members of a rock band during after hours. In 1844, the closest thing to Joseph's life exposure is our rock stars' round-the-clock experiencing of contrasting realities—from tiny family pond to oceans of adorers; from humble shack to the White House in D.C.; from the supreme accomplishment of the Book of Mormon to a humiliating eleventh-hour rescue from a firing squad; from deep commitment to one wife to the heady comparisons between a series of wives; from rustic prophet to leader of a world church. Such transformations include an incredible range of lives in a succession of worlds—each with its own point of view, morals, and hierarchies. Many find the center cannot hold. Some gifted people who've packed in that much combine the disarming mix of sophistication and sense of primitive entitlement Joseph showed in Quincy's memoir.

Dressed in striped pantaloons and a linen jacket "which had not lately seen the washtub," showing a three-day beard, Joseph took his guests through the drenching rain into the chilly, "comfort-less" inn and on a search for a room where they could talk. All were filled with sleeping disciples. Finally, Joseph found a room where only one Mormon was softly snoring. He pulled a blanket over the man's head and drew chairs to the fire. Smith pelted his visitors with stories of Nauvoo's industrial successes, his city's unusual charter and the persecutions that had made it necessary.

The men did not have much in common when it came to religion. Before Joseph spoke of his theology, he took the two to the back kitchen, where they all had breakfast with a group of workers. The prophet cheerfully went on talking and changed into a broadcloth suit in everyone's presence. Then they returned

to the first room, where the bed was now made and the fire co-
zily built up. Dr. Goforth was there. Hyrum joined them, as did
Sidney Rigdon and Brigham Young, showing the leadership's
interest in the visitors. In his "wild talk," as Quincy called it,
Joseph denied the existence of the Trinity, displayed his familiarity with scriptures, and boasted about his gift for revelation.

Quincy listened skeptically to Joseph's claims about "his miraculous gifts of understanding all languages." The prophet
showed them "proof" by taking down a Bible and reading parts
in Hebrew, which he then translated. "There!" he would exclaim
in language Quincy found "homely." "I have proved that point as
straight as a loon's leg."

Quincy suspected a setup, and when they followed Joseph to
his hall of curiosities, he grew even more dubious. Joseph took
them to see four Egyptian mummies he'd bought from an itinerant peddler, claiming that they came with parchments that con-
cerned "the earliest account of creation." These were the same
scrolls found in the basement of the Metropolitan Museum of
Art in New York City a century later and identified as common
Egyptian funerary texts. The prophet's debunkers love this coincidence as a spectacular example of his being an emperor
with no clothes. Even without living to see the scrolls exposed,
Quincy subtly and without reproach clearly believed they were
fakes. He showed it in his story of Joseph's crowing about the hi-
eroglyphics, which his inspired translation revealed as "the handwriting of Abraham" and "the autograph of Moses." The story is

beautifully told to let the reader experience the full outrageousness of Joseph's claims and theatricality.

Quincy had not read the Book of Mormon, so he could not know that Joseph's inspired translation had produced a work of religious genius. Given the mind-blowing brilliance of that scripture, Joseph had reason to believe in his powers as a certain kind of holy translator. But he also played fast and loose with his artistic gift here. Translating God was the work of a shaman. Translating ancient parchment was that of a scholar. Did it not occur to him that someday someone would be able to literally translate the scroll he was using in a work of daring improvisation? No, it did not—either that or he did not care about the risk he was taking.

Quincy and Adams could not know that the tattered old funerary hieroglyphs inspired one of Joseph's most radical ideas, one of several that make Christians argue that the Mormons are not Christian. The Book of Abraham, now part of the official Mormon scriptural canon, explores the notion that God created the universe out of preexisting and eternal matter instead of creating it ex nihilo. If Quincy and Adams had come a month before, they might have heard Joseph delivering his renowned funeral sermon for Elder King Follett. They could have been in the huge crowd that heard Joseph elaborating on the likeness between man and God and Jesus Christ. All had the same nature; all would continue to evolve through eternity. The archmandarins might then have had their chance to experience the genius that burned inside the whirlwind.

The weather finally cleared on the day of their actual visit, and Joseph took Quincy and Adams outside. Quincy was impressed by the "diligent workers," the city of "handsome stores and comfortable dwellings." He found the temple "a wonderful structure," "odd and striking." But seeing Joseph surrounded by adoring acolytes, Quincy thought of the inmates at McLean Asylum for the Insane, of which he was a trustee. He'd met men there who thought God had appointed them His representatives on earth. They felt they were sane, everyone else insane. "If the blasphemous assumptions of Smith seemed like the ravings of a lunatic," Quincy wrote, "he had at least brought them to a market where 'all the people were as mad as he.'"

Later in the visit, Quincy confronted Joseph by saying he had more power than was safe with one man. Joseph answered, "In your hands or that of any other person, so much power would, no doubt, be dangerous. I am the only man in the world it would be safe to trust with it. Remember, I am a prophet!" Quincy took care to emphasize that the last sentence was spoken "in a rich, comical aside." Quincy called this Joseph's characteristic tone. It was "half-way between jest and earnest." Adams used the same phrase, "half-way between jest and earnest," in his diary. In other words, the New Englanders corroborated one another's view of Joseph's irony. I hear it coming off the page myself; and to me it is the proof that the best in Joseph is still morally alive.

When a world-famous prophet says, "Remember, I am a prophet," in a rich, comical tone, he is making fun of his audience's expectations; he is making fun of his own. He is joking around and also deadly serious. He is showing disinterest and stoicism. He knows he has worth, but for both better and for worse people don't know the whole truth. Yes, God used him to create the Book of Mormon, which he could never have written himself. Yes, God chose him to found a church, something else Joseph could never have done on his own. He'd been part of miraculous acts and events that were beyond his abilities. None-theless, they raised him among his followers to a level just below God. Joseph who saw the divine comedy in the universe—as well as the human comedy in and around him: Joseph had the irony that went with the dramatic incongruities in his life. That irony is behind his famous cry to his followers a few days after Quincy and Adams left, "You don't know me—you never will. You never knew my heart. No man knows my history. I cannot do it: I shall never undertake it. I don't blame any one for not believing my history. If I had not experienced what I have, I would not have believed it myself."

He was not mad when Quincy and Adams met him, he was maddened. Maddened by his conflicts—between the man who didn't want to apologize to his wife and the prophet who may have misread God's signals about polygamy; between the leader who had let a tiger loose and the seer who knew the tiger was coming back to eat him; between the visionary who saw God and the revelator who'd given God a prop. It was only by the sheerest luck he wasn't arrested during the arch-mandarins' visit. After he dropped Quincy and Adams at the Mississippi boat dock, Joseph returned to charges that had been brought against him for defamation and adultery in the courts at Carthage, a town just outside of Nauvoo. The dissenters' strategy was to expose his crimes in a court Joseph did not control. They won a grand jury indictment against him for perjury and for practicing polygamy. He went into hiding twice in May to avoid the police. Before finally going to court voluntarily, he denied the charges to his loyal congregation, and then lucked out because one of the prosecution's material witnesses did not appear.

The dissenters in the community had started a new reformed Mormon church. They quickly intensified efforts to bring Joseph down by purchasing a press and preparing an issue of a newspaper, the *Nauvoo Expositor*, which would report his hypocrisies and crimes. Joseph knew what was coming. The dissenters could raise three hundred supporters in their meetings now, and gossip was no stranger to the streets of the holy city. It crossed into the surrounding counties, where strong feelings had been building against the Mormons for their growing political power and endless controversies with none more inflaming than their plural marriage.

Inside the community, Joseph still had thousands who remained loyal, among them Jesse Harmon and Anna Barnes. They were quintessential stalwarts. Jesse was by now the Colonel of the Nauvoo Legion. In his journal, Milo expressed what could easily have been his parents' opinion on why those outside of Nauvoo might be ready to persecute the Saints again. "In the Spring of 1844 the tide of emigration in to Nauvoo had for a time been gradually increasing, and had caused a Spirit of Jelousey to arise in the breasts of our eneymies they feard [*sic*] that if they left us thus alone all men would believe on us and the Mormons would take away their place and nation, and hold the balance of power."

The only issue of the *Nauvoo Expositor* was published on June 7, 1844. There were seven essays, each dealing with a different aspect of Joseph's tyranny, his disrespect for the separation between church and state, and his pursuit of unholy matrimony in the form of vile "whoredoms and abominations." Joseph called a city council meeting which declared the *Expositor* "a nuisance." Joseph chose Jesse to lead the police in the destruction of the press and the entire issue of the newspaper. He may have thus singled out Jesse because he would have wanted a man he could completely trust, and Jesse had by this time accepted Joseph's teachings on polygamy. When the men at the newspaper said they would not give up their key to the printing press, the officer with Jesse said, "I have 'a key' that will fit." Then he took a sledgehammer and smashed down the door. Milo was one of the police force "called upon to remove and destroy the press type and all libelous prints." Others threw the printed papers and fixtures into the street and burned them.

The flames spread to people's feelings, their tempers, their rhetoric. In Nauvoo, women went door to door to pass the word. Men rushed to gather in mobs. Dissenters threatened to burn Joseph's house and the Temple. In the outlying counties, some organized to disarm the Mormons in their midst; others wanted to drive all outlying Saints into Nauvoo. Joseph and Hyrum were headlined as "Hellish Fiends" in *The Warsaw Signal*, which also urged anti-Mormons to arm against the "Devils." Joseph had attacked liberty of the press! The most sacred principle of the democracy! People were urged to take up arms against the Mormons and their prophet, who had no respect for the law. On June 17, Joseph, Jesse, and Hyrum, along with fourteen others, were arrested on a writ issued by the Carthage court, on complaints of their fomenting a riot. They were released in Nauvoo municipal court, where the writ of habeas corpus countered all others.

The mayor's office issued a declaration of martial law for Nauvoo on June 18. The next day Joseph gave the order to have a picket guard lining all the roads out of the city; he asked Major Jesse Harmon to see that brethren be posted on all streets and alleys inside the city as well. Joseph ordered the foundry to start turning out artillery, though he also made it known that "there would not be a gun fired on our part during this fuss." Within days, three or four thousand armed Mormon men were patrolling the streets.

Governor Ford feared Illinois would soon reprise the Missouri horrors. He went to Carthage to investigate the situation around the court and jail. The tiny town had been taken over by armed citizens from the three surrounding counties. If their anger flamed, the county militias would be stoking the general bonfire in a flash. Ford wrote to Joseph saying he must come to

Carthage and face charges for destroying the press. "If you by refusing to submit, shall make it necessary to call out the Militia, I have great fears that your city will be destroyed and your people many of them exterminated."

Fawn Brodie believes that Joseph failed to deal with the challenge because he lacked the courage to face up to the consequences of his behavior. He could not bring himself to simply go public with polygamy, so he destroyed the *Nauvoo Expositor* press. But then he would go neither to court nor to war. Bushman portrays Joseph as a very complex victim of circumstance. He was called to introduce polygamy by God. He attracted criticism and legal challenges. Convinced that his authority was from God, he violated worldly law by destroying the *Expositor* press, but then hesitated when the world overreacted. I believe Joseph froze, that he was absolutely conflicted and broke the law because there was nothing cleansing he could do as a prophet or anything right he could do as a man. Like Brodie and Bushman, I think that destroying the printing press brought on his death, but I feel it also put him to the ultimate test. Would he stand and take responsibility? Would he save his people and face the hostile forces he'd called down on them all?

When he received Ford's letter with its ultimatum, Joseph knew that if he stayed in Nauvoo, many Mormons would die along with him. He felt going to Carthage would be fatal. After some more discussion, Joseph thought he saw a middle way. The state wanted only Hyrum and him. If they got out, the Mormons in Nauvoo would be safe. Meanwhile, he had been sending messages to President John Tyler in the hopes of getting federal assistance. Joseph and Hyrum could cross the country and find help in Washington, D.C.

They quickly arranged a boat for their trip to the Iowa side of the Mississippi. The river was so full, Joseph, Hyrum, and Willard Richards had to frantically bail out waves coming over the sides with their boots. The Destroying Angel of Mormondon, Porter Rockwell, rowed though he could barely see; the night was dark and the wind blew his long hair across his face. They scrambled onto dry land with no means of travel and no sure idea where they'd go if they had horses. For the next twelve hours, Joseph cast about in confusion. Part of him wanted to escape, though even in that desire, he showed his conflicted state. He wrote Emma asking where she'd be so he could join her. At the same time, he also wrote two young sisters, swearing them to secrecy and asking them to make their plans to meet him in Cincinnati.

In the early morning, a posse rode into Nauvoo. They found Emma at the governor's mansion and told her Ford would send troops to guard the city and search for Joseph until he was found. The Legion, by Joseph's order, had been dismissed. Nauvoo was unarmed. People were terrified. Heber Kimball's wife wrote, "Some were tyred almost to death to think Joseph should leve them in the hour of danger. Their [Joseph's and Hyrum's] giving themselves up, is all that will save our city from distruction."

Emma had the responsibility for calling Joseph back or not.

When Ford guaranteed Joseph's safety and a fair trial if she did, Emma wrote to her husband who, having read her letter, pushed it away and said, "I know my own business," by which he implied he now meant to go on to D.C., if he could get outfitted for such a journey.

One of the men who'd brought the letter from Emma spoke up, "You always said if the church would stick to you, you would stick to the church, now trouble comes and you are the first to run."

Another in the group joined in. The two men charged Joseph with being a coward.

"If my life is no value to my friends, it is of none to myself," Joseph replied.

He looked at Rockwell to see whether there was any sympathy there. Joseph asked Rockwell what he should do.

"You are the oldest and ought to know best," Rockwell told him. "As you make your bed, I will lie with you."

Joseph turned to Hyrum and said, "Brother Hyrum, you are the oldest, what shall we do?"

"Let's go back and give ourselves up," Hyrum said, "and see the thing out."

These were dramatic moments when Joseph decided whether he would or would not step up. When he spoke, it was not the ironic Joseph whose words were written into history. It was the affectionate Joseph, the familial Joseph, the antiauthoritarian, first-among-equals Joseph, a man who did not want to die, but turned his fate over to the will of the group. He had shaped these followers, now he acquiesced to whatever shape they felt his fate should take. He turned to his brother and said, "I will go with you, but we shall be butchered." Hyrum replied: "No, no; let us go back and put our trust in God, and we shall not be harmed. The Lord is in it. If we live or have to die, we will be reconciled to our fate."

I have been in the jail cell where Joseph and Hyrum were killed. Years before we made the documentary, after I'd first been so intrigued by reading about Joseph, I drove to Nauvoo from Bloomington, Illinois, where I was living. This was the early 1990s. Joseph's "beautiful city" on the Mississippi was hardly developed as a tourist site. It was a large field with an occasional house or a ruin of one standing by an empty street. There may have already been a visitors' center, something very modest. The temple was a collapsed remnant of stone and wood. Mainly, though, there were the poetry and ghosts of an old prairie settlement—one surprisingly touched by elegance here and there in the brick outlines of the town houses. Even the great silver river rushing by in the background looked like a thing of beauty, and not, as I well knew, a mighty potential destroyer of efforts to establish Zion. As I walked along the street, serenity was all around me, not the struggle, violence, and desperate prayer of Joseph's last days after he returned to face trial in Carthage.

I felt time reeling back, back through the blood-soaked years of his adulthood to his life as a boy. I wondered if Joseph, going home to say good-bye to his wife and children in 1844, remembered the days of meeting Moroni or learning to translate the gold plates. Did those halcyon days give Joseph the faith to meet his own death? Some courage took him through the door into his home to his family—when, as Emma later told a friend, "I felt the worst I ever did in my life, and from that time I looked for him to be killed."

On June 24, Joseph and Hyrum went to Carthage, with Jesse Harmon and twelve other men involved in destroying the *Nauvoo Expositor* press. I drove there on my visit to see where Joseph's life ended. I can see the twentieth-century road clearly in my memory now, can easily erase the paved streets and parked cars, can go back into the jail museum and imagine it as a dark, dirty frontier jail. I imagined how all the men stank from not having bathed, the tension, the extreme emotion of destroying a newspaper in a free country and then fighting with friends, cousins, brethren, and sisters in the terrible explosive stew Joseph had mixed together in God's name at the end. That God felt as real to me as the irreverent God Joseph served as a boy. But the God that Joseph called down on himself at the end was God, the Furious; God, the Tipper Over of Tables; God, the Very Particle Accelerator Itself.

When Joseph and the first group of lawbreakers straggled in, Carthage was filled with restless, armed militiamen, drilling idly. For those who arrived from Nauvoo, the trip ended in an unnerving anticlimax. All except Joseph and Hyrum were released for lack of evidence. Jesse Harmon went back to Nauvoo with the other prisoners who had been set free. Later even the

Smith brothers were allowed to go home, where they helped Governor Ford persuade the Mormons to disarm. Joseph and Hyrum then returned once more to Carthage to face new charges of treason. They were put up in a modest hotel.

Joseph was steadied overnight by Hyrum's company. His brother had always been a strong shoulder. His kind heart had been a comfort. Hyrum had been the only person who could help relieve the pain in the leg infected by typhus. He would carry Joseph during the day when the infection hurt too much for him to walk. When he couldn't sleep, Hyrum would take his younger brother's throbbing leg onto his lap, pressing his own hands against the hot skin to relieve the pain. If Joseph slept that night in Carthage, it was because Hyrum was nearby.

In the morning, the brothers went before a judge and were found guilty of treason. They were jailed. Four friends came to be with them: Willard Richards, John Taylor, Dan Jones, and John Fullmer. During the evening Hyrum read from the Book of Mormon. Joseph bore testimony to the guards of its divine authenticity. He said he was in jail for prophesying that which had miraculously happened: "the restoration of the Gospel, the administration of angels, and that the kingdom of God was established on earth." Joseph and his men rested as they could during the night, which was broken by a gunshot. They were up at five a.m.

Jesse Harmon had a twelve-year-old nephew, Henry, who lived in Carthage. He had heard the rumors that Joseph and Hyrum would never leave jail alive. On the Thursday morning when Joseph and his friends passed their time nervously in jail, Henry found ways to slip through the streets. The boy climbed into the cupola on the top of the courthouse, where he could view movement all around town. He saw John Fullmer leave, and then later Dan Jones as he was sent away from the jail after he asked the guard outside the building about the gunshot. The man told Dan there had been so much trouble getting "Old Joe" into jail that the Carthage Greys would never let him get out alive. Then the same guard wouldn't let Jones back into the prison.

I sat in the room where Joseph spent his last day. There were no bars on the upstairs window. The men looked down on the town square. The time dragged, I'm sure. Allies smuggled guns in for Joseph and Hyrum. In the melancholy of the fading afternoon, John Taylor sang "A Poor Wayfaring Man of Grief." Once, twice. Soon after, he looked out the window and saw a line of men coming around the jail, their faces painted black. From his place in the cupola, Henry could see the same sight as these dark men filled the square, wearing their jackets inside out so that the insignia of the Illinois militia would not show. Henry ran out of the building and raced to the jail just as the Greys had broken in, their guns blazing as they ran upstairs to the room where Joseph and the others were held prisoner.

Inside, in the room where the men were shot, I listened to words from Willard Richard's diary about hearing the thunder of footsteps on the stairs, the shouts of Joseph and Hyrum, the guns firing through the door. Hyrum was struck and staggered back. A shot then hit him in the face. He fell, crying, "I am a dead man," which he was. On the recording, Joseph's voice covers his brother's, saying, "Oh dear, brother Hyrum!" John Taylor collapsed, badly wounded. Willard Richards, trapped behind the door as it was pushed open, escaped injury. Joseph emptied his gun, and then as his assailants poured toward him, he leapt up on the windowsill. He was shot simultaneously from behind and from below as young Henry watched from across the way. I remember so clearly the creaky, pious voice on the tape saying, "The prophet froze for a moment on the sill. Then he cried, 'O Lord my God,' and fell into the street."

TWELVE

Except Ye Be Converted, and Become as Little Children

I want to be a nineteenth-century Mormon. I love the pioneer era. I love everything scandalously starting afresh, all connected and confused: God, nation, community, family purpose, daily work, practice. Alfred North Whitehead said, "Apart from God every activity is merely a passing whiff of insignificance." Without God, life is a list of activities, separated by commas. I have the dream that a completely meaningful life must have been possible for religious settlers on the frontier. I have the illusion that their lives were fundamentally different than mine, that they burned in their aspirations until the fire had consumed them all. There is a mild but real despair in the spaces between the unconnected parts of my life: between polishing a silver spoon with my married initials and doing my boyfriend's laundry for him to pick up later; between weeding my garden and reading a Paul Krugman editorial; between learning new software and figuring out if Joseph's parts fit together after he was blown apart by the Book of Mormon.

I believed he grew in irony, but I couldn't understand exactly how he balanced it with his faith. Maybe he didn't. His life ended tragically and his flaws played their part in his demise. Maybe his irony had been a flaw. Somehow I felt it was a strength. Part of his magnetism, a way to be steadfast in his faith by seeing God as doubled the way everything else in life is. What do we know that isn't both what it seems to be in any moment and yet the opposite in another beat? And living in these constantly changing circumstances, moods, political horrors, superprivileges, incomprehensible darkness moseying slowly into material for skits for *Saturday Night Live*, alternating this way between the divine and its other, how else can we hold on to faith except through irony? Our contradictory world was beyond faith and doubt. Joseph showed us we could live in it with faith and irony.

But I also wondered whether Joseph's message for me was hidden in plain sight: in my local Mormon ward. Conversion came from the heart. Conversion was faith, irony, and surrender. Joseph helped my unbelief, but I still had not answered whether he gave me what I needed to believe. Could I become a member of his church? I was anxious about going to services. I didn't know if I should mention having worked on the PBS film. Some Mormons loved it; some did not. If I said nothing, it might seem like I was staying undercover. I had Joseph in common with Mormons, but worried my interest in his irony might hurt their feelings. This didn't seem like their doctrinal type. Faith in my own innocent and sincere desire won out.

The first meeting I attended was the annual Children's Service. It said so on my program, but there were no decorations, nothing to inflame my suggestibility. The walls were unadorned, the wooden pews were spare. There was a lectern where the altar usually stood in Christian churches; seats ran up the back behind the dais with room for a small organ in the middle. The hymn numbers were posted on the wall to one side. The table where young deacons prepared the bread and water for communion was at the far right, covered with a white cloth. At the start of the service, when the bishop asked the congregation to manifest approval or disapproval of a new calling or a ward decision, members raised their right hands. It was a little like a small town meeting of stockholders in a company devoted to the business of the Holy Ghost. I liked the no-frills approach. It seemed like we were dealing with essentials, focusing on what exactly the Holy Spirit stripped of all fancy trappings was about.

My first service turned out to be dangerously inflaming after all. Not right away. First there were prayers and communion and hymns. There were personal testimonies by members who'd been tapped by the bishop to speak about their experiences of God in family life. It was like an NPR program: the people's voice was heard. Their words were both ordinary and eloquent. These were men and women like me, struggling to express their experiences with the Holy Spirit. At a certain point, a flock of utterly charming children were arrayed around the lectern, combed and groomed by caring parents and dressed in Juicy Couture and Tory Burch fashions. They sang hymns about "sharing families through all eternity" with such tender sweetness I had to lash myself to the mast. I reminded myself of all the reasons against sudden conversion: my strongest impulses were the least reliable; I was always a fellow traveler, never a member; I wasn't sure I was a Christian; my politics were on a crash course with the Mormons. I couldn't vote for Mitt Romney. There wasn't room here for a convert who supported gay marriage in this church. (I wasn't eager to mention that I'd had a relationship with a woman, but I didn't feel it would be held against me if I wanted to convert. The Mormon Church forbade its members from having gay relationships in the present, not the past.)

As I sat in church during the Children's Service, listening to these darling little boys and girls, the thought that I might become a Mormon made me feel a simple, rich happiness, almost a relief, as if I'd always felt this, as if I'd always known, "Except ye be converted, and become as little children, ye shall not enter the kingdom of heaven." I was wise enough to prepare for my sentiment not to last. When I was back in my observing mind, the faith of a naïve child would not suffice. Somehow my critical faculties would also have to be satisfied in this pilgrimage toward faith.

I kept going back to services at my Mormon ward during the fall. I felt a strong religious spirit there. Though I was searching for something to feed my reason, I assumed there would be time to get answers (or not) to my political questions. For now I just wanted to float openly in this new medium. I might not be as intensely Christian as the Mormons, but I still might turn out to be some sort of Christian. Homosexuality and the politics surrounding same-sex marriage were my worst problem with the church. Yet even there, my experience with black converts to Mormonism helped me hold my horses for the moment. There were many highly intelligent, well-informed black converts who joined the church before the 1978 revelation opening the priesthood to "all worthy male members of the Church" regardless of "race or color." In our interviews for the film, in answer to the question of how they could join a racist church, their refrain was always, "God trumps politics."

These black converts had not liked being excluded from the priesthood, but they felt that God's urging to convert overrode their reservations. These men and women did not fit the secular world's idea of a minority person suffering from false consciousness. They made the ordinary race-conscious liberal seem like the one with intellectual blinders. Granted, homosexuals' situation in the church was much less promising than that of the blacks had been. The Mormon theology of gender is fixed for all eternity; unless you are male or female you cannot participate in the exaltation of godhood. It is for now an incontrovertible aspect of the religion, whereas the racial taboo had no clear derivation, no fixed anchor. Still, I put my political loyalties aside, if only temporarily. I was getting something I needed from the Mormons' concentration of faith in their services. I felt the spirit there. Maybe in the end spirit could trump reason. *Le cœur a ses raisons que la raison ne connaît point.* Pascal's moral might be enough to underwrite an important change in me.

My friend from the Family History Center introduced me to

the Gospel Principles class for adults. It combined those investigating the church, missionaries, and members who, as it said
on the cover of our text, wanted "knowledge of their Redeemer
and the very points of his doctrine, that they may know how to
come unto him and be saved." A very intelligent, funny young
woman taught us. Before we got into the first lesson, the non-
Mormon husband of a new convert shot up his hand and asked
if she was going to talk about Mormon underwear. People burst
out laughing. Our teacher said sympathetically, "Please, please,
he's worried that he could walk in the house and find people in
their sacred garments." She suggested that he and his wife talk
a little more on the subject in private.

Intrigued by the course description, I also started sitting in
on a University of Virginia class called "Faith and Doubt in the
Modern Age." The course description for Religion 2380 said the
course would consider whether belief in God was "wishful thinking," "neurotic," "inherently immoral," or perhaps just "a primitive stage in human development"; how fear and guilt related
to it, and whether one could be simultaneously "rational and a
believer." I did not think I would have difficulty holding two
opposed ideological streams in my head. That's how I'd always
lived, seeing there were two sides to everything, recognizing that
in the end I would have only my own peculiar preferences. I
wanted to know the arguments here, the wherefores and why-
nots so I could learn how to express belief in a way that I could
respect. The University of Virginia students, I soon learned,
called the course "Doubt and Doubt" because the reading list

was so heavily weighted in the direction of atheism: Hume, Freud, Comte, Nietzsche, and Feuerbach versus Kierkegaard, James, and Bonhoeffer.

There was value in reading the atheists for me since the process helped me sort out the different streams of my own unbelieving. They'd been in the air I'd always breathed. God as a barely transparent father figure = Freud. Man inventing God from fear of own self's power = Nietzsche. God as projection of man's infinite nature = Feuerbach. I considered these ideas completely natural. As compelling as they were, however, they didn't put an end to the possibility of God. They uncovered illusions, but God loomed imperturbably on. Going back to the heavy-hitting atheists felt like I'd cleaned my cluttered attic and made room for the arguments on behalf of belief. Most of these did turn out to be variations on *"Le cœur a ses raisons . . ."* The exceptions were modern thinkers who embraced the scientific method and felt they had to be able to answer doubt with scientific logic. William James was rigorous, but not the most rigorous. Still, I favored him. In *The Will to Believe*, he wanted to convince those sticklers who couldn't choose God until there was absolute proof of His existence. James knew there was no such thing. But he had to act. A person must choose: James accepted "the risk of acting as if my passional need of taking the world religiously might be prophetic and right."

The atheist philosopher Antony Flew was the most rigorous logician on our "Faith and Doubt" reading list. There were moments when Flew's syntax was so convoluted about such things as the "endemic evil of theological utterance" that I wanted to stop arguing the topic with myself at this depth. It was bottomless. If logic was the end-all and be-all, I preferred to do what Richard Dawkins was constantly exhorting us to do: spend the hours wasted on religion in the study of science. I knew that there were many beautiful things I could learn about modern science, and I feared I would never be able to make a true or false statement about religion if it had to be constructed in any way like this torture chamber of Flew's: "For if the utterance is indeed an assertion, it will necessarily be equivalent to a denial of the negation of that assertion." There had to be an easier way.

As Dr. Ferreira, the professor of "Faith and Doubt," had said at the start of her course, "Faith has nothing to do with intelligence. If you believe, there will always be people smarter than you who don't. If you don't believe, there are always people smarter than you who do." This was my mantra as I tried to attend the LDS Gospel Principles class more consistently. I had my ups and downs. There were a lot of Mormon doctrines. Almost everything was governed by doctrine: God, Christ, history, how we should pray, "the still small voice" by which Mormons know the Holy Spirit, repentance, death, exercise, the eternities. The doctrines were very literal, and the doctrines were *true*. People often concluded their testimonies by saying, "I know this church is *true*," meaning God definitely has a body of flesh and bones. He loves us, has a Plan of Life for each of us. There were doctrines for eternal family, exaltation, chastity, children, the importance of genealogy. There were times when I appreciated the doctrines for cleaning up all the cobwebby aspects of life. Not that I believed them, but I saw they served a purpose. As a convert, our teacher told us she had come to love Mormonism because it had answers for every question.

There were other times when the doctrines freaked me out. When we came to the battle in the preexistence, I actually had a crisis. Maybe it was because I'd started to investigate with the missionaries. Since two male missionaries could not meet with a single woman without another person present, my Gospel Principles teacher and her husband had kindly invited us to meet in their home. They were all extraordinarily sweet to me. I'd had moving experiences of this Mormon quality when I went out with the missionaries for the documentary. The drama of its impact increased when I was a participant. They asked me about my sense of God. I did have one, but then I had problems with the idea that He had a body. They asked me to pray to find out if it was true. I wasn't sure it would work, but it seemed fair. Still I felt we were on a tightrope, that it was very straight and very taut, and it wouldn't take much for their beliefs to unbalance me or my honesty to unbalance them. I had by then mentioned my role in the PBS film, and there seemed to be no problem with that. I was relieved. I didn't want my exploration to end. I still found their faith compelling.

Then the battle in the preexistence looked like it might be too much for me. Joseph received bits and pieces of this in revelations during his lifetime. Between his day and 2010, those pieces had been hammered and refined and finally woven into a doctrine that covered God's decision to send Christ to earth as the Savior eons before history started. According to current Mormon theology, when Satan heard that God had chosen to send Christ, he was furious. He felt *he* should have been chosen. "War broke out in heaven about who should come to earth as God's representative," our teacher explained, and went to the whiteboard. At this point, I felt the unmistakable stirrings of an oncoming anxiety attack. She wrote "Christ" in black on one side and "Satan" on the other. She then wrote "2/3rds" under Christ and "1/3rd" under Satan to indicate the fractions of the unborn spirits who fought on the different sides during this battle in the preexistence. It was as if we were studying Charlemagne's troop count in his battle against the Moors. I could feel sweat on my face. Finally, we were told that Satan's followers had been sent out of heaven, never to enjoy mortal bodies. We who were sitting there in our mortal bodies had supported Jesus Christ in the battle of the preexistence. By continuing to follow Jesus, we would be able to return to God after death. Now the worms in my eyes began to counterrotate, the surest sign I was in the throes of cognitive dissonance. I had no higher degree of anxiety.

My first duty was to get out of the classroom without crashing into one of my classmates. I did not want to hurt anyone. But when the worms counterrotated, it was hard to tell whether I was coming or going. Among other things, my terror of the preexistence bode ill for any comfort I might draw from the Mormon afterlife, which was to die for. Friends and family would be there, and probably some of the houses I'd had to leave, one that

I missed in particular. But now I found that something deep inside did not respond—just did not believe—in any life before or after this one constructed along human lines. I made it to my car, made it home, and e-mailed my friend from the Family History Center that I needed to talk to her. She found time for me. I didn't mention the worms. I told her the description of the pre-existence made me nervous. I asked my friend if I was supposed to believe it literally. She said I was. She added that I shouldn't get too hung up on doctrine. I need concern myself only with feeling that the church was true. When I felt the gospel was true, the doctrines would be true to me, too. That was what mattered.

Maybe I had hit the wall. This might be the end. I prayed, asking if it was, and, to my surprise, got a sign while I was having a glass of wine with my young friend Annie, a professor in the University of Virginia English department. I told her about my Mormon search, and she told me about Joanna Brooks, a remarkable scholar of literature who also writes about current political and cultural issues. Brooks, a fifth-generation Mormon whose great-great-grandmother crossed the plains as a child, grew up in a conservative family and went to Brigham Young University. Although her writing has established her as a liberal, feminist, gay-friendly Mormon, she feels the LDS Church is home. Her first book, *American Lazarus*, changed the way the national academic world viewed religion and communities of color in the eighteenth century; conferences have been built around this prizewinning book. Brooks is associated with the well-known *Mormon Stories* podcast; she permablogs in *Religion*

Dispatches and writes for newspapers and magazines across the Mormon–non-Mormon spectrum, everything from *Sunstone* to *The Washington Post*.

Joanna Brooks is also the woman behind askmormongirl .com. This site includes her blog, and she invites all questions about Mormonism and promises "unorthodox answers from an imperfect source." It makes for delightful reading. Here are some sample questions:

> *"Proselytizing makes me uncomfortable. What should I do?"*
>
> *"Are Mormons really as happy as they seem? What's with the perkiness?"*
>
> *"I'm a Mormon mom, and I don't want my gay daughter to bring her girlfriend home. Am I being unfair? What about my beliefs?"*
>
> *"Ouch! I've just survived a Facebook fight with a fellow Mormon. Can you help develop a Mormon netiquette code?"*
>
> *"I'm about to be baptized. And boy do I have some questions."*

I felt this could be the right Mormon place to air my anxiety. I wrote askmormongirl.com, describing my job on the film, my near-conversion on the road to Richmond, and my great discomfort over the battle in the preexistence. My question was: I don't think I'm a literal believer; can I still be a Mormon?

Parts of her answer:

Let me get this straight: you're a smart, funny secular intellectual who fell in love with Joseph Smith through Fawn Brodie and decided to get serious about Mormonism after writing for PBS's Mormon documentary? Holy. Moly. . . . You've come in through the out door! . . . I'm thrilled you are here!

The vast majority of Mormons active in the LDS Church today are literalist and orthodox in their beliefs. . . . Church can be a lonely three hours . . . and many try to remedy their lonesomeness by plugging into Internet communities of like-minded Mormons, or dialing into blogs like this one or Feminist Mormon Housewives, or listening to the Mormon Stories podcast.

I'd encourage you to consider: what do you understand by the word believe? Some etymologists hold that the word believe shares the same Teutonic or Gothic linguistic roots as the word love . . . Could it be that be-loving Mormon doctrine or Mormon history is a form of be-lieving? . . . Is believing more like hands closed around a concept, or hands empty but open and turned palms up in seeking and gratitude? Or is it some mixture of both?

Joanna Brooks's words pushed me to be more present with the missionaries. I was fascinated with Mormon history, and felt I wasn't be-loving enough toward Mormon beliefs. I had to

go beyond my limitations at my next meeting with the missionaries. We met at the house of some young law students. I almost
fainted when the elder's first question was what date I wanted to
set as my day for baptism. I was interested, even eager to learn,
but I was far from ready to be baptized. If I were to pick a date,
I said, it might be five years from now. My missionaries' faces
fell. People usually chose a date within a few months of starting
to investigate. But I'd hardly gotten adjusted to the idea of doctrines. Our attractive, warm, young host stepped in. He told the
story of being on his mission in Guatemala. The people he was
teaching could not speak a lot of English—enough, though, to
understand the power of the Book of Mormon. After only a few
months, these Guatemalans were sufficiently touched to be baptized. I was older, better educated, more probing. I would need
more time, he said to both me and the missionaries. I hoped I
would last through another meeting. I was hanging by a thread,
but I agreed to meet again.

When the boys arrived at my house a week later, I was practicing my good-bye speech. I'd planned to start our visit by saying how much I'd learned, but that I didn't think I was a real
candidate. Yet as soon as I saw they'd brought a third elder for
correctness' sake, I felt my farewell crumbling on my tongue. It
would be too rude to express in front of a stranger. Meanwhile,
Elder Gibney (not his real name), the older of the boys I was
used to seeing, had a new confidence to him.

While many young Mormon missionary men seem like
they've been sent by central casting—tall, pink-cheeked, very

handsome—Elder Gibney was medium height, pale, with a severe crew cut. He had introduced himself to me as a "mama's boy," meaning that he loved his mother very much and felt warmly (and appropriately) toward older women like me. I did not hold this against him; in fact, I held it more against my stiff-upper-lip WASP culture, which had inculcated in me the sense that it wasn't good for a boy to be a mama's boy. Today, however, Elder Gibney had rather a patriarchal firmness about him. After we prayed, he told me that this was the day I was supposed get a lesson in the Plan of Life. But the boys had thought and talked about our last meeting, and they felt I needed a lesson in faith. We would be studying Alma 32 (in the Book of Mormon), the verse which says, "If ye have faith ye hope for things which are not seen, which are true."

It was the very verse for me. I was touched that they had done such a good job of understanding my problems. Our lesson went swimmingly, ending in their asking me whether I had faith in Joseph Smith's words. Whether I had faith in their unseen truth. I did. We agreed our next lesson would be about Joseph as a holy prophet. I felt we were on a new copacetic track. It wasn't clear where it would lead, but they'd helped me get onto their wavelength. At our next meeting, the elders had arranged to watch a church video of Joseph's life with the young married couple who'd had us to their house before. I felt quite close to these two by now. When the young wife compared Joseph's three-part trinity with the "dysfunctional Christian trinity," I was tickled by her choice of words. Having gone on his mission first, the husband was now a college student. He gave me a paper he'd written for his English class about Joseph's belief in progression to Godhood. I loved this boy's willingness to put his religion out there in a secular community college. I hope the compliment had been returned by his teacher.

There was a certain buoyancy between us as we sat down to see the Joseph video. Though the film left out some complexities, I felt I could embrace its point of view. Elder Gibney asked me if I felt Joseph was a holy prophet of God. I said I did. In the contented I-rest-my-case silence that followed, the young husband gave me a hug. I usually shrink from feel-good hugging, but this was lovely. We made our next date and separated. When the five us came back together again (once more at the couple's apartment), we started out on the high where we ended. There was laughter, glasses of water, joking about the world's mistaking Angel Moroni for Angel Macaroni. News of the young wife's pregnancy. Excitement that rounded into seriousness that led to the first prayer. Afterward, Elder Gibney talked about my fascination with Joseph. I was grateful for it to be acknowledged. Then he basically said, "Joseph is not the point of the whole effort. Christ is. Joseph restores Christ."

Our pace slowed. I admitted to not getting Christ. They said Mormonism was centered on Christ and the atonement. They said that if I read the Book of Mormon I would come to see this was true. I told them I'd been worried about this. They explained that Christ was perfect. Jesus already knew I had problems with the atonement and did not fault me for it. I skipped any mention of the time I'd spent in a fury with Jesus. I tried rather timidly to explain that I'd read the Book of Mormon and came away feeling that it could support more than one view of Christ. In my case, it supported my feeling that Christ's time had passed; that God's absolute power had gone out of the world, leaving us amid a battle of religious books, each one contending for its particular, partial truth. The missionaries explained the necessity of Christ's existence. He was the only one who could atone for our sins. I said that I could take Joseph as my prophet, but not Christ in the sense they wanted me to. Fortunately, they were not offended. It was an error, but not a sacrilege. We went on like this, but it felt good somehow, as if we were all being honest. Our honesty did not rip a hole in our closeness. We made an appointment for the next week, and I asked them all to come to dinner beforehand.

When they came, there was an unexpected excitement in the air. This was the night. I was going over or I wasn't. I emptied my mind and served them water, chicken, roast vegetables, and rice. The second elder, a very young-looking boy, prayed over our food. Elder Bierer's (not his real name) first meeting with an investigator had been his first meeting with me. He was from Utah, so green in our early encounters I once was afraid he was going to cry. But he'd picked up steam, revealing that he had a booming voice, one for the ages, one that came from somewhere deep down in his personal basement. When he said grace, we could have been early Christians gathered in a cave church in 50 AD. As we ate, they asked me about my life for the first time:

where I came from, what church I'd grown up in, if I had children. I sketched in some details: rootless childhood, traveling with Dad's career in the CIA, marriage, writing, two daughters, divorce. It felt like I was inadvertently drawing attention to our differences, how we were each other's other. Then I described how I'd had a Joseph-related, near-conversion experience on the road while I was working on the film.

They radiated Mormon goodness, a warmth so thick it seemed like they'd swallowed sweaters. I knew this warmth was belief. Their souls would never grow cold. My own ached with longing as we left the table to go have our discussion in the living room. We were instantly going at the problem of Christ hammer and tongs. In my average conversations with secular friends, the subject of God could cause eyes to glaze over in an instant. I was amazed by the missionaries' emotional focus. The young husband explained how the "light of Christ" was possible before baptism. Everybody was entitled to that light, but Mormon baptism intensifies that relationship. Their warmth met my coolness. I was not rejecting their words. I could not understand them. Whenever they said the word "Christ," it was as if I saw a subtitle in Chinese. I did not feel anger. I felt incomprehension. I would have liked to understand the root of their belief, but I just could not. I actually begged them to help me. They responded genuinely, showering me in urgent bulletins: Christ's atonement means we can be saved from sin! Christ's resurrection brings resurrection to us all! Christ led a perfect life!

Our back-and-forth was incredibly intense. I wanted to know.

They wanted to teach. The room was like a sauna of truthful reaching from the heart. I felt there was the sheerest veil between us. We were so close to real connection. Hoping to break through the barrier, I said that whenever they said, "Christ," I saw the letters written in a Chinese subtitle. It didn't have meaning for me. Elder Bierer boomed, "It's like this ballpoint pen." He held up his black Bic and took off the top. "You are the pen without the top. You have the Holy Spirit without your top on. We all do. But Christ, baptism in Christ, completes you. Then you are whole." He put the top on his Bic. It was one of the most adorable things I'd ever heard, but I'd hit the wall. I wasn't going through.

"I don't get it," I said finally, sitting back in my chair. "Nothing you say rings a bell inside."

There was a long, serious pause.

Finally, my Gospel Principles teacher said quietly, "You remind me of teaching the Muslims. You have no need for a Savior."

I was amazed . . . honored. She showed respect for my religious search, and she did not fault me for not being able to embrace hers. She was also right in seeing that I could not understand the Savior because I felt I had no need of him. It was a surprise to learn this about myself.

Elder Bierer, all of eighteen, thin as a blade of grass, looked at me so kindly. He made me feel a childlike gratitude even before he spoke. He said in the voice of the Proclaimer, "You are so different than us, from such a different background. I think you should be commended for the effort you have made." The word "com-mend-ed" came out like three bangs on a huge kettle drum.

I was going to be away in the coming weeks for work. While I was gone, both elders would be transferring to their next post in another town. No one mentioned another meeting. Before we all finally said good-bye, I asked my Gospel Principles teacher if she'd been comfortable enough on my straight-backed Empire sofa. She'd hurt her tailbone in a fall the previous weekend, and I had seen her squirming during our meeting. She said, "I felt no pain. I felt the Holy Spirit was present."

I was touched by her words. I'd felt it, too. But I couldn't convert. I loved the missionaries' belief, but I didn't share it. I just hoped I could find a way to keep Joseph close to me.

THIRTEEN

Sanctified Flesh

In Nauvoo things unraveled quickly after Joseph's death. I have put myself into the scene many times. It had so many makings for the ending of a wrenching film about the American dream, a lasting film, one with layers and layers that I could watch and slowly understand over time. But what would that dream be, I always asked as I imagined myself in the cast of extras, running along the street and catching sight of Milo, my cousin, being played by some unknown youngster. Milo was among the police on the streets the day Joseph's and Hyrum's corpses were brought back into town under a blanket in the back of a horse-drawn wagon. Which American dream did the tumultuous end of Joseph's life sum up? The one about the frontier religious visionary whose nature was so controversial he died at the hands of a mob? Or the one about a new American church that was too strong for its own good? Or the one about the first nineteenth-century Mormon woman to cross-dress as a man so she could escape her fate as a plural wife? That would be me, of course, who always dressed in men's clothes in my imaginary role as an extra in Nauvoo. I could relate to Joseph only as a tomboy, not as a woman. He was not threatening, really, or attractive to me in a "Be still, oh my heart" way. He felt more like a kindred spirit.

As the prophet's body passed through Nauvoo, Milo must have held a few of his widows back from the wagon carrying his corpse. Some of these women wept, among them a few mothers with children who might be Joseph's. Their uncertain status was just one of the many threads that would unravel in the wake of his murder. His personal practice of celestial marriage would create havoc among his family members, widows, friends, followers, and students for years to come. Emma, first among his widows, simplified her situation by turning her back on what had been too painful. She denied that Joseph ever practiced polygamy. She had been in a movie about being the dedicated wife of an upright American prophet. She stayed on location and never went to Utah.

During the uncertain time after Joseph's death, Jesse Harmon was the doorkeeper of the carpenter shop, in charge of completing woodwork on the temple. It still wasn't finished in early December, but the Mormons began holding sacred ceremonies around the clock in hopes of giving proper blessings to all those who were going on the trek. Jesse and Anna, along with Milo and their daughter, Sophronia, took part in the special rituals of "endowment" in the temple on December 16, 1845. Jesse took his first plural wife, Margaret Allen, aged twenty-one, on February 6, 1846. Anna was forty-nine. There is no record of how Jesse and Anna reached the decision to invite another wife into their marriage. As part of Joseph's inner circle, Jesse was probably taught the principle by the prophet himself and urged to teach it to his wife. That nicety may have been skipped under pressure; what proper manners were, let alone procedure in courtship before (and during) a plural marriage, were among the least-worked-out parts of Joseph's polygamy. All we know about Anna was that she was "very sweet and gentle and spiritual." Maybe she was wonderfully accepting of her husband's decision.

Unfortunately, there are no descriptions either of the marriages between Hulda Barnes, then thirty-eight, and Sophronia Harmon, then twenty, to Heber C. Kimball on the same day, February 3, 1846. I have the impression there was a marriage ceremony for each woman, both probably in some awe of their groom, who by then was large and bald and forty-three years old. He had long been a close associate of Joseph and Brigham's, a colorful, stalwart character, among the most savory of the prophet's savory admirers, and a fiercely dedicated member of the Mormon leadership. When Brigham Young took over as president after Joseph's death, Heber was next in the Quorum of Twelve. He was also legendarily the most romantic polygamous patriarch. He was theoretically supposed to love his wives equally, but even after he had taken forty, he could not stop loving his first wife most. He had more than a hundred children with his other wives, and dutifully visited and supported them, but he could never wait to get home to Vilate.

Joseph saw plural marriages as both the most celestial and the most practical part in a network of Mormon connectedness. Hulda and Sophronia were unprotected, single women, and so marrying them was one of Heber's duties as a good frontier polygamist. Ordinary life on the prairie was hard enough, but for a young virgin and a spinster to cross the wilderness alone was beyond dangerous. Heber lent Hulda and Sophronia the official protection of his family, which may, even under the circumstances, have been cold comfort. In February 1846, Hulda, along with Milo and his new wife, joined the vanguard of western emigration with Heber's company. They were a party of twelve to fifteen wagons as they crossed the Mississippi on ice, heading for Council Bluffs.

Jesse and Anna, along with her sister wife, Margaret, and their children made slow progress. They did not leave Nauvoo until September. The autumn was bitter; the winter worse. Their daughter, Sophronia, was traveling with her family, and she grew so sick in the severe weather that they had to lay by. Once the party did continue, Jesse, Anna, and Milo's two brothers also fell ill with the "extreme fatigue and exposure." By the time they arrived at Milo's small, newly built house, they were "too sick to help each other."

Anna died first. She was buried at Winter Quarters near Council Bluffs while Milo was away selling a wagon so he could buy eatables. He heard of his mother's death as he returned home with a new supply of food. When he got back, Sophronia was failing. Anna had died on January 16, 1847. Her only daughter died on January 30 and was buried near her mother in the Winter Quarters graveyard. In the pitiless cycle of death and animal spirits, Milo's father and brothers recovered and threw themselves back into the challenges of slogging through snow and fierce winds into the mountains. Milo's party was among the first pioneers to break through to Emigration Canyon in Utah. In his journal, he extolled the sight of the valley drenched in sun, and praised the brethren who met them as all looking "beautiful, godlike, handsome and cheerful."

The Harmons were there to become gods, too. Milo wrote that their "religious sentiments compelled" them through the hostile wilderness, losing wife and sister, into a primitive landscape where their religious drama would be staged on stone. They'd start to become gods by digging sand with their bare hands to plant their potatoes. Jesse spent twenty years building up his family's life in Salt Lake City and then was ordered on a mission to southern Utah. As he left, he married his third wife, Nancy Calkins. For what it is worth, he was sixty-six, Margaret was forty-six, and Nancy was twenty-one. Milo did not practice polygamy. Neither, as far as I have been able to find out, did his brothers. But as nineteenth-century Mormons, they would have held it as a true principle. After 1852, when Brigham announced Mormon polygamy to the American public, the Harmon boys would have been hated for their adherence to Joseph's religion.

Statehood was withheld as long as the Mormons practiced polygamy. Officially the Mormon Church ended it in three different ukases issued between 1890 and 1921. While the larger part of his church set it aside, Joseph's polygamy endured into the twenty-first century in a range of small religious groups and independent families. It became so much more complicated and entrenched than people east of Texas realize. Polygamous families are not small. Four Heber Kimballs equal four hundred children. The modern polygamists' story is endlessly rich, messy, and dramatic. It would take a Faulkner to capture the history-isn't-dead-it-is-not-even-past consciousness among these American polygamists. In Utah, their suffering, ardor, and strength of character (and weakness, too) cry out for a depth of sympathy and moral complexity that our mainstream culture has never extended. Amid the broken families and bizarre lives, there are noble figures, extraordinary people, some of whose dynastic lines have been in place since Joseph's time. These men and women have refined the principles of celestial marriage over decades and practice a discipline as severe as any Benedictine monastery's.

The Timpsons of Centennial Park are such people. Their family consists of a husband and three wives: David, Ellie, Alyne, and Elda Mae. They have fifteen children. The adults are serious, stalwart, educated, amazingly frank about their practice. Joseph Smith is central to their religious life, and their whole life is religious. I met the Timpsons in 2004, in the research phase of working on the film. That was the year Warren Jeffs became the face of contemporary polygamy when he was charged with welfare fraud and for sexually abusing underage girls and boys.

It was my job to find polygamists who could make the best on-camera case for plural marriage to a national PBS audience. It was a dodgy and confusing situation in which to find connections. The shadowy fundamentalist world was split into groups, some savory, some not. How was I going to find the "good" polygamists? Gradually, I heard more and more about Centennial Park as a model fundamentalist community. I went from contact to contact in a careful, wary dance. Fortunately, Centennial Park was looking for the right media opportunity, and I got an audition. I went to an unpretentious office building off a dusty road near Salt Lake City to meet a member of Centennial Park's priesthood council.

This is where I first met Claude Cawley, a man with several wives, who exuded a great fondness for Joseph Smith. Claude had a dignity I did not usually associate with small-town American businessmen (which he was). I began to associate his dignity with his long commitment to unpopular causes. Claude loved polygamy, it had given him everything; yet the world despised the source of his spiritual richness. Claude had an integral role on the Centennial Park priesthood council, which he described at some length. He emphasized repeatedly how the council was the indispensable authority in his group's fundamentalist practice. It provided their prophet with checks and balances and was what Warren Jeffs threw out in favor of his one-man rule. When Jeffs did this, he lost his authority and descended into personal psychosis.

Authority was of utmost importance to Claude. Just the way he said the word communicated a world of depth and wisdom, a depth he taught me came from Joseph, who had received it from God, and a wisdom that arose from having been practiced in the chain of authority passed from Joseph to John Taylor from whence it left the Mormon Church's official line of presidency. The lineage then continued through the Woolleys, Broadbent, Barlow, Musser, and Johnson, all the prophets who went underground to keep Joseph's law alive. I would hear the names on this list invoked solemnly by other men from Centennial Park, usually members of the priesthood whose forefathers held to the true grail generation after generation in the growing shadow of Salt Lake's Goliath.

The divide between the official church and the fundamentalists over polygamy is still deeply painful to the people of Centennial Park. Men who became the prophets and who led the official church in the early twentieth century, men like Joseph F. Smith and Heber J. Grant, had enforced the end of polygamy—though they themselves had plural wives. They used their power to make sure the practice did not continue, and in so doing diminished the first prophet's proper place in their church. Claude mentioned to me more than once that no one in the official Mormon Quorum of Twelve or First Presidency received their authority in the line from Joseph. There were several men in the Centennial Park priesthood council who had.

As a result of our first interview, Claude gave me contact information for the Timpsons. By happenstance, I met their matriarch, Guinevere, before I met the young family. She had joined the Centennial Park Action Committee, a group of women who were making themselves available to the press. We agreed to meet on their home ground. I first drove five hours south from Salt Lake City to St. George, where I stayed in a motel on a highway like those outside cities all over America. Once I got onto Route 53 out of Hurricane en route to the remote Arizona Strip, I was quickly in a world that was unlike any place I'd ever been. Route 53 ran through wasteland and sage brush, rising to a series of plateaus surrounded by stern, red mountains. It was a judgmental landscape that asked whether you were ready to meet your Maker. The sun was relentless. When my cell stopped working, I pleaded for God's forgiveness and help.

About an hour out, there were signs of civilization. The storage containers began to gather on the side of the road, broken equipment, shacks, huge power sources, streets, and well-built residences. Colorado City was on its knees to my left and Centennial Park was on its knees farther ahead on the right. I turned into Centennial Park, a work-in-progress with its unfinished network of paved streets, a handsome charter high school, and a no-holds-barred mixture of mansions, huts, and ample middle-class homes.

I went to the meeting place, a simple, utilitarian building where twenty women were slowly gathering around a large rectangular table. The room was unusually quiet, possibly because these women had so often been vilified, sensationalized, or studied by the press. They were almost never portrayed as human beings. I knew something about forbidden fruit. I didn't see anything inherently wrong with mine. I didn't see anything inherently wrong with plural marriage. I started by asking them to describe the core of beauty in polygamy, which the world could not see.

A lovely old lady sat close to the front on my left. This was Guinevere Timpson, a woman with an aristocratic face and gray hair piled in a Victorian roll on the top of her head. She was the first to raise her hand and speak. "I hate the word 'polygamy.' Polygamy is the way people live in the world. Celestial marriage is so high above, people can't comprehend it." She was passionate, and she knew well what she wanted to say. She had the authority of age and her intelligence; no one interrupted. "As you do it, so you sanctify your flesh. As you go on to your other life after death, you will progress and progress so you'll have a character like god and you'll associate with other gods. You have to have knowledge, faith, justice, mercy, and love. Those are the attributes of god. These are the principles the Savior taught us, and as you develop this in your character in life you go beyond your little selfish self."

I felt Joseph Smith himself could not have been clearer about the work of their religious virtue, of how hard it is to sacrifice possessive love, yet how high the reward for doing so can be. When I finally met David Timpson at his Centennial Park office, I told him about the remarkable woman, Guinevere, who had spoken at the meeting. He nodded respectfully and told me that she was one of his mothers. I was confused. He patiently led me to understand that Guinevere was one of David's father's thirteen wives, and so *a* mother to David. His birth mother was Donna, a lively woman and dedicated companion to Guinevere, her aging older sister wife.

David was a handsome, blond, young middle-aged businessman and entrepreneur. Along with his jeans and tieless shirt, he wore his authority and gravitas lightly. He told me he hoped greater respect for polygamy would develop through media coverage of Centennial's model religious practice. He encouraged me to be searching in my work in his home. There was, however, one question he and his family wouldn't answer. I could not ask how they scheduled David's nights with his wives. It was the question TV interviewers sprang on polygamists without warning for live, on-camera excitement.

David does not fit any polygamist stereotype. Neither do his wives, Ellie, Alyne, and Elda Mae. All of these women are beautiful and stylish dressers. Ellie is an administrative assistant at Masada Charter School. Elda Mae works in Title One at the Mohave County public school. Alyne is the primary mother at home. Each of the Timpsons is what once was called a rugged individualist: very strong and outspoken about how they live and why. They are serious about their religious practice. The family has prayers together morning and night. On Saturday evenings, Elda Mae teaches a scripture class to the toddlers; Ellie teaches one for children eight and up. On Sundays, David teaches classes for three different age ranges in the morning, and the whole family spends the afternoon at church. As befits a religion in which marriage is so central, there is gravity in the adults' manner with one another, but they are also curious and funny. They all enjoy gourmet food and know fine wines. (The fundamentalists believe Joseph's Word of Wisdom was health advice, never meant as an absolute taboo. The mainstream church imposed restrictions on alcohol, coffee, and tea at the beginning of the twentieth century as they worked to overcome their image as uncontrolled polygamists.)

When I asked about the fundamentalists' recent representation on television, the Timpsons preferred *Sister Wives* to *Big Love*, which they felt was "sick." *Sister Wives* was natural, yet reverent, and of special interest because the patriarch and his four wives had recently gone to court to legalize polygamy. The Timpsons were horrified by *Big Love*'s portrait of polygamous domestic life, which left out so much of its spiritual dimension. The stereotype the Timpsons most despise is the abusive one commandeered by Warren Jeffs. The Timpsons suffered it first-hand through members of their families who were hurt during Jeffs's horrific progress.

David, Ellie, Alyne, and Elda Mae all grew up in Colorado Park and watched Jeffs come to power. Many of their family lines go back through Colorado Park to Short Creek, as the community was first called when it was founded in 1934. All of the Timpsons' parents and grandparents practiced plural marriage; Ellie's family's practice goes back six generations to Joseph Smith. The famous Short Creek raid in 1953 drew a major line between a prelapsarian Utah polygamy and its battle-scarred present. After the 1953 raid, when the police overwhelmed the town, arrested the men, and sent the children into welfare, some fundamentalists wrapped themselves in the secrecy that drove their communities in on themselves.

The world knows about the dark side of those communities,

but not much of the joy and honor. The Timpsons' parents remembered the raid, and their lasting fear was in the background of daily life. Nonetheless David, Ellie, Alyne, and Elda Mae all report childhoods full of learning, culture, and music, and often having enough brothers and sisters to make up two softball teams. All of their parents were committed to the education of their children. David read everything as a boy, including a biography of Babe Ruth that turned him into a passionate Yankees fan. Ellie, still a voracious reader, first heard *The Hobbit* when her father read it aloud to all his children. One of Elda Mae's mothers was a successful businesswoman and an assistant mayor of Ogden. She married Elda Mae's father when she was sixty-six, thereby giving all the family's daughters a striking example of a feminist.

"I wasn't sitting there thinking I have to share my toys," David said. "We used to write plays because we had enough kids for the cast. It was a royal time for us." The fact that their families lived off in the middle of a wild landscape meant hours of the sort of exploration I'd adored as a child. "My mother allowed us to be free," Ellie told me. "We had large fields and mountains by our house. These weren't farm fields, these were wild fields with sagebrush. . . . We were able to roam freely. . . . The earth here is red. It must have been a horror to clean up. But she let us go." Elda Mae had such a happy family life, she had no desire to be anywhere else. "I wanted to be home. We had older sisters who could gather you up, and we'd be sitting around—the family, maybe twenty of us—listening to a book.". For Alyne, having mothers, plural, was the saving grace during troubled times with her birth mother.

The Timpsons' childhood joys were inextricably entwined with their prophet, Joseph Smith. His name was often invoked in their prayers. The children sang a hymn about him. Joseph was such an integral part of their teaching and awareness that Ellie said she didn't remember "discovering" him. He was the air she breathed and also the holy architect of the relationships that made her family special. In the mainstream Mormon Church, giving up polygamy seems to have distanced people from Joseph. The Timpsons hold him close; they hold him personally dear. They spoke of Joseph as fondly as people do of Thomas Jefferson in Charlottesville—so fondly, it's as if (depending on where you are) he had just stepped into the next room.

Last spring, after I signed the contract for this book with Penguin, I made another visit to Centennial Park. I wanted to spend time with the Mormons whose love of Joseph was closest to mine. I was too old to take up polygamy, but I wondered if I could learn something about holding on to Joseph from the way they did. They lived in a remote place, but not in isolation. How did they deal with the stream of negative writing about Joseph, much of it because of his attempt to introduce polygamy?

When I asked Claude Cawley if he read secular biographies of Joseph, he said he'd read Fawn Brodie. (David had bought a copy of Richard Bushman's *Joseph Smith: Rough Stone Rolling*, but hadn't had a chance to read it yet.) Claude had learned some things from Brodie, but felt she had an agenda. I told him that she seemed to be in the camp that thought Joseph had just introduced polygamy to satisfy his unusually strong sex drive. Claude laughed at that and replied, "Joseph did have an unusually strong sex drive. That was a good thing." The body was a beautiful gift, he explained, but polygamy required everyone to subordinate their sex drive in service to God. (David, Ellie, Alyne, and Elda Mae all said they felt sex for its own sake was not part of Joseph's polygamy. The sex projected onto Joseph was in the eye of the beholder, not the practice.)

There are many psychoanalytic theories about Joseph's behavior, one in particular by Dr. William Morain about his need to introduce plural marriage. He argues that Joseph suffered post-traumatic stress as a result of the surgery on his leg when he was eight. Later, as an adult, Joseph dreamt of an angel who came to him with a raised sword, threatening to kill him if he did not bring the principle of polygamy to his people. Dr. Morain connects the knives in the surgery and the knife in the dream. According to his theory, Joseph was unconsciously compelled to rework the trauma of his terrifying early experience through polygamy. I asked Alyne what she thought of this theory. She displayed her right, as a rugged individualist, not to subject her religion to intellectual analysis. She hooted loud enough to make me laugh; then she added, "You've got to be kidding!"

Alyne remembers Joseph Smith coming into her life when she was four. That was the year she began thinking about Joseph going into the grove and praying to know which church was true. That was the year her father married her second mother, the woman who began to read stories about Joseph to the children in the family. Alyne's birth mother doesn't seem to have taught her doctrine, but she asked her seven-year-old daughter the only question whose answer really mattered. One day as she brushed Alyne's hair, her mother asked, "What do you want? What do you want in your life, Allie?" Before she could even think, the little girl said, "I want my salvation." When Warren Jeffs exploded Colorado City, Alyne's primary drive to find God, coupled with Joseph's example of finding Him for himself, set her on her own path. She gradually broke from her parents in Colorado City and settled in Centennial Park.

Though the Timpsons aren't that interested in secular critiques of Joseph, they share some of the outside world's censure of his treatment of Emma. A lot of people I talked to in Centennial Park had read Linda Newell and Valeen Avery's *Mormon Enigma: Emma Hale Smith*. The women readers felt deeply for Emma and, I would say, mourned the fact that Joseph lied to her so much. They recognized sorrowfully that there was a cloud over Joseph's introduction of polygamy. But they all believed celestial marriage involved God's highest law.

David Timpson, who is widely read in Mormon history, had a different take. He had no doubt that Joseph was completely in love with Emma. "It was probably the trial of his life to embrace a doctrine that broke her heart." For David, Joseph is "overwhelmingly loving" and "honest." It pained Joseph to lie to Emma; and it pained Joseph that he had to hold himself back for her sake while pushing men around him forward. But David believes

Joseph was "under the gun." The angel who gave Joseph this command was not part of a dream. "It was not a revelation nor a dream. It was an experience. It was real." God was also absolutely real to Joseph. "His greatest revelations were about the identity of God. In Joseph Smith's quest, he received revelation after revelation about the process this character went through to become God." Celestial marriage was central to this process.

Practiced properly, polygamy prepares men and women to become gods by helping them overcome their selfish possessiveness as lovers, spouses, and parents. Not everyone is ready for the challenge of polygamy in this lifetime. Not all members of the Centennial community are called to live in plural marriages. A couple must pray to be given an opportunity to share their marriage with another wife. The priesthood council also prays as they search for the right woman to join a particular marriage. A couple's prayers are not always answered, and when they are, the new relationship involves many responsibilities. In response to the inevitable question about why plural wives can't have as many husbands as their husbands have wives, the answer is they are free to practice polyandry. But they will have to find that New Guinea for themselves. Polygamy is the gateway to Joseph's celestial marriage as it exists in Utah.

If Joseph's polygamy seems too heavily balanced in favor of the man, remember his polygamy is not about falling in love. It is about working on a relationship as a group endeavor in the eyes of God. As David told me, "The outside world assumes men are the cause of plural marriage to get more sex. To be blunt with you, I get less of that in plural marriage than in monogamy. Polygamy stretches you. The focus in our family is not on creating a dreamy romantic situation. In the family, I like to say, I'm not about plural monogamies. We're partners in life and we have to work on that." The man must become more understanding rather than less when he has two wives.

In the Timpsons' plural marriage, David has had to get to know three women as individuals; the women have had to trust one man with more space than comes naturally for them to give. When I asked Ellie, David's first wife, how easy it was to accept another woman into her marriage, she laughed and said, "It's not the run-of-the-mill American experience, is it?" Yet as unlike marriage on Main Street USA as hers is, Ellie has a core of self-reliance that most women would admire. She told me she consciously resisted the kind of dependence their situation fostered. There would be no likening of their household to a harem! She demanded respect and believed David gave it. Yes, it was difficult "to have your husband sleeping with another woman in the next room." It wasn't easy. But it was worth the spiritual growth. "It's not that we're superhuman women. What makes it possible to come up to that commitment is our faith in God. It's a commitment we have made to God. That's where our faith is placed. It's not that we love our husbands so much. They're just men, too, in the end."

When I visited last spring, the Timpsons' children ranged in age from nine months to seventeen years. Ellie, Alyne, and Elda Mae all feel having several mothers was a great advantage. Now as David's second wife, Alyne celebrates her role as the mother at home with the children. "I welcome every child in this house whether I bore it or not. They are all David's children. I'm thrilled to death having my sister wife's child to care for. Maybe this is egotistical of me. I want that child. I want that child to love me. I've never gone through issues of resentment toward a child."

Elda Mae is the widow of David's brother, who died in a car accident. In polygamous communities, it is customary for a brother to marry his brother's wife under such circumstances. Elda Mae made the transition from being the only wife to being one of three. She wanted to do it because the Timpsons stress character work in their daily discussions of religion. If the children are fighting, the mothers ask them to relate their anger to scripture. Husbands and wives must also live their beliefs on a daily basis. Elda Mae told me that "there are times when there are words. You ask, 'Is this truly what you want?' I live with a husband who is accountable as I am accountable. He's not just a man to have a good time with. . . . If there weren't a religious focus, I wouldn't do it."

The Timpsons love entertaining. On the last night of my visit, I had dinner with the family—David, Donna, Ellie, Alyne (with her nine-month-old baby on her lap), Elda Mae—and a young couple from the neighborhood. We all sat at the long table in the expanded dining area near the kitchen. While we sipped a Washington State Pinot Noir, the Timpsons' children lined up to greet me. As David told me their names, these young creatures came and shook my hand or gave me a friendly hug. Afterward, David went to the stove to cook his signature béarnaise sauce, which we had with grilled salmon and asparagus. As we ate, conversation turned again to Joseph Smith. The young husband from next door said he was reading a book about Joseph that turned him into a saint. He wanted the real man, the real prophet, warts and all.

I realized suddenly that Joseph *had* found his place in a grown-up American dream here in Centennial Park. The real Joseph had earned a place in the American dream of lessons learned. He had found it here at the Timpsons' table. It was not our most dramatic or glamorous national dream, but one that had gained respect amid our failures as a country in recent years and our problems during the recession. Joseph was very much part of the extravagant, early America, a place where many with his untutored talents flew too close to the sun. But the Timpsons were the product of six generations of struggling with Joseph's most unruly celestial aspiration. They'd made sense of plural marriage; they'd brought discipline to it; they were perfecting their love for one another and becoming gods step by step. It was as if some part of Joseph had been maturing among these fundamentalists in the 167 years since his death. Now, against all odds, through the hard moral work of unrelenting adherents like the Timpsons, through their tenacity—a quality they shared with mainstream Mormons—their persistent dedication to their highest ideals over decades, Joseph's once scandalous polygamy might even be accepted as an alternative form of marriage.

FOURTEEN

A Dead Prophet, a Corpse,
and a Woman Who Will Die

The years while I worked on the PBS film and then afterward thought about Joseph Smith and about writing this book were all years when Tovi was slowly declining. He was lucky in many ways. He could live on his own. His particular case of Parkinson's was slow-moving. He never got the tremor. For some years, he could put on the kinds of fireworks and feasts that he felt were his particular calling as the god of revels. People did not know how to live or celebrate life's wonders! He did. He would show them the magnificence everywhere. Those were years when he could still canoe. He would use his huge patience to lift his leg slowly, slowly over the side in shallow water, and then I'd pull the boat out and all but tip it over by leaping impatiently over the gunwale. We had some spectacular trips down the James in successive autumns when the trees were flooded with color, and we could hear wild turkeys calling from beyond the brush along the banks.

When his balance got too iffy for the canoe, he concocted an electric bike with a friend. For a while, he could ride it around looking like a cross between Mary Poppins and Babar the Elephant. Then, after he began using crutches, he loved cooking for the hummingbirds. He'd boil their sugar and water, fill the feeders, and sit for hours watching the ferocious creatures dive bomb the red plastic flowers for syrup. Tovi wouldn't speak of his decline. It was almost as if he didn't notice it. He took a scientific interest in Parkinson's and loved to discuss aspects of the illness with his doctors during his regular appointments. He was so entertaining and articulate about it, one of his doctors took Tovi on rounds with him to encourage other Parkinson's patients. But Tovi never complained about his own Parkinson's. He regarded complaining as "overmasticating that which a person had already chewed too much."

I noticed the subtleties of his decline—big and small: his slowing pace as we walked, his growing loss of interest in the world, his snooziness (which actually also had the catlike charm of an elderly tom catching a few winks whenever he felt like it). Though I complained to my friends about feeling responsible, he was actually very self-sufficient and independent. I regularly nagged him about his working out his medical game plan. Actually, I thought it would make me feel better even if he didn't care a fig about the damn thing. I secretly sympathized. Why should he spend his remaining time planning for what couldn't be predicted? Who knew how he'd die? Whether it would take forever or happen in a flash? Even when I secretly prayed for a million dollars to fall from the sky so he could have the best care ever,

I knew the only things money could buy would be fancier and fancier ways to superficially hide his decline. As soon as he stood up or tried to put on his clothes, his Parkinson's would announce itself.

I wasn't going to join, but I still sometimes went back to the Mormon Church. I got some relief from feeling the Holy Spirit there. No reassurance about the afterlife, but some feeling I could lay down the burden of my own grumpy egotism about the pain of living with Tovi's decline. Once after an absence of a few weeks from church, two new missionaries introduced themselves as I came in the door. It was part of their job to be available to potential investigators. As soon as these young women heard my name, they recognized me as an old investigator. I was apparently on a list of people with unfinished business, the sort of person they would have contacted even if I hadn't returned to church. They immediately asked if they could visit. I told them I was no longer a likely candidate, but they still wanted to come. When they arrived, we got right into it. I described my experience with the former missionaries, how it had culminated in the dramatic but fruitless meeting about Christ. Both girls had encouraging words on how just believing that I could believe in Christ could bring me finally, slowly but surely, to him. One said I just needed to pray and ask God if it was true that Christ was the Son of God.

We fell into a conversation about what they meant by "true." I had many experiences, I said, which were utterly true in the moment. But the feeling of that reality didn't last. These missionary girls said if God sent a sign saying something was true then it was true completely and forever. I asked them if they'd heard about the scientific method. Would their sense of truth ever be changed by evidence to the contrary? They said if God indicated something was true, there wouldn't be evidence to the contrary. I described my God moments and how I'd try to pack them into a sort of . . . sort of a snowball. But they melted away even if I prayed, asking God if they were true. One of the girls said haltingly, well, that was good, but I had to try and pack them into a nonmelting snowball before I prayed. We all roared with laughter, but we also agreed not to meet again at the end of the meeting. If I was going to enjoy their church, I had to play by their rules. I had to adopt their beliefs. I understood that.

Once I was not in relation to any religious structure, I drifted. I felt my life had been changed by exploring Joseph and his church. Yet the only reality I'd gained was seeing myself in some of the results of the Pew Forum's U.S. Religious Landscape Survey. These findings were the ones suggesting that while mystical experience was on the rise, commitment to doctrine was down. Across the board, Americans might not practice religion as seriously as their Puritan ancestors; only a little more than half of them attended church regularly and prayed daily. Yet polls showed that more than ninety percent of Americans believed in God and an afterlife. There were new patterns of conversion or "affiliation," as the Pew survey called it. People's spiritual needs weren't so deeply invested in a set of teachings. Seekers were even put off by judgmental teachings, the reason many people cited for leaving their childhood faiths. They continued to describe themselves as religious or converted to another faith because they'd had mystical experiences such as moments of intense religious insight.

What I took away from Joseph was love of Joseph. I'd been through the wars with him, the craziness of life, and he'd affirmed for me that God was part of it all: the upside-down and backward surrealism of our illusions, desires, losses, misfortunes, horrors, joys. But that was Zen, this was now. If I tried reading the Bible, I couldn't get what I wanted. Then, gradually, I began to lose hold of my precious God moments: the *shazam!* moment in the car, my revelation about God in the Book of Mormon, and the *ker-thunk* that went with the coincidence of having Mormon ancestors. Yet as these seemed to fade, a strange, primitive urgency arose in me. I began to obsess about "loving thy neighbor." It felt like an early developmental stage was suddenly asserting itself. It was a dumb and gullible and especially loved doctrine about obedience, about how we should obey without understanding and how no commandment was too small or too great to obey. I saw how different I might have been if my inner waif had not had her religious upbringing interrupted by moving to Washington, D.C.

The phrase "Love thy neighbor" began to consume me in relation to Tovi. My distress with his decline began to increase. Though there was no urgent reason to feel he was near the end, I started going crazy watching the process that would end with his death. I died his death all the time. Even before he had to go up a size or two in his clothes, I saw changes: the skin of his face was extra dry from one of his medications; he wasn't as strong; he didn't care so much about his appearance. Maybe I can credit myself with not always saying something to Tovi. Instead I called the social worker in the Parkinson's clinic and asked what I should do. He just said it was common for Parkinson's patients to lose interest in how they looked. It would get worse. And if he was tending toward a cluttered living space (he was), then that could reach dangerous levels (it did). I died Tovi's death every time his legs got more rigid or his face was maskier. He never complained. He was grateful for everything. If the sun was out, he would praise it. "Oh, for this wondrous morning, washed in the light of the Lord," he once exclaimed—he who never went to church—as he stepped out the door of his apartment.

For all my talk of conversion in the last few years, for all my fascination with Joseph and his beliefs, for all of my experience of God, I had less natural grace than Tovi did. Even after we reached a point when our lives began sometimes going in different directions, he never complained. When it was difficult to take him out of town on visits to my children and grandchildren, he would stay home and watch old movies and videos of the Three Tenors on his flat-screen TV. He went out for BBQ luncheons with his club called ROMEOs (Retired Old Men Eating Out). In his prime he had acted as Santa Claus for a number of New York men's clubs. In his role as Saint Nicholas, he'd handed out endless loving cheer and presents to all the children who came. Now he was kind to the child in himself. When I couldn't be with him, he cooked his favorite recipes like slumgullion and mashed potatoes; he ordered pizzas from Domino's; he ate lots of ice cream and cake. He didn't complain.

I did. I complained to my friends that he wouldn't even say the words "assisted living." He wouldn't plan for his further decline. It was as if he was never going to die. He never mentioned it at all. He wouldn't. I was terrified of his death, but, honestly, even more terrified of my own. I think that's why I was so obsessed with "Love thy neighbor." As Tovi declined, he became more of a neighbor, a stranger carving his own lonely path. What could I do for this neighbor who had to walk his walk in his own way as he moved toward his end? What should I not do for my old sweetheart, my companion? In our later years, once we made our arrangements, he never asked to be taken in, but I often felt he should have been. I often felt my neighbor was not getting the proper tender, loving care. And that, perhaps if I gave it, I would not notice my own death in his as I so often did. Meanwhile, this stranger's way of never saying the word "death" and my unmet need to talk about it all the time were combining to build a wall between us.

I tried to make an appointment with the therapist on Tovi's medical team. She did not call me back. Again I cast about for some wisdom I had taken in from Joseph, and I realized that the one concrete result of studying him was now knowing I had religious need. I had uncovered a hunger for religion. But since I myself did not have belief, I needed to be around people who did. So I tried the only representative of Christ with whom I had some connection. In my wanderings, before I started going to the Mormon Church and in between my visits there, I'd sometimes gone back to an Episcopalian church in town. The minister was a very literate person; his sermons were intelligent; he had convinced me he was a believer; and he often said from the pulpit that anyone in need should call and make an appointment with him. I did.

I wore a skirt, blouse, and Sunday shoes out of respect for the institution. I was as calm as a nuclear explosion and erupted as soon as we sat down. I tried to say twenty-six things at the same time. I personally feel unnerved when a stranger comes in—whether male or female does not matter—and pours red-hot emotional chili in my lap. I did not think the youthful, dark-blond minister looked very happy. As my smoking ashes settled, he said coolly, "Let me see if I understood you correctly. You are in a relationship from which you are getting nothing, but toward which you feel obligated."

"Not *nothing!*" I cried. New nuclear detonations while I tried to express that I should take Tovi in, but couldn't. Money, the fact I worked in my bedroom, on and on, a million reasons. What did Christ expect of us? It was killing me that I was killing Tovi. And he was killing me by dying.

"You know," he said, playing to the public image of Episcopalians as above the fray. "You know, I am supposed to go to the old-age home several times a week. I don't always want to go. Sometimes I let myself stay home and have a martini."

"Dealing with Tovi is not the same as the old-age home," I whispered furiously.

"What do you want me to do?" the minister asked, and I feared he was only as much of a believer as I was.

I said, "I want you to be Christ's lawyer. I want you to argue loving thy neighbor from his point of view. What did he expect of us when he said it? How much did he feel we had to give? What if your friend turns into a neighbor? What if his illness estranges you because it reminds you that you're on the way out, too? What then?"

"First, Christ does not need a lawyer," he sighed. "Christ is the mediating figure, mediating between us and what there is to know."

"What did he know about loving? What does he offer between 'Love thy neighbor' and 'Greater love hath no man than the one'—what's the quote? 'The one who lays down his life for his friends'? Christ left his family, told others to follow him. What does he know about the day-to-day grind of loving?"

"You can't just follow Christ's call to love for morality's sake."

This was more my type. The minister was trying, I could see that. Hadn't I long ago decided he and I were in the same tradition? Couldn't I live and let live, die and let die?

"You have to find a way to let God work on your resistance so that it turns to love."

He had a point. He'd been kind enough to make it without criticizing me. He could have pointed out that I wanted "love thy neighbor" to feel good. It didn't.

Our silence continued without growing easy. He asked if there was anything else I needed help with.

"I don't think Christ knows us," I said honestly enough. But I was probably also trying to needle him. "He's not modern. Just take books. Christ hasn't read anything. He hasn't read *Origin of Species*. He doesn't know about Einstein. Christ doesn't even know he has to argue for himself as one authority among many."

The minister grunted slightly, almost companionably. He said, "Christ knows everything. He already knows everything you know, everything mankind will ever know. Christ's read all the books that will ever be written. . . . But maybe he skipped Darwin because Christ himself *was* the origin of the species."

Funny, I observed to myself, how *The New York Review of Books* never mentioned that as an acceptable argument against evolution. I had the sense not to speak my mind. I knew I had problems compromising with my traditions. I needed to be more reasonable. We said a polite good-bye, and I left.

As I walked home, I reminded myself how I could always find a sacred pleasure in Joseph's early story. I always felt a youthful joy when I thought of Joseph and the angel, the plates, the hat (O Lord, thank you for that hat!), the reformed Egyptian. The boy's imagination gave me hope in things unseen. When I passed the pathetic parking lot behind the bank, I did not ask myself, as I often did, why my eyes ever had to fall on such dullness. I saw with my spiritual eyes, as they used to say in Joseph's day, and what I saw was as beautiful as the gold plates themselves.

History is still wondering about the state of Tom's and Huck's eyes on the night they met Joseph and stayed in Palmyra so long ago. That was the night they'd gone round and round about whether there really were any gold plates. Whether Joseph had imagined them or buried some sort of plates "hisself." That's when Huck said, "You can't pray a lie. I know that."

And Tom replied, "If he didn't see them for real, he's going to catch it."

Now, in some accounts, the two boys actually made a model out of tin that night. They went back and buried this model, but they were pretty frightened of what they'd undertaken to do. They might be godless boys, but they were superstitious. They got back up to the top of Cumorah Hill at dawn. There was an owl hooting, animals stirring, and even a fat snake that slithered right under their noses as they were digging the hole. They stopped to smoke and get up their courage, and then turned back to their work. It was getting late in the morning, and they were afraid of being seen by someone who knew about Joseph and his holy gold plates. They'd ruin everything for the friend they were trying to rescue. And what if Joseph himself caught them!? By the end Tom and Huck were all stirred up, their nerves on fire when they pulled out a last big rock and shoved the plates into the earth. Suddenly, the whole hill began to tremble; the trees around them swayed horrifically and there was a deep, unearthly rumble from the bowels of the earth. Well, they hurled dirt over the plates and got out of there so fast, they were falling all over themselves and each other; and then, golly, if there wasn't an oversized creature with bulging eyes bearing down on them. The next thing Huck started screaming about "a toad with a sword." That got Tom screaming, too, so they were both screaming as they passed me, "A toad man, rusty sword, struck."

Like every story on the Mormon record, this one has inspired archive upon archive of scientific research. Church results show there was, in fact, a rare earthquake that morning on August 2, 1827; but there's secular scientific research that shows there wasn't even a tremor. There's psychological testing on both boys. Church studies show they were out of their minds, and there's secular research proving they weren't. The research is so conflicting that each side cancels the other. Basically, there's no way to establish what Tom and Huck were doing on Cumorah Hill that morning.

My story hasn't yet been recorded, but now I think it should be. My story is a dream, a waking fiction in which I am with Joseph in Palmyra as he makes the model of the plates. I am dreaming this dream as I walk down the street in Charlottesville, thankfully going over Belmont Bridge with its view of Albemarle County's misty blue foothills. As I walk, I see Joseph standing at a worktable, cutting pages out of tin with shears. He is a "ragged fellow" with "patched trousers" and "suspenders made out of sheeting." He wears a dirty calico shirt. His "uncombed hair" is "sticking through holes in his old, battered hat." He has a "careless" air. In a somewhat appealing way, he seems "like a low bred sort of chap." When I try to speak, no words are audible; but he replies, also in silence. He never looks up at me. We're both irreverent, we joke about our ages. He's 205 in 2011.

I'm 167 years older than he is. Though I laugh at this, Joseph does not. I remember how his friend Pomeroy Tucker said that Joseph was "proverbially good-natured . . . and yet never known to laugh." *Never* seems strong. But the fact that he had a jesting spirit, was ironic, yet did not have a big *har, har, har l*augh could be meaningful. He saw God constantly, after all; he was serious about his irony.

I knew about that. I was a bit like that myself, took funny things seriously. I often felt humor was the last refuge of the transcendent. Comedy gave me relief, was touching and serious, sometimes terribly so. Yet even when the comedy was unbearable, God's pulse was there. Actually, it's when religion was most pious, righteous, and preachy that it just seemed dead. Making a model of the plates was an example of serious irony. No wonder he didn't laugh. It was not a laughing matter. Faith and irony, belief in God and amazement that we felt belief in God; faith and irony, one after the other, on and on forever. How could it be other? We know nothing. We die; we end, and what can religion do about it? It can feed and calm our tender need, our tender openness to faith, followed by our tender irony.

Tovi died on August 1, 2011. I had been with my brother after he had a hip replacement operation in Boston. Tovi hadn't answered my calls, but that wasn't so unusual. If we had lived together, maybe I wouldn't have gone away. Or maybe he would not have felt so abandoned when I did. If I'd been the sick one, I would have done what he did. I wouldn't have returned his calls. I found him Monday morning when I went down to his apartment. He was laid out like a big fallen tree in his little office. I could see him through the door on the left as I came in. He must have gotten up from his computer after sitting for a long time; and in that effort, the medical personnel later said, his blood probably gushed effortfully upward through his arteries, breaking off the clot that would have caused a pulmonary embolism. It probably took all of five seconds. There were no signs of struggle. His hands were open and relaxed.

I knew instantly that he was dead. It wasn't a bad feeling, but it was an indescribable one. Tovi, Tovi . . .

I'd say that I felt "glad," but it wouldn't be exact. It was almost like hunger or desire. I was hungry to know who he was in this state. I wanted to understand his corpse. I was glad to finally get my hands on death. I'd say that he looked "wonderful," and somehow I had that feeling, but he was so far beyond the ordinary uses of "wonderful." I was upset every time I heard the word coming out of my mouth later, when I could not stop talking about the experience of finding him. But still I kept saying, "He looked wonderful."

His color was "good." His color was pale, almost beautiful; I actually have to use the word "radiant" to describe the color over his large, naked shoulders and chest. He was wearing his American flag suspenders, blue shorts, and white socks. He had been dead for a while, but he was a lovely color, lying on his back so the blood was probably pooling underneath.

"Tovi, Tovi," I kept saying and asking what happened. I said over and over how sorry I was that I hadn't been with him. He didn't seem to care. We were close again finally. His death, which had driven such a wedge between us, was no longer divisive. That's why I hungered for the feel of him and touched his hands, stroked his face. This was it: the thing he didn't want to mention, and the thing I wanted to talk about night and day. His pale, radiant face was riveting. His blond hair was tossed back; his wrinkles were relaxed, though something about his expression looked ancient. His mouth was open in awe, and his chin was grizzled with white stubble. Even before his living face came into his dead one, something around his darkened eyes preserved his youthfulness.

Then suddenly his living face *did* come into his dead one. His blue eyes were shining in their dark sockets. He was smiling a huge, celebratory grin. But it was his blue, blue eyes I could not take my own away from. They shone with generosity and joy. He seemed to be saying, "You won't believe this! It's fantastic here! Fantastic!" I could see his magnificence, his *divinity,* and felt his reassurance. I should not worry: so much on earth was small and everything on the other side was immeasurable. All was forgiven. Tovi was with me for another second. His eyes dimmed, his smile faded, and I felt some motion of the man's spirit in the quiet room. Then he was dead again, his old jester's face sharply angled upward in a beseeching attitude.

Amen. So be it; truly.

ACKNOWLEDGMENTS

Helen Whitney, old friend and inspiration, at the top of any list of my life-changing guides and without whose bestowal of opportunity this book would have never emerged . . . Kathleen Ford and Kenny Marotta, talents divine, stalwart companions in the literary trenches . . . Jessica Tuck, who only gives 250 percent and "always gets to the heart of a story and makes it sing" . . . Trudy Hale, under whose roof and in whose aura a significant part of this book was written . . . Tracy Barnes and Liz Rodgers, in whose guest room Chapter Eight was written, and with whom I've enjoyed many spirited exchanges, witty dust-ups, and fruitful reconciliations over the subject of Joseph Smith . . . Lindsay Edgecombe, agent of change . . . Levi Peterson, who asked me to write something about my experience working on "The Mormon" documentary. I wrote an essay for *Dialogue* which became the first chapter of this book . . . Lesley Karsten-DiNicola, ever an enthusiastic supporter and honest reader of parts of this book before it was conceived as such . . . John and Abbie Rowlett, always for their friendship, and for reading "Faith and Irony" when it was an untamed essay and offering their uncritical interest and helpful comments . . . Adrienne Ghaly, for helping me take "Faith and Irony" to the next stage . . . Lynn Powell and Anna Clare Stinebring, for helping me finish "Faith and Irony" by sharing their rich and subtle, art-soaked insights . . . Ernie Drucker, Andy Kaufman, and Annie Stafford, for conversations about art, religion, and the world . . . Polly Aird, Lavina Anderson, Will Bagley, Alison Booth, Jo Lynn Harline (genealogist), and James Lucas, for their help in dotting my Mormon "i's" and crossing my Mormon "t's" . . . The 2nd Ward of the Charlottesville Church of Jesus Christ of Latter-Day Saints for being so welcoming . . . Tovi, who has been such a sustaining presence both here and from the great beyond.

NOTES

Page   Two. The Return of the Repressed

22   *"Asael's Universalism was a form"*: Richard Lyman Bushman, *Joseph Smith: Rough Stone Rolling* (New York: Alfred A. Knopf, 2005), p. 16.

23   *"conversion was compelled"*: Donald Scott, "Evangelism, Revivalism, and the Second Great Awakening," p. 1, nationalhumanitiescenter.org/tserve/nineteen/nkeyinfo/nevanrev.htm, revised November 2000, accessed December 3, 2011.

24   *"would not subscribe to any particular system of faith"*: Lucy Mack Smith, *History of Joseph Smith, By His Mother, Lucy Mack Smith*, ed. Preston Nibley (Salt Lake City: Bookcraft, 1956), p. 46.

25   *"This field is the world"*: Ibid., p. 47.

25   *"the agony of my soul"*: Ibid., p. 66.

25   *Joseph was interested . . . "But so great"*: Joseph Smith, *History of the Church of Jesus Christ of Latter-Day-Saints* (Salt Lake City: Deseret Book Company, 1978), vol. 1, p. 3.

Three. The Angel, the Plates, and the
Power of Joseph's Charms

40   *"Conversion was an experience"*: Donald Scott, "Evangelism, Revivalism, and the Second Great Awakening," p. 1, nationalhumanitiescenter.org/tserve/nineteen/nkeyinfo/nevanrev.htm, revised November 2000, accessed December 3, 2011.

42   *"pretend that he sees them"*: Grant Palmer, *An Insider's View of Mormon Origins* (Salt Lake City: Signature Books, 2002), p. 176.

48   *And then, just when he believed his soul . . . angel Moroni*: Several sources feed the story of Joseph's encounter with Moroni, the gold plates, and the boy's moral apprenticeship in the years before he finally took them out of the ground. There are the colorful affidavits written by Joseph's friends and neighbors, which were published in *Mormonism Unvailed* [*sic*] in 1834, and there is Joseph's magisterial account, which was canonized in 1838. The affidavits include some details and plot twists that never made it into the canonized account. Many of Joseph's neighbors portray the boy and his family as first finding a magnificent store of gold, which, as it fails to appear, becomes a heavenly treasure. Joseph Smith Sr., reported, among other things, that a spirit told his son he could recover the plates only if he wore all black clothes and rode a black horse with "a switch tale [*sic*]." Willard Chase describes Joseph digging the plates up for their monetary value. But a toad the size of man was in the box, which toad leapt up and struck him in the side of the head, bringing Joseph back to his moral senses. The voices of the affidavits tell a folk story of enchantment. They reveal context. Joseph's official account leaves out the details I've mentioned here. He lifts the central events into a religious rite of passage for the ages. I've kept some of the unofficial folk elements because they help communicate the charm of Joseph's sacred story.

Four. La Vita Nuova

61   *"a fraud and conjurer"*: Christopher Hitchens, "Romney's Mormon Problem," http://www.slate.com/articles/news_and_politics/fighting_words/2011/10/is_mormonism_a_cult_who_cares_it_s_their_weird_and_sinister_beli.html, posted November 17, 2011, accessed March 24, 2012.

71   *"Is the pen a metaphorical penis?"*: Sandra M. Gilbert and Susan Gubar, *The Madwoman in the Attic: The Woman Writer and the Nineteenth-Century Literary Imagination*, 2nd ed. (New Haven, CT: Yale University Press, 2000).

Five. Joseph Smith Couldn't Have Written the Book of Mormon

79   *"Yet when the converts began to file off"*: Joseph Smith, *History of the Church* (Salt Lake City: Deseret Book Company, 1978), vol. 1, p. 3.

Page

81   *It was the first time the state and the Christian religion had been set apart*: Daniel Howe, *What God Hath Wrought: The Transformation of America, 1815–1848* (New York: Oxford University Press, 2007), p. 146.

82   *"I happened to think of what I had heard"*: Peter Ingersoll's affidavit in Eber D. Howe, *Mormonism Unvailed* [sic]: *Or, A Faithful Account of That Singular Imposition and Delusion* (Painesville, OH: Eber D. Howe, 1834), pp. 236–237.

83   *"He must not lie"*: Martin Harris, quoted in Richard Bushman, *Joseph Smith: Rough Stone Rolling* (New York: Alfred A. Knopf, 2005), p. 51.

84   *"I frequently fell into many foolish errors"*: Smith, *History of the Church*, vol. 1, p. 9.

84   *"he could not stop thinking"*: Oliver Cowdery, quoted in Bushman, *Joseph Smith*, p. 51.

84   *"the angel told him he must quit the company"*: Martin Harris, quoted in Bushman, *Joseph Smith*, p. 51.

85   *Emma, a remarkable young woman . . . "often got the power"*: Linda King Newell and Valeen Tippetts Avery, *Mormon Enigma: Emma Hale Smith, Prophet's Wife, "Elect Lady," Polygamy's Foe, 1804–1879* (Garden City, N.Y.: Doubleday, 1984), p. 18.

86   *1813 New York statute:* Quoted in Dan Vogel, *Joseph Smith: The Making of a Prophet* (Salt Lake City: Signature Books, 2004), where it is cited as *Laws of the State of New York, Revised and Passed at Thirty-Sixth Session of the Legislature*, 2 vols. (Albany, N.Y.: H.C. Southwick, 1813), 1:114, sec. I.

88   *"acknowledged he could not see in a stone"*: Peter Ingersoll's affidavit in Howe, *Mormonism Unvailed* [sic], pp. 235–236.

89   *"the severest chastisement"*: Joseph Smith, quoted in Lucy Smith, *History of Joseph Smith, By His Mother, Lucy Mack Smith*, ed. Preston Nibley (Salt Lake City: Bookcraft, 1956), p. 100.

90   *"the gold plates are the hinge"*: Author telephone interview with Richard L. Bushman, May 10, 2011 (notes in author's possession).

92   *"mearly instructed in reading"*: Joseph Smith, *The Essential Joseph Smith* (Salt Lake City: Signature Books, 1995), p. 26.

92   *"somewhat partial to the Methodist sect"*: Grant H. Palmer, *An Insider's View of Mormon Origins* (Salt Lake City: Signature Books, 2002), p. 44.

Page

96   *"For behold, you should not have feared"*: Joseph Smith, comp., with additions by his successors in the Presidency of the Church, *Doctrine and Covenants of the Church of the Latter-day Saints: Containing Revelations Given to Joseph Smith, the Prophet* (Salt Lake City: The Church of Jesus Christ of Latter-day Saints, 1952), Section 3, 7–8, pp. 4–5.

96   *"The speaker stands above"*: Bushman, *Joseph Smith*, p. 69.

97   *"These days were never to be forgotten"*: Oliver Cowdery, quoted in Vogel, *Joseph Smith*, p. 166.

98   *"He could not pronounce the word Sariah"*: Emma Smith, quoted in Newell and Avery, *Mormon Enigma*, p. 26.

99   *"Joseph Smith could neither write nor dictate"*: Ibid.

Six. Back to the Future

107   *"'It came to pass' was his pet"*: Mark Twain, *Roughing It*, ed. Harriet Elinor Smith and Edgar Marquess Branch (Berkeley: University of California Press, 1993), p. 107.

108   *"ignorant and impudent"* . . . *"gift of tongues"*: Alexander Campbell, "An Analysis of the Book of Mormon with an Examination of Its Internal and External Evidences, and a Refutation of Its Pretenses to Divine Authority," *Millennial Harbinger*, Bethany, Virginia, February 7, 1831; www.lds-mormon.com/campbell.shtml, accessed December 4, 2011.

110   Book of Mormon *"must either be true or false"*: Orson Pratt, "Divine Authenticity of the Book of Mormon," *Orson Pratt's Works* (Liverpool, England: R. James, 1851), pp. 1, 2; lib.byu.edu/digital/mpntc/az/S .php, accessed March 25, 2012.

112   *I opened the Book of Mormon at random*: Joseph Smith, Jr., trans., *The Book of Mormon: An Account Written by the Hand of Mormon, Upon Plates Taken from the Plates of Nephi* (Salt Lake City: The Church of Jesus Christ of Latter-day Saints, 1981), p. 188.

113   *the signs at his death will include*: Ibid., p. 400.

119   *"Christ is not some figure down the road"*: Jonathan Cott, ed., *Bob Dylan: The Essential Interviews* (New York: Wenner Media, 2006), p. 276.

Page

Seven. Past-Life Digression

127   *WGBH began giving out reels:* Alex Beam, "A Mormon President? I Don't Think So," *The Boston Globe*, March 5, 2007, accessed March 23, 2012.

134   *"twas in our humble cottage" that a "pilgrim of God arrived":* Appleton Milo Harmon. Autobiography and Diary, 1850–1853 (extracts). http://www.pa-roots.org/data/read.php?338,296840, revised December 15, 2007, accessed April 30, 2012.

137   *"Anna was a kind and loving wife":* Raymond W. Madsen A. G., *Life Story and Ancestry of Jesse Perse Harmon, 1795–1877: Patriot, Soldier and Pioneer* (Raymond W. Madsen A. G., 2000), p. 14.

138   *"that unabashed assumption of superiority":* Edward Morgan, quoted in Richard Howland Maxwell, "Pilgrim and Puritan: A Delicate Distinction," Pilgrim Society Note, Series 2, March 2003, copyright 1993, 2003 Richard Howland Maxwell. www.pilgrimhall.org, accessed March 23, 2012.

139   *"originated in the European pulpit":* Sacvan Bercovitch, *The American Jeremiad* (Madison: University of Wisconsin Press, 1978), p. xi.

Eight. Joseph Through the Particle Accelerator

142   *"eagle-eye" . . . "there was something in his manner":* John D. Lee, *Remembering Joseph: Personal Recollections of Those Who Knew the Prophet Joseph Smith*, ed. Mark L. McConkie (Salt Lake City: Deseret Book Company, 2003), p. 43.

142   *"It must not be supposed":* Thomas Ford, *A History of Illinois, from Its Commencement as a State* (Urbana: Illinois University Press, 1995), p. 249.

144   *Only then would the Mormons . . . "exiles from the Old World":* Terryl L. Givens, *The Book of Mormon: A Very Short Introduction* (New York: Oxford University Press, 2009), p. 31.

145   *"Wherefore, I the Lord, knowing":* Joseph Smith, comp., with additions by his successors in the Presidency of the Church, *Doctrine and Covenants of the Church of the Latter-day Saints: Containing Revelations Given to Joseph Smith, the Prophet* (Salt Lake City: The Church of Jesus Christ of Latter-day Saints, 1952), section 1:17.

Page

147 *"I said it Ironically"*: Joseph Smith, *The Essential Joseph Smith* (Salt Lake City: Signature Books, 1995), p. 200.

148 *"He was looking ahead"*: Mary Rollins, quoted in Todd Compton, *The Sacred Loneliness* (Salt Lake City: Signature Books, 1997), p. 207.

148 *"Each sentence was uttered slowly"*: Parley P. Pratt, in Mark L. McConkie, ed., *Remembering Joseph: Personal Recollections of Those Who Knew the Prophet Joseph Smith* (Salt Lake City: Deseret Book Company, 2003), p. 256.

148 *being able "without premeditation"*: William E. McLellin, in McConkie, *Remembering Joseph*, p. 257.

148 *"speaks by the Spirit"*: Ezra Booth, Letter I, in Eber D. Howe, *Mormonism Unvailed [sic]: Or, A Faithful Account of That Singular Imposition and Delusion* (Painesville, OH: Telegraph Press, 1834), p. 177; www .solomonspalding.com/docs/1834howb.htm, revised August 17, 2006, accessed March 23, 2012.

149 *If "placing the Bible"*: Ibid., p. 182.

149 *"A new commandment was issued"*: Ezra Booth, Letter VII, in Howe, *Mormonism Unvailed [sic]*, p. 206; www.solomonspalding.com/ docs/1834howb.htm, revised August 17, 2006, accessed March 23, 2012.

149 *"This too we proved to be false"*: Ibid., p. 208.

150 *"Have you not frequently observed"*: Ibid., p. 203.

152 *"In regard to D. P. Hurlbut"*: Benjamin Winchester's Last Testimony (1900); www.solomonspalding.com/docs/1900winc.htm, revised January 2, 2010, accessed March 20, 2012.

153 *"Whether or not Elder Hurlbut was meeting the local Mormon girls"*: Dale R. Broadhurst, "Benjamin Winchester's Last Testimony," p. 15; http://www.solomonspalding.com/docs/1900winc.htm, revised January 2, 2010, accessed March 20, 2012.

153 *"to root out cases of 'fornication' among the Saints"*: Dale R. Broadhurst, "Crisis at Kirtland," Part 2: "Meetings in the Mission Field: Licit and Illicit (Mar–Apr 1833)," p. 31; http://www.olivercowdery.com/hurlbut/ Hcrisis2.htm, revised April 2, 2001, accessed March 19, 2012.

154 *"He wept like a child"*: Dale R. Broadhurst, "Crisis at Kirtland," Part 4: "Smoke and Mirrors (1833)," George A. Smith, quoted in "Divine Origins of Mormonism." *Journal of Discourses*, vol. VII, London & Liverpool, 1860, p. 113; http://www.olivercowdery.com/hurlbut/ Hcrisis2.htm, revised April 2, 2001, accessed April 30, 2012.

Page

155   *Brother D. P. Hurlbut was boasting to friends:* Ibid., p. 45.

156   *That one was an undated document in Joseph Smith's hand:* Ibid., p. 40.

Nine. Contradiction Is Not a Sign of Falsity

169   *"Every night before retiring to rest":* Joseph Smith, *History of the Church*
       (Salt Lake City: Deseret Book Company, 1978), vol. 2, pp. 64–65.

171   *"descended into a tangle of intrigue and conflict":* Richard Lyman Bush-
       man, *Joseph Smith: Rough Stone Rolling* (New York: Alfred A. Knopf,
       2005), p. 322.

172   *a diagnosis of "Imposter" . . . "struggle between two dominant identities":*
       Fawn M. Brodie, *No Man Knows My History: The Life of Joseph Smith
       the Mormon Prophet* (New York: Alfred A. Knopf, 1945), p. 418.

173   *He urged his followers to become all they could be:* Joseph Smith, *The
       Essential Joseph Smith* (Salt Lake City: Signature Books, 1995),
       pp. 232–245.

175   *"They might rail and slander him":* Brigham Young, quoted in "History
       of Brigham Young," *Desert News*, February 10, 1858, p. 386.

Ten. The Pure Products of America

177   *Missouri had been treating the Mormons like wartime enemies:* Richard
       Lyman Bushman, *Joseph Smith: Rough Stone Rolling* (New York:
       Alfred A. Knopf, 2005), p. 354.

178   *"Had the army been composed":* Lucy Smith, *History of Joseph Smith,
       By His Mother, Lucy Mack Smith*, ed. Preston Nibley (Salt Lake City:
       Bookcraft, 1956), p. 289.

182   *the prophet said the president had treated him with disrespect:* Uncle
       Dale's Readings in Early Mormon History, Misc. New York City Pa-
       pers, 1840–1849 Articles, *New York Journal of Commerce*, March 27,
       1840.

183   *"The river enclosed a position":* Josiah Quincy, *Figures of the Past from
       the Leaves of Old Journals* (Boston: Little, Brown, 1910), p. 388.

186   *Joseph's most unsavory admirer, John C. Bennett:* A potentially even
       more unsavory admirer among Smith's intimates was Joseph H. Jack-
       son. A non-Mormon with a mysterious past, Jackson came to Nauvoo
       in 1842. Like other antagonistic confidants of the prophet, Jackson
       claimed that he worked his way into Smith's inner circle to gather

material to expose this unworthy charlatan. To do so, he successfully presented himself as a priest in his effort to "become one" with Joseph. In his exposé, "A Narrative of the Adventures and Experience of Joseph H. Jackson, in Nauvoo, Disclosing the Depths of Mormon Villainy," published in August 1844 in *The Warsaw Signal*, Jackson claimed to have enjoyed privileged information from the prophet about his sexual adventures and depravities. Jackson's essay details Smith's callousness toward his wife behind her back; his corrupt clique of older women who educated younger ones to the joys of spiritual marriage; and his cynical, not to say depraved, desire to seduce his niece and sister. For his part, Smith claimed that Jackson, a notorious counterfeiter, tried to assassinate him. Both Fawn Brodie and Richard Bushman barely quote Jackson's unsavory essay, finding him too unreliable to believe. Will Bagley, the respected author of *Blood of the Prophets: Brigham Young and the Massacre at Mountain Meadows*, regards Jackson's essay as an insightful perspective on the prophet's compulsive behavior. I think the piece is a hoax. It is strangely brilliant, almost too slick in its style and its perfectly damning portrait. In the end, I find Jackson's Joseph is too consistent to be plausible.

191   *"By later summer 1843"*: Linda King Newell and Valeen Tippetts Avery, *Mormon Enigma: Emma Hale Smith, Prophet's Wife, "Elect Lady," Polygamy's Foe, 1804–1879* (Garden City, N.Y.: Doubleday, 1984), p. 147.

192   *"rather her blood . . . run pure"*: Emma Smith, quoted ibid., p. 170.

193   *the Mormons were "a ruined people"*: William Marks, quoted at http://www.josephsmithspolygamy.com/JSImproperProposals/16ImproperProposalsAccusations/DaughterWilliamMarks.html, p. 1, accessed December 7, 2011.

193   *In public, Joseph raved against his accusers*: Quoted in Joseph Smith, *History of the Church of Jesus Christ of Latter Day Saints* (Salt Lake City: Deseret Book Company, 1978), vol. 6, pp. 408–409.

Eleven. Faith and Irony

196   *an official familiarity, "such as a crowned head"*: Josiah Quincy, *Figures of the Past from the Leaves of Old Journals* (Boston: Little, Brown, 1910), p. 381.

197   *a cordiality "with which the president"*: Ibid.

201   *"If the blasphemous assumptions of Smith"*: Ibid., p. 397.

Page

201   *"In your hands or that of any other person"*: Ibid.

202   *"You don't know me"*: Joseph Smith, *The Essential Joseph Smith* (Salt Lake City: Signature Books, 1995), pp. 232–245.

203   *"In the Spring of 1844"*: Appleton, Milo Harmon. Autobiography and Diary, 1850–1853 (extracts). http://www.pa-roots.org/data/read.php? 338,296840, revised December 15, 2007, accessed April 30, 2012.

204   *Milo was one of the police force:* Ibid., p. 12.

205   *"there would not be a gun fired"*: Raymond W. Madsen A. G., *Life Story and Ancestry of Jesse Perse Harmon, 1795–1877: Patriot, Soldier and Pioneer* (Raymond W. Madsen A. G., 2000), p. 31.

206   *"If you by refusing to submit"*: Thomas Ford, quoted in Richard Lyman Bushman, *Joseph Smith: Rough Stone Rolling* (New York: Alfred A. Knopf, 2005), pp. 545–546.

207   *"Some were tyred almost to death"*: Vilate Kimball, quoted in Linda King Newell and Valeen Tippetts Avery, *Mormon Enigma: Emma Hale Smith* (New York: Doubleday, 1984), p. 188.

208   *"You always said if the church would stick to you"*: Reynolds Cahoon, quoted in Newell and Avery, *Mormon Enigma*, p. 188.

208   *"If my life is no value to my friends"*: Joseph Smith, quoted in Newell and Avery, *Mormon Enigma*, p. 188.

208   *"You are the oldest"*: Newell and Avery, *Mormon Enigma*, p. 188.

208   *Joseph turned to Hyrum . . . "Let's go back"*: Joseph Smith and Hyrum Smith, quoted in Joseph Smith, *History of the Church of Jesus Christ of Latter Day Saints* (Salt Lake City: Deseret Book Company, 1978), vol. 6, pp. 549–550.

209   *"I will go with you"*: Ibid., p. 550.

210   *"I felt the worst I ever did"*: Emma Smith, quoted in Newell and Avery, *Mormon Enigma*, p. 189.

211   *Joseph bore testimony to the guards:* Smith, *History of the Church of Jesus Christ of Latter Day Saints*, vol. 6, p. 600.

Twelve. Except Ye Be Converted, and Become as Little Children

222   *"For if the utterance is indeed an assertion"*: Antony Flew, "Theology and Falsification," http://www.infidels.org/library/modern/antony_flew/theologyandfalsification.html, accessed March 26, 2012.

Thirteen. Sanctified Flesh

241   *This is where I first met Claude Cowley"*: All quoted conversation with Claude Cowley and the Timpson family in this chapter comes from my personal interviews with these people in 2004, 2005, and 2011.

Fourteen. A Dead Prophet, a Corpse, and a Woman Who Will Die

267   *Joseph was "proverbially good-natured"*: Pomeroy Tucker, *Origin, Rise, and Progress of Mormonism*, pp. 16–17; www.solomonspalding .com/docs1/1867TucA.htm, revised August 23, 2006, accessed March 18, 2012.

BIBLIOGRAPHY

Anderson, Richard Lloyd. *Investigating the Book of Mormon Witnesses.* Salt Lake City: Deseret Book Company, 1981.

_____. *Inside the Mind of Joseph Smith: Psychobiography and the Book of Mormon.* Salt Lake City: Signature Books, 1999.

Bloom, Harold. *American Religion: The Emergence of the Post-Christian Nation.* New York: Simon & Schuster, 1992.

Bradley, Martha Sonntag, and Mary Brown Firmage Woodward. *4 Zinas: A Story of Mothers and Daughters on the Mormon Frontier.* Salt Lake City: Signature Books, 2000.

Broadhurst, Dale R. "Crisis at Kirtland." OliverCowdery.com, 2001.

Brodie, Fawn M. *No Man Knows My History: The Life of Joseph Smith the Mormon Prophet.* New York: Alfred A. Knopf, 1945.

Bushman, Richard Lyman. *Joseph Smith: Rough Stone Rolling.* New York: Alfred A. Knopf, 2005.

Butler, Jon. *Awash in a Sea of Faith: Christianizing the American People.* Cambridge, Mass.: Harvard University Press, 1990.

Compton, Todd. *In Sacred Loneliness: The Plural Wives of Joseph Smith.* Salt Lake City: Signature Books, 1997.

Covington, Dennis. *Salvation on Sand Mountain: Snake Handling and Redemption in Southern Appalachia.* Cambridge, Mass.: Da Capo Press, 2009.

Day, Dorothy. *The Long Loneliness: An Autobiography of Dorothy Day.* San Francisco: Harper & Row, 1981 (originally pub. 1952).

Flanders, Robert Bruce. *Nauvoo: Kingdom on the Mississippi.* Urbana and Chicago: University of Illinois Press, 1965.

Ford, Thomas. *A History of Illinois, from Its Commencement as a State in 1818 to 1847.* Urbana: University of Illinois Press, 1995.

Foster, Lawrence. *Religion and Sexuality: The Shakers, the Mormons, and the Oneida Community.* Urbana: University of Illinois Press, 1984.

Gibbons, Ted. *The Road to Carthago*. Provo, Utah. Maasai, 1990.

Givens, Terryl L. *The Book of Mormon: A Very Short Introduction*. New York: Oxford University Press, 2009.

———. *By the Hand of Mormon: The American Scripture That Launched a New World Religion*. New York: Oxford University Press, 2002.

Gordon, Sarah Barringer. *The Mormon Question: Polygamy and Constitutional Conflict in Nineteenth-Century America*. Chapel Hill: University of North Carolina Press, 2002.

Hall, David D. *Puritans in the New World: A Critical Anthology*. Princeton, N.J.: Princeton University Press, 2004.

Hardy, Carmon B. *Solemn Covenant: The Mormon Polygamous Passage*. Urbana: University of Illinois Press, 1992.

Hardy, Grant. *Understanding the Book of Mormon: A Reader's Guide*. New York: Oxford University Press, 2010.

Harmon, Appleton Milo. Autobiography and Diary, 1850–1853. http://www.pa-roots.org/data/read.php?338.296840.

Howe, Daniel Walker. *What God Hath Wrought: The Transformation of America, 1815–1848*. New York: Oxford University Press, 2007.

Howe, Eber D. *Mormonism Unvailed* [sic]: *Or, A Faithful Account of That Singular Imposition and Delusion*. Painesville, Ohio: Eber D. Howe, 1834.

James, William. *The Varieties of Religious Experience: A Study of Religious Experience*. New York: Barnes & Noble Classics, 2004.

Lester, Julius. *Lovesong: Becoming a Jew*. New York: Arcade, 1995.

Lobdell, William. *Losing My Religion: How I Lost My Faith Reporting on Religion in America and Found Unexpected Peace*. New York: HarperCollins, 2009.

Madsen, A.G., Raymond W. *Life Story and Ancestry of Jesse Perse Harmon, 1795–1877: Patriot, Soldier and Pioneer*. Raymond W. Madsen A.G., 2000.

Marquardt, H. Michael, and Wesley P. Walters. *Inventing Mormonism: Tradition and the Historical Record*. San Francisco: Smith Research, 1994.

Marty, Martin E. *Religion and Republic: The American Circumstance*. Boston: Beacon Press, 1987.

McConkie, Mark L., ed. *Remembering Joseph: Personal Recollections of Those Who Knew the Prophet Joseph Smith*. Salt Lake City: Deseret Book Company, 2003.

Morain, William D. *The Sword of Laban: Joseph Smith, Jr., and the Dissociated Mind*. Arlington, Va.: American Psychiatric Publishing, 1998.

Newell, Linda King, and Valeen Tippets Avery. *Mormon Enigma: Emma Hale Smith, Prophet's Wife, "Elect Lady," Polygamy's Foe, 1804–1879*. Garden City, N.Y.: Doubleday, 1984.

Ostling, Richard N. and Joan K. *Mormon America: The Power and the Promise.* San Francisco: HarperSanFrancisco, 1999.

Palmer, Grant H. *An Insider's View of Mormon Origins.* Salt Lake City: Signature Books, 2002.

Pew Forum on Religion & Public Life, U.S. Religious Landscape Survey. http://religions.pewforum.org/, 2010.

Philbrick, Nathaniel. *Mayflower: A Story of Courage, Community, and War.* New York: Viking, 2006.

Quincy, Josiah. *Figures of the Past from the Leaves of Old Journals.* Boston: Little, Brown, 1910.

Quinn, Michael. *Early Mormonism and the Magic World View,* 2nd Ed., Revised. Salt Lake City: Signature Books, 1998.

Rust, Val D. *Radical Origins.* Urbana and Chicago: University of Illinois Press, 2004.

Shipps, Jan. *Mormonism: The Story of a New Religious Tradition.* Urbana: University of Illinois Press, 2000.

Skousen, Royal. *The Book of Mormon: The Earliest Text.* New Haven and London: Yale University Press, 2009.

Smith, Joseph, Jr. *The Essential Joseph Smith.* Salt Lake City: Signature Books, 1995.

————— *History of the Church of Jesus Christ of Latter Day Saints,* vols. 1–7. Salt Lake City: Deseret Book Company, 1978.

————— *The Pearl of Great Price.* Salt Lake City: The Church of Jesus Christ of Latter-day Saints, 1952.

————— comp., with additions by his successors in the Presidency of the Church. *Doctrine and Covenants of the Church of the Latter-day Saints: Containing Revelations Given to Joseph Smith, the Prophet.* Salt Lake City: The Church of Jesus Christ of Latter-day Saints, 1952.

————— trans. *The Book of Mormon: An Account Written by the Hand of Mormon, Upon Plates Taken from the Plates of Nephi.* Salt Lake City: The Church of Jesus Christ of Latter-day Saints, 1981.

Smith, Lucy Mack. *History of Joseph Smith, By His Mother, Lucy Mack Smith,* ed. Preston Nibley. Salt Lake City: Bookcraft, 1956.

Stegner, Wallace. *Mormon Country.* Lincoln and London: University of Nebraska Press, 1972.

Steinke, Darcey. *Easter Is Everywhere.* New York: Bloomsbury USA, 2008.

Twain, Mark. *Adventures of Huckleberry Finn.* New York: Barnes & Noble Classics, 2003.

—————. *Adventures of Tom Sawyer.* New York: Barnes & Noble Classics, 2003.

_____. *Roughing It*. New York: Viking Penguin, 1981.

Van Wagoner, Richard S., and Steven Walker. "Joseph Smith: 'The Gift of Seeing.'" *Dialogue: A Journal of Mormon Thought* 15, no. 2 (1982), pp. 48–68.

Vogel, Dan. *Joseph Smith: The Making of a Prophet*. Salt Lake City: Signature Books, 2004.

Waterman, Bryan, ed. *The Prophet Puzzle: Interpretive Essays of Joseph Smith*. Salt Lake City: Signature Books, 1999.

INDEX